The President
&
Economic Policy

D1548034

The President
&
Economic Policy

Edited by
JAMES P. PFIFFNER

A Publication of the
Institute for the Study of Human Issues
Philadelphia

Manufactured in the United States of America
1 2 3 4 5 89 88 87 86

Library of Congress Cataloging in Publication Data

Main entry under title:

The President & economic policy.

   Includes bibliographies and index.
   1. United States—Economic policy—Addresses, essays,
lectures.   2. United States—Politics and government—
1945–   —Addresses, essays, lectures.   3. Presidents—
United States—Addresses, essays, lectures.   I. Pfiffner,
James P.   II. Institute for the Study of Human Issues.
III. Title: President and economic policy.
HC106.5.P685   1986   338.973   84-19746
ISBN 0-89727-063-0
ISBN 0-89727-064-9 (pbk.)

For information, write:

Director of Publications
ISHI
210 South 13th Street
Philadelphia, PA 19107

Preface

The 1980s have been a time of turmoil in U.S. economic policy. The soaring inflation of the seventies and increasing unemployment presented this country with unacceptable alternatives. The election of Ronald Reagan in 1980 led to a large "supply-side" tax cut and a major reversal of fiscal priorities along with the largest deficits in U.S. history. The tight monetary policy of the Federal Reserve Board helped bring inflation under control, but also led to the deepest recession since the 1930s. The strong economic recovery of 1983 and 1984 brought the nation out of its recession, but real interest rates remained relatively high, and deficits in the $200 billion range were projected for the rest of the decade. No national political consensus emerged on the priorities among various economic goals, nor was there an intellectual consensus on the proper means to achieve those goals.

The chapters that make up *The President and Economic Policy* were prepared for this volume by political scientists who are experts on the economic issues they consider. As might be expected, their analyses concentrate primarily on the political aspects of these issues. Not all of the authors agree with one another. We did not strive for internal consistency, but rather to promote debate through a better understanding of the main issues facing the United States and the economy.

By way of introduction, Chapter 1 presents an overview of the major fiscal concerns facing the U.S. government in the 1980s. The argument is made that our problems are caused, in large part, by our failure to make difficult tradeoffs. The unwillingness to face our problems before they erupt into crises is the fault of politicians who promise easy solutions and citizens who are looking for easy answers. Among the major issues discussed are the size of the deficit, Social Security financing, defense spending, monetary policy and international debt.

Part 1 focuses on the link between the public and economic policy. This link is necessarily indirect since election outcomes are determined by many more issues than economic ones. Yet concern with the economy is important in any national election and recently has come to dominate national electoral politics. In Part 1, both William Keech and Stephen Weatherford take up the hypothesis of the political business cycle, which postulates that presidents take a short-term perspective in trying to manipulate the economy in order to maximize their votes in the next election.

In Chapter 2, Professor Keech surveys the evidence from the complementary perspectives of empirical theory and common sense. He concludes that the evidence for and against the assumptions of the political business cycle is not conclusive. But he argues that rigorously examining the evidence leaves us in a much better position to understand the relationship between politics and the economy.

In Chapter 3, Professor Weatherford also examines the arguments and evidence, and concludes that presidential economic policy decisions are determined by a range of considerations broader than short-term vote maximization. He maintains that narrow electoral considerations are mediated by the economic ideology of the president and his political party as well as by prevailing economic ideas about the role of the government and how it can affect the economy.

Part 2 deals with the role of the president in fiscal policymaking. Charles Jacob, in Chapter 4, presents an overview of presidential economic decision-making since World War II. In considering each president's approach to economic policy, he emphasizes the interplay of the president and his values with the institutions of presidential economic policymaking. In Chapter 5, James Anderson looks at the machinery of fiscal policymaking in the presidency. He describes in detail President Lyndon Johnson's economic policymaking apparatus, including the Council of Economic Advisers, the Bureau of the Budget and the Department of the Treasury, and how influence on policy was shared among them. He also discusses developments since the Johnson years, including President Ford's Economic Policy Board and President Carter's Economic Policy Group.

In Chapter 6, the budget battle of 1982 is described as a historic clash between competing political and economic priorities. Ronald Reagan's budget victories were remarkable in that he and OMB Director David Stockman engineered a major shift from domestic to defense spending and the largest tax cut in U.S. history within seven months of taking office. The victories of President Reagan in these historic battles are attributed to careful planning and skillful execution by the new administration. Nevertheless, luck did play a role, and the victories were won at the cost of other neglected priorities.

Gary Freeman argues, in Chapter 7, that the role of the president in Social Security policymaking, which was limited in the past, is increasing due to the financing crisis of the late 1970s and early 1980s. What used to be characterized by low-visibility, subsystem politics has recently increased in importance to the point where the president, Congress and the public are actively involved. This crisis has presented politicians with difficult trade-offs between concerns for the budget and the economy on the one hand and electoral concerns on the other. Professor Freeman argues that these circumstances will continue to result in active involvement by presidents in Social Security policymaking, in contrast to the episodic involvement that characterized the first four decades of the system's existence.

Fiscal policy involves the ways in which the government's taxing and spending policies affect the economy, and Part 3 deals with the taxing portion of the fiscal equation. John Witte points out in Chapter 8 that while presidents have become more active in this area, tax policy continues to be dominated by Congress. He goes on to argue that presidential success in tax policy formulation depends heavily on being in tune with long-term pressures for tax reduction and increasing tax expenditures. He criticizes political science approaches that are based on analyses of aggregate data on economic outcomes to the neglect of the political actors who make the decisions.

In Chapter 9, Susan Hansen argues that the president and Congress are careful to disguise efforts to increase government revenues by a combination of incremental, automatic and illusionary techniques. Despite the highly publicized changes in the tax code, the tax burden and income distribution have remained remarkably stable in the United States. She also argues that tax cuts seldom have the effects on the economy or revenues that are anticipated. While the budget becomes increasingly less controllable, tax revenues become increasingly earmarked. She concludes that "Presidential administrations can be evaluated in part by how fast they learn that they cannot provide a 'free lunch,'" and that "tax cuts are no panacea for hard questions of budgetary priorities and fiscal management."

Although the president does not directly control monetary policy, the control of the money supply plays an important and sometimes dominant role in the impact of government policy on the economy. The Federal Reserve Board sets monetary policy, and despite its nominal independence, seldom strays far beyond the bounds of presidential preferences. Part 4 contains two chapters on the Fed and its relation to the broader political system.

Alberta Sbragia, in Chapter 10, examines the intellectual debate between the "monetarists" and the "Keynesians" over what policies ought to be followed by the Fed. She argues that neither prescription for the appropriate rate of growth of the money supply has solved our dilemma over the balance between fighting inflation and promoting economic growth. She concludes that the range of choices available to presidents or chairmen of the Fed is quite narrow, and that there are no theories that constitute viable alternatives to the monetarist and Keynesian approaches. In this way presidents are constrained by a lack of ideas rather than by other institutions or political forces.

In Chapter 11, John Woolley takes up the question of the institutional and political independence of the Fed from the president and Congress. He argues that the actions of the Federal Reserve System cannot be understood separately from the political and economic context within which it operates. In doing so he traces the vicissitudes of politics and monetary policy over the past several decades. He concludes that despite formal independence, the Fed does not usually operate outside the consensus of the dominant political coalition.

Although the main purpose of this book is the analysis of the substance and the formulation of U.S. economic policy, there are some important methodological implications. Professor Keech presents an overview of the political business cycle and examines the assumptions upon which several different approaches are based. Three other contributors explicitly point out the shortcomings of drawing conclusions based merely on the analysis of aggregate data describing economic and political outcomes. Professors Weatherford, Woolley and Witte all argue that in order to understand public policy outcomes in the U.S. one has to look beyond the correlation of aggregate data. Each argues that to understand economic policy we must examine the people and institutions that make it and the political and economic context within which they operate. This is not to denigrate aggregate data analysis, but merely to argue that a full understanding necessarily entails taking into account the political and institutional context of decision-making as well as the statistical outcomes.

This book presents no solutions to our economic problems. There is by no means a consensus about what economic policy ought to be in the United States today, even among those who agree on the goals that ought to be pursued. It is hoped, however, that these discussions will help clarify the issues so that economic policymaking can be analysed with a more informed understanding of the issues.

JAMES P. PFIFFNER

Contributors

James E. Anderson is Professor of Political Science at the University of Houston. He is the author of *Politics and the Economy* (1966) and *Economic Policy-Making* (1970). His latest book is *Managing Macroeconomic Institutions: The Johnson Presidency*.

Gary Freeman is Associate Professor of Government at the University of Texas at Austin. He is the author of *Immigrant Labor and Racial Conflict in Industrial Societies: The French and British Experience, 1945–75* and of articles on the politics of the welfare state in Europe and America.

Susan B. Hansen is Associate Professor of Political Science at the University of Pittsburgh. She has also taught at the University of Michigan, the University of Illinois and Washington State University. She is the author of *The Politics of Taxation* (1983) and of articles on taxation, public opinion and women's politics.

Charles E. Jacob is Professor of Political Science at Rutgers University. He is the author of *Leadership in the New Deal* (1967), *Politics in New Jersey* (1979) and *The Election of 1980* (1981).

William R. Keech is Professor of Political Science at the University of North Carolina at Chapel Hill. He is author of *The Impact of Negro Voting: The Role of the Vote in the Quest for Equality* (1968, 1981) and co-author of *The Party's Choice* (1977). His teaching and research interests are in the theory and practice of representative government.

James P. Pfiffner is Associate Professor of Public Affairs at George Mason University. He has worked at the U.S. Office of Personnel Management and has been a Research Fellow at the Brookings Institution. He is the author of *The President, the Budget, and Congress: Impoundment and the 1974 Budget Act* (1979), *Taking Over the Government: Presidential Transitions since 1960* (1985), and of articles on the presidency, public management and the budgetary process.

Alberta M. Sbragia is Associate Professor of Political Science and Director of the West European Studies Program at the University of Pittsburgh. She is the editor of *The Municipal Money Chase: The Politics of Local Government Finance* and of a forthcoming book on the relationship between local governments and the financial community in the United States and Britain. She has been a Visiting Research Fellow at the Centre for the Study of Public Policy at Strathclyde University in Glasgow, and she was Visiting Professor at the Harvard School of Business in 1983 and 1984.

M. Stephen Weatherford is Associate Professor of Political Science at the University of California, Santa Barbara. He is the author of *Presidential Control of the Economy* (1985) and of several articles on the interplay of economic policy and political interests.

John F. Witte is an Assistant Professor in the Political Science Department and the Center for Public Policy and Administration at the University of Wisconsin-Madison. He is author of *Democracy, Authority and Alienation in Work* (1980) and *The Politics and Development of the Federal Income Tax* (1985).

John T. Woolley teaches in the Political Science Department at Washington University, St. Louis. He has been a Research Fellow at the Brookings Institution and a Research Assistant at the Woodrow Wilson International Center for Scholars. He is the author of *Monetary Politics* (1984) and of several articles on the politics of macroeconomic policy.

Contents

Introduction: The Crisis of Confidence in U.S. Economic Policy

JAMES P. PFIFFNER

During the 1980s the United States has experienced a crisis of confidence in economic policymaking that went beyond the dismal economic performance of 1981 and 1982. Economic performance depends as much on the expectations of investors and consumers as it does on physical infrastructure. The crisis of confidence was due to unrealistic expectations on the part of the public, overpromising on the part of presidential candidates, and the failure of the president and Congress to choose among competing fiscal policy priorities.

This chapter will examine public expectations and presidential promises and how they foster delusions of a quick fix for our economy and the consequent refusal to make hard choices. It will then trace how the U.S. came to have a $200 billion deficit along with 10 percent unemployment and the greatest number of business failures since the Great Depression. Economic recovery in the 1980s called for choosing among fiscal priorities, and several alternatives will be examined in tax policy, the social security system and defense policy. Finally, some of the dilemmas facing the U.S. in monetary policy and the international arena will be discussed.

The author would like to thank John Erickson, Pat McInturff, John Odell and Michael Reagan for comments on an earlier version of this chapter.

THE PUBLIC AND UNREALISTIC EXPECTATIONS

National public opinion polls have shown a marked disaffection with government institutions and policies over the past several decades. Those who trust the government to do right always or most of the time dropped 43 points from the 1960s to the 1970s. Americans believe that government is too big and taxes are too high. When asked whether overall government spending should be reduced, consistent majorities reply in the affirmative, but when presented with specific policy trade-offs, the majority of respondents reply that the government spends too little in most policy areas (only foreign aid, welfare and space exploration are losers). Thus Americans want lower taxes, but are not willing to cut spending.

This contradiction might be explained in part by the public's belief that the federal government wastes a lot of money. This belief is fostered by a constant parade of politicians all campaigning on the platform that government is wasteful and that they will clean up the mess as soon as they are elected. These people are bound to be disappointed when they get the chance to put their ideas into action. David Stockman, President Reagan's Director of the Office of Management and Budget, complained in 1981 that he had to educate the people in the White House about the realities of budget cutting: if you want to produce significant savings, you have to cut programs. "They really thought you could find $144 billion worth of waste, fraud and abuse."[1] How can the American people be faulted for believing that budget cutting can be painless if the people in the White House believe it? This is not to imply that waste or slack does not exist in government. The point is that sometimes it is hard to find, must often be dealt with at the micro-level, and frequently masks differences of opinion about priorities.

A more likely explanation for the contradiction in the public mind between wanting increased services with lower overall spending is that most people think that some public programs constitute a "waste" of tax dollars. That is, some people believe that the very fact that the government is involved in some policy areas, whether subsidies to business or welfare or foreign aid, constitutes a waste of the taxpayers' money, whether or not the program itself is well or poorly managed. Thus many assertions that the government "wastes" money are merely disagreements about public policy priorities. A more widespread recognition of this would greatly clarify public debate.

The tax revolt of the late seventies grew out of the widespread belief that difficult choices among priorities were not necessary. In part voters and public officials were reacting to very real growth of governmental taxes and spending, but the tax revolt also reflected the unrealistic expectations that taxes could be cut with little impact on public services.

California rode the crest of the tax revolt with its passage of Proposition 13, the initiative that constitutionally cut local property taxes by half. More than 25 states imposed property tax limits on local governments during the 1970s, and nine indexed their state tax systems to the consumer price index. At least 12 states limited their increase of expenditures to some specified rate or the increase in some economic indicator. With the recession of the early 1980s, many states had to backtrack because of decreased revenues and increased expenditures. Cutting taxes during a period of economic expansion may not prepare revenue systems for the decreased revenues and greater welfare payments of recessionary periods. Forty states have raised taxes since 1978. By 1983 California was faced with a $1 to $2 billion deficit which was not paid back until the economic recovery in 1984.

The main focus of the tax revolt at the federal level was the campaign to amend the constitution to require the balancing of the federal budget each fiscal year. In 1985, 32 of the 34 states necessary had passed resolutions calling for a constitutional convention to consider such an amendment. In 1982, the Senate passed a resolution calling for a balanced budget amendment. The House, however, failed to pass the resolution during the 97th Congress.

While many objections were raised to the proposed amendment, the most serious was that it would deprive the country of one of the few weapons it has to fight a declining economy. In a recession, in order to pump more money into the economy to stimulate production and put idle workers and factories back to work, the government spends more than it receives in revenues, thus causing a deficit. Without this option the economy in a recession might slide into a depression. While President Reagan presided over the largest deficits in U.S. history and argued that any increase in taxes to reduce them would slow the economy further, he nevertheless endorsed the Senate's proposal to amend the constitution.

Using what John Kenneth Galbraith has called the "archeological excuse," presidents tend to blame the state of the economy on their predecessors. Both Presidents Carter and Reagan took office declaring that they inherited the worst economic situation since the Great Depression. They were both right in claiming not to have created the economies they inherited; there is plenty of blame to go around. But blaming the state of the economy on one's predecessor tempts presidential candidates to think they can control the budget and economy, and as we have seen, this is hubris.

What happened in the seventies and early eighties should provide a lesson in politics as well as economics. Voters may react as they have in the past and look for a new candidate who will promise another economic panacea. But a new realism should set in that neither presidents nor the U.S. government can fully control the economy, and that promises to do so are overblown. This does not mean that voters should not hold presidents responsible for their economic policies; they should. But we should not expect a "quick fix," and presidential candidates should not promise one. The question is whether a politician who promises less can get elected.

After leaving office and reflecting back on his presidency, Jimmy Carter judged that the worst part of being president is "the complexity of the job versus the demand for simplistic answers from the public and media."[2] But can any candidate resist such simplicities and still be elected? We must expect more from both voters and candidates in order to answer in the affirmative.

THE PRESIDENCY AND OVERPROMISING

The United States has come to expect leadership from the president in times of crisis, and the economic situation in this decade certainly qualifies as a crisis. But have contemporary presidents provided the sort of leadership that is required, and if not, why not? The answer is that they have not, and the reason is a combination of overexpectation on the part of the public and inflated promises on the part of presidential candidates.

The federal government has taken an active role in the U.S. economy since the 1930s, and the Employment Act of 1946 formalized that role. The optimism that the economy could be "fine-tuned" with the use of fiscal tools guided by Keynesian theory was dispersed when the 1970s brought "stagflation"—rising inflation and low economic growth at the same time.

Public expectations of what the government and the president could do reached a high point with the promise of the Great Society to win the war against deep-seated social problems such as poverty, hunger, racism, ill health and illiteracy. Disillusionment set in when these problems persisted despite high levels of federal spending. The national traumas of the Vietnam war and Watergate produced a reaction against the "imperial presidency."

Presidential candidate Jimmy Carter, riding the tide of discontent, campaigned against big government and the Washington insiders. He promised honesty, reform and a balanced budget by the end of his first term. There was no hint that the U.S. economy might be driven by forces that a president could not control. But a stimulative fiscal policy to get the country out of the 1974–75 recession and a second oil shock in 1979 left President Carter with a deficit that could not be reduced, much less eliminated, during his first term.

Conservative Republican Ronald Reagan campaigned against President Carter in several important ways that were similar in approach if not in degree to those of candidate Carter. He ran as an outsider against the "mess" in Washington and promised to balance the budget by the end of his first term. He argued that government itself was part of the problem and that its functions should be cut back in principle, as well as in order to save money. One of this main themes was that President Carter had mishandled the economy. He cited rising inflation and asked whether voters felt better off in 1980 than they did before Carter took office. The assertion was that Carter was responsible for the state of the economy, and the implication was that a President *could* control the economy, if he only chose wise policies.

This exaggeration of the possibilities of presidential power led candidate Reagan to promise that he could return the nation to economic growth and a balanced budget. His formula for an economic turnaround included a large income tax cut, reduced spending on social programs, greatly increased defense spending, and a restrictive monetary policy to keep the lid on inflation. Within his first eight months in office President Reagan was successful in getting Congress to pass virtually all of his economic program, but by 1982 the early optimism about the president's ability to control the economy had dissipated in the deepest recession since the thirties.

The main reason that presidents cannot control their budgets is that they cannot control the economy which greatly affects the government's budget and determines the size of the deficit. Yet in trying to get their budget proposals passed, presidents make optimistic assumptions about the performance of the economy and ignore the

effect of economic performance on uncontrollable government expenditures. Since the level of revenues, expenditures and the deficit
are so dependent on the performance of the economy, they make
optimistic assumptions about the future in order to minimize the size
of the deficit. Presidents Ford, Carter and Reagan all consistently
based their budget proposals on assumptions that turned out to be
overly optimistic.[3] That is, ironically, one of the factors that has bol-
stered the credibility of the Congressional Budget Office which has
often come up with economic projections that are more realistic than
those of the president and OMB.

The effect of the economy on uncontrollable expenditures is the
key reason that presidents cannot accurately predict the size of the
deficit for the next fiscal year. Uncontrollable spending consists of
prior year contracts, interest on the national debt and entitlement
spending. This third category includes social security, military and
civilian pension programs, and welfare expenditures, most of which
are indexed to the consumer price index. Expenditures for these programs cannot be reduced without changes in the law, and they are
very volatile because expenditures depend on the state of the economy. As inflation increases, so do benefits.

The rates of inflation, unemployment, interest and GNP growth
have a great, and largely uncontrollable, impact on the size of the
budget. For instance, when the rate of inflation in 1981 rose by 1
percent, outlays in 1982 increased by about $6 billion. An increase in
unemployment by 1 percent added about $9 billion to outlays due to
increased unemployment benefits paid out, as well as increased outlays for social security, food stamps and public assistance. But increasing unemployment has a compounding effect on the deficit by
decreasing tax revenues at the same time spending goes up. Thus the
1 percent increase in unemployment could increase the deficit by $25
billion. The high interest rates which plagued the economy in the
early 1980s meant that the government had to pay more to finance the
national debt. A rise of interest rates of 1 percent in 1981 meant an
increase in outlays for 1982 of $4.5 billion.[4]

As the economy is caught in a syndrome of increasing inflation,
unemployment and interest rates, it also faces decreased economic
growth. When the economy expands it can absorb increased outlays
without too much dislocation, but when total production does not
grow, the effect can be devastating to the federal budget. The impact
of a 1 percent decrease in growth can increase the deficit by $19 billion
because of fewer taxes paid and greater outlays for unemployment

and other programs. National budget-making suffers from the inability to predict the performance of these economic indicators.

HOW THE U.S. CAME TO HAVE A $200 BILLION DEFICIT

During most of its history the United States has balanced its budget and has run deficits primarily in times of war or recession. The acceptance of Keynesian economics early in this century led to the belief that deficits were useful economic tools that could be used to stimulate a slack economy and put unused resources back to work. A corollary to this was that when the economy recovered and full employment was approached, the budget should run a surplus in order to pull money out of the economy and dampen inflationary tendencies. Thus the budget was to be balanced over business cycles, not necessarily every fiscal year.

The problem was that after 1950 the budget seldom ran a surplus, in good economic times or bad. Democrats traditionally argued that deficits were not inherently inflationary and that the national debt was decreasing from the post-World War II level of 80 percent of GNP. President Johnson refused to make the difficult choice between guns for the Vietnam war and the butter of his Great Society, and his tax surcharge came too late. Running deficits (despite a small surplus in 1969) during this period of relatively high employment (unemployment averaged 3.6 percent), along with an accommodating monetary policy, touched off the inflationary spiral that was not completely broken until the recession of 1981–82.

Traditional fiscal conservatives and Republicans have consistently denounced deficit spending by the federal government. When President Nixon was in office, he tried to control inflation by wage and price controls, but when they were lifted, inflation resumed, greatly aggravated by the rise in oil prices engineered by the Organization of Petroleum Exporting Countries (OPEC) cartel. President Ford fought the inflation with fiscal and monetary restraint, but the economy fell into what was then the worst recession since World War II with unemployment at 8.5 percent.

When President Carter took office, he pursued a stimulative fiscal policy that brought unemployment down to 5.8 percent in 1979, but which also helped increase inflation to 9 percent in 1978, and after the second oil shock, to over 12 percent. During this time Ronald Reagan and other fiscal conservatives were lambasting the Democrats for their fiscal policy which ran deficits that the Republicans said directly led to inflation. They argued that deficit spending absorbed investment capital that could be used for industrial expansion in the private sector. Heavy borrowing by the government also put a high demand on financial markets and caused interest rates, already high because of inflation, to rise. These were the arguments of traditional fiscal conservatives in the U.S., and they helped Ronald Reagan defeat Jimmy Carter in 1980. Then came the great supply-side conversion of Ronald Reagan.

During his 1980 campaign for the presidency Reagan embraced the supply-side proposals of economist Arthur Laffer and Congressman Jack Kemp. They originally advocated an income tax cut of 33 percent. Instead of increasing the deficit by decreasing revenues, the tax cut was supposed to stimulate investment and production in the private sector and thereby increase revenues from the taxes generated by the economic expansion. Thus deficit spending in the short run would be quickly wiped out. With increasing productivity and monetary restraint, inflation would fall and interest rates would quickly follow. When President Reagan took office, he staffed important economic posts with economists who believed in the supply-side predictions.

Economic policy in the first year of the Reagan administration was based on the optimistic predictions of the supply-siders, despite warnings from economists from the traditional liberal and conservative perspectives. When David Stockman ran the initial budget data with econometric models that contained the built-in assumptions of mainstream economists, the projected deficits came out too high. So he inserted into the models the much more optimistic assumptions of the supply-side economists.[5] The new projections were used to defend and pass the administration's budget and economic program for fiscal year 1982.

The Reagan budget program that was finally enacted called for the largest peacetime arms spending program in history ($1.6 billion over five years), the largest tax cut in history ($750 billion over five years), and the largest cuts in social programs in U.S. history. All of this was promised with an FY 1982 deficit of $45 billion that was to shrink to 0 in 1984. The problem was that the economy did not react the way the supply-siders predicted, and the economic program began to unravel almost as soon as it was passed.

The monetary part of the plan called for restraint from the Federal Reserve Board to keep the supply of money growing at a moderate pace so that inflation would not increase from the stimulative fiscal policy. The combination of a tight monetary policy and high interest rates (with the prime rate at 20 percent in the spring of 1981) slowed the economy so suddenly that it fell into the deepest recession in half a century. Inflation was brought down to about 5 percent in 1982, but interest rates remained artifically high because lenders feared a quick reflation of the economy. Unemployment zoomed to more than 10 percent along with the greatest number of business failures since the Great Depression.

In 1982, it became clear to many that the supply-side miracle was not going to happen. Due to the recession and the Reagan fiscal policies, the deficit for FY 1982 was $110.7 billion and the projections for FY 1983 and 1984 were about $200 billion. The administration's fiscal posture was such that not even an economic recovery would significantly reduce the deficit. For the first time optimistic economic forecasts did not promise a balanced budget in the near future. The national debt, which passed the $1 trillion mark in 1981, threatened to double by the end of the decade.

When Martin Feldstein took over as the Chairman of President Reagan's Council on Economic Advisers, he warned that the growing deficits of the Reagan administration must be curbed. "We now see that unless there is dramatic action the U.S. will experience an unprecedented series of deficits during the years ahead. . . . The long-term consequences of such deficits are just not acceptable."[6] He argued that the high deficits would absorb funds needed for private sector investment. They would also keep interest rates high and strengthen the dollar, which would make U.S. goods more expensive in foreign markets and make foreign goods that much more attractive to U.S. buyers. This lower demand for U.S. goods would increase unemployment and the U.S. trade deficit. Feldstein backed off from the supply-side faith in "self-financing tax cuts,"[7] and criticized the supply-side and monetarist "extremists" who "predicted that inflation would be reduced without raising unemployment."[8] His CEA predecessor Murray Weidenbaum admitted that the belief that "the way to cut spending was by cutting taxes was wishful thinking."[9] President Reagan, however, resisted cuts in his defense buildup and any tax increases despite the consensus among many of his top aides that some flexibility was necessary.

Many economists argued that the $200 billion deficit was not dangerous to the economy as long as the recession lasted and there were slack resources. The danger was that as recovery progressed and only part of the deficit was eliminated, the remaining deficit of $100 to $200 billion would have inflationary and crowding-out effects, thus increasing interest rates and limiting investment in the private sector. A bipartisan group of former Cabinet members wrote an open letter to President Reagan in January 1983, urging him to take steps to reduce the deficit from 5.6 percent of GNP to 2 percent of GNP by 1988. They called for reductions in defense spending, cuts in entitlements and a consumption-based tax.[10]

FISCAL POLICY OPTIONS

Ronald Reagan had long led and echoed public feeling that taxes were too high, and when he came to office he made good on his promise to lower them. The Kemp-Roth proposal for cutting income taxes by 33 percent was modified to a cut of 25 percent spread over three years. Business depreciation allowances were greatly increased, and "tax leasing" allowed successful companies to reduce their tax burdens. The highest rate of tax on investment income was reduced from 70 to 50 percent, and the capital gains tax was further reduced. In addition individual tax brackets would be adjusted to correct for inflation, beginning in 1985, in order to eliminate "tax bracket creep." In the bidding war between Democrats and Republicans other provisions that were designed to help special interests were added to the Economic Recovery Tax Act of 1981. The total loss to the treasury would be more than $1 trillion from 1983 to 1988.[11]

In 1982 it became clear that the economic recovery promised by President Reagan's supply-side economists was not going to materialize and that deficits were going to be in the $200 billion range in 1983 and 1984. In the summer of 1982 President Reagan, despite his staunch stand against tax increases, was pursuaded by his advisors to push for a "revenue enhancement" that was enacted in August with bipartisan support in Congress. The Tax Equity and Fiscal Responsibility Act of 1982 restored about 25 percent of the revenue lost from the 1981 cuts, with about 55 percent of the revenue coming from the corporate tax reductions.

The projected gap between revenues and expenditures over the period 1983–88 exceeded $1 trillion, with a 1988 deficit of $249 billion, or more than 5 percent of GNP.[12] The Reagan administration's 1984 budget proposed to reduce this gap with tax increases and cuts from domestic spending, but included further increases in defense spending. The tax increases amounted to about $200 billion from 1984 to 1988, with $117 billion of it coming from a contingency income tax surcharge and an excise tax on oil to take effect if the projected budget deficit for 1986 exceeded 2.5 percent of GNP.[13] The rest would come from Social Security and other tax increases. The fiscal 1984 proposals also called for outlay reductions of about $130 billion over the four-year period, including about $90 billion in entitlement programs and $60 billion in non-defense discretionary spending. Defense spending would be increased by about $75 billion. These proposals would still leave an FY 1988 deficit of between $115 billion and $160 billion.[14]

Thus any attempt to reduce the projected deficit from 5.5 percent of GNP in 1988 to the 2 to 3 percent range would entail significant tax increases along with serious spending cuts. The following sections look at the two big-ticket items in the U.S. budget: Social Security and defense spending.

The Social Security System

The Social Security system of the 1980s bears little resemblance to the New Deal intention of supplementing private pensions and family savings; it now is the primary source of retirement income for many Americans, and it comprises 25 percent of the budget. Since 1935, Old Age and Survivors Insurance (OASI) has been supplemented twice: with Disability Insurance (DI) in 1956, and with Hospital Insurance (HI; Medicare) in 1965. The system is funded on a pay as you go basis, and benefits to individuals far exceed their contributions, in contrast to an annuity-type plan.

Over the years coverage of workers was expanded and benefits were greatly increased. In 1972 benefits were increased 20 percent (ironically to keep revenues from accumulating at too great a pace and causing a drag on the economy), and benefit levels were indexed to the consumer price index. These and several other factors explain the great growth of the social security system and why it was running out of money in the early 1980s. Demographic changes are a major factor. The ratio of workers to beneficiaries has decreased from 16 to 1 in 1940 to 3.3 to 1 in 1980; By 2035 it will be 2.0 to 1. In addition life expectancy past age 65 has increased from 12.3 years in 1940 to 16.6 years in 1980, and continues to improve. People are also retiring earlier, in part because of incentives built into the social security system. These factors have combined to produce a short-term financing crunch in the mid-1980s and a long-term imbalance that necessitates significant, though not necessarily drastic changes in benefits and financing.

The short-term crunch was a shortfall of $150 to $200 billion during the early 1980s that was due to the factors cited above, which were exacerbated by a deep recession that cut into the payroll taxes that finance the Social Security trust funds. In 1982 the OASI Trust Fund paid out more than it took in and had to borrow from the disability and hospital funds. The hospital trust fund was solvent in the early 1980s, but would be in critical trouble by the end of the decade unless some method were devised to contain hospital costs.

The long-run problem would become critical in the second decade of the next century when the ratio of workers to retirees will be less than 3 to 1. The accumulated reserve will hold the system together until about 2025 when there will be a large gap between income and benefit payouts (using the Social Security Commission's intermediate assumptions about economic growth, which some say are too optimistic).

There is a large range of alternative modifications to the system that would reduce the short- and long-term threats to its solvency. The main controversy is between those who want to increase Social Security payroll taxes (mostly Democrats) and those who want to reduce benefits (mostly Republicans). To deal with the short-run problem, tax increases scheduled to go into effect in 1990 could be moved up to 1984. These would have to be raised further in the coming century if benefits were not changed.

There are a number of options for decreasing benefits and phasing in the changes so that the elderly poor would not be hurt and the burden of benefit reductions could be distributed over several age groups. The yearly cost of living allowances could be indexed to the growth in wages or productivity rather than the CPI. This would make retired persons share the burden of a poorly performing economy and reduce the imbalance of income to benefits for the system when inflation rises faster than wages, as was the case in the later 1970s and early 1980s.

The retirement age could be increased gradually, at 3 months a year beginning in 1990, to 68. A portion of Social Security benefits could be subject to the income tax, as are private retirement systems. The rates could be set so that those in need would not be hurt. In addition federal and other government workers could be gradually integrated into the system. Some combination of the above options could be put together that would make the system solvent and protect those in greatest need.

The main obstacle to all of these changes is political. The elderly and others feel very insecure about Social Security benefits, and those opposing any change at all constitute a formidable political force, as President Reagan learned the hard way when his administration proposed benefit reductions in 1981 and was stopped by Congress. Some politicians have aggravated the situation by implying that their opponents wanted to scrap the whole system when in fact they had favored relatively minor benefit reductions.

Part of the problem is what Rudolph Penner calls the "Panama Canal Syndrome"—we bought it, we payed for it, and it's ours. The myth that retired persons are merely receiving what they paid into the system plus interest is fostered by using terms such as "insurance," "contributions" and "pension," when in fact Social Security is an intergenerational tax transfer program. Retired persons withdraw all that they contributed to the system within several years, and with average life expectancy, eventually receive many times what they contributed, particularly if they have dependents.

Another stumbling block to reform was the belief that most elderly people are poor. The percentage of elderly that have incomes below the poverty line has decreased from 35 percent in 1962 to 16 percent in 1982, due in part to Social Security benefits. And 20 percent of the elderly have family incomes over $30,000. But the main point here is that any reform of the benefit structure can, and should, make special provision for those in greatest need. Some fear that these changes will attach to Social Security the stigma of welfare. But the fact remains that Social Security retirees withdraw much more from the system than they contribute and that the taxes of the working generation provide the funds to finance the system. Unfortunately the issue has become so politicized that our ability to deal with the solvency of the system is in serious jeopardy.

The Greenspan Commission (the National Commission on Social Security Reform) appointed by President Reagan to propose a solution to the financing crisis announced its bipartisan plan in January 1983. The proposals would provide about $170 billion from 1983 to 1989. The changes included delaying the COLA (cost of living allowance) for six months, taxing some OASDI benefits of higher-income beneficiaries, speeding up scheduled tax increases, increasing tax rates for self-employed workers and including new federal employees in the system.[15] These proposals would deal with the OASDI financing crisis in the 1980s. The hospital insurance fund imbalance in the late 1980s and the long-range imbalance in the retirement funds were not addressed. Most of the Greenspan Commission proposals were adopted by Congress and signed by President Reagan.

Defense Spending

Defense spending as a percentage of total budget outlays had been slipping during the 1970s, and by the election of 1980 public opinion favored a defense buildup. President Reagan had campaigned on a platform of strengthening U.S. defense in order to close the "window of vulnerability." When President Carter proposed a 5 percent increase in his lameduck budget, Reagan upped his to 7 percent.[16] He was committed to sending a signal to the Soviet Union that the U.S. was willing to incur greatly increased defense expenditures. He argued that any meaningful negotiations between the two superpowers could only be made from a position of strength. What he proposed in 1981 was the greatest peacetime buildup of arms in U.S. history. The increase in spending authority of $1.6 trillion by 1986 amounted to more than a 7 percent real increase when inflation dropped sharply in 1982. Defense expenditures increased from $136 billion in 1980 to $187 billion in 1982, amounting to a 38 percent increase (12 percent in real terms). Budget authority (commitments for future spending) rose even faster.[17]

OMB Director David Stockman did not scrutinize the defense budget as much as he wanted to in 1981 when the initial Reagan budget was being prepared, and the Pentagon got what he termed a "blank check." After the initial budget battle was over, he intended to return to closer scrutiny of the Pentagon to attack what he thought was a "swamp of waste," and he had convinced several White House colleagues that some defense cuts were necessary, but he was not able to convince the president, who made the final decisions. He admitted that "the defense numbers got out of control. . . ."[18]

The big-ticket items in the defense budget included the MX missile (about $35 billion), the B-1B bomber (about $30 billion), the F-18 fighter (about $40 billion), the M-1 tank (about $20 billion) and the Nimitz-class aircraft carrier (about $10 billion). Research, development and production of these advanced defense systems amounted to a big chunk of the five year buildup. One of the problems with the scaling back of any of the defense increases is that the main costs for these systems fall in the "out years," that is, when they have been fully developed and production begins. Such cuts will not help reduce the deficit in the short run. Large short-term cuts would come in operations, maintenance and training which would reduce the readiness of U.S. forces. There was a general consensus in the defense community that this would be unwise.

But if we are going to reduce longer-term costs, reductions in budget authority must be made quickly, because the longer they are delayed the more wasteful it will be to change our minds. It will be argued that the sunk costs will be lost and unit costs will rise. Defense contractors will have geared up, and thousands of jobs will be at stake in many congressional districts.

The main criticisms of the Reagan defense buildup were that it was not focused and that it cost too much. Some critics argued that the Reagan administration merely let the services pursue their "wish lists" and failed to choose among competing priorities or make strategic choices other than increasing overall spending. Others argued that the speed of the buildup would create bottlenecks and inefficiencies in defense industries.

Even those who shared President Reagan's concern about U.S. defense readiness and favored significant increases in spending criticized him for going too far. They were concerned about the impact of large deficits on the economy, but they were also afraid that the president's rigidity and refusal to consider scaled-back increases in defense might destroy what former Defense Secretary Harold Brown called the "fragile consensus" that an arms buildup was necessary. They feared that widespread public support for increased defense spending could easily be reversed if the public came to view defense spending as the main threat to economic recovery. Such a reaction could result in roller-coaster spending on defense, which in their view would be worse than a slower, steady buildup of 3 to 5 percent sustained over a number of years.

William Kaufman, a defense analyst at the Brookings Institution, summed up the feelings of many critics by relating the story that John Jacob Astor said to the bartender when the Titanic hit the iceberg: "I asked for ice, but this is ridiculous."[19]

IMPROVING ECONOMIC PERFORMANCE

Monetary Policy

The main dilemma of monetary policy, and of the Federal Reserve Board which makes it, is how to engineer the delicate balance of allowing the money supply to grow enough to foster economic ex-

pansion but not fast enough to spur inflation to unacceptable levels
This was a particularly vexing problem during the seventies when the
U.S. experienced "stagflation"—rising inflation in a period of reces
sion. The main tools of the Fed and its Open Market Committee are
the buying and selling of U.S. securities and the setting of the dis
count rate in order to control the money supply.

The oil shock of 1973 and an expansive fiscal policy (defici
spending) created inflationary pressure in the U.S. economy. The Fed
"accommodated" these pressures by increasing the supply of money
and the federal government tried to fight the deepening recession by
a stimulative fiscal policy. The result was a growing inflation that
topped 12 percent in 1979 and 1980.

When Paul Volcker was appointed Chairman of the Fed in 1979,
he promised to try to bring inflation down by strict control of the
money supply rather than by trying to maintain interest rates at a
particular level. The new Reagan administration approved of this
restrictive monetary policy and saw it as an important part of its
overall economic program. Control of the money supply would keep
inflation down while the government was pursuing an expansive
fiscal policy through decreased revenues and greatly increased defense spending that was only partially offset by domestic spending
cuts.

The result of high deficits and the continued tight monetary policy was high interest rates, with the prime rate at 20 percent in January 1981. These high interest rates played a major role in reduced
economic activity; factories were running at less than 75 percent of
capacity, unemployment rose to more than 10 percent and businesses
were failing in record numbers. The auto, steel and housing industries were particularly hard hit.

With the economy in such bad shape there were increasing calls
from both ends of the political spectrum to force the Fed to expand
the money supply more rapidly. Supply-siders felt the tight monetary
policy had undermined the recovery they had promised, and liberals
felt that the level of unemployment was too high a price to pay for
reducing inflation. Each felt that in a slack economy increasing the
money supply posed no great threat of renewing inflation immediately.

There have been calls in the past for increased responsiveness of
the Fed to the Congress or the president, particularly in bad economic
times. But these threats to rein in the Fed have been backed by little
follow through. In part this is because the Fed was deliberately designed to be independent, with board members serving fixed terms of

14 years. This structure was meant to remove it from "politics," to let the "technical experts" make monetary decisions and to absorb political hostility that would otherwise be directed at the officials in the two elected branches. Another reason that past efforts at control have not been enacted is that the Fed does not act all that independently, despite the outcries of those who disagree with it. The Chairman of the Fed has often consulted with presidents and members of Congress.[20] As Herbert Stein has said, from the perspective of the executive branch: "the Federal Reserve is an independent duchy but shouldn't be confused with such foreign powers as the House Ways and Means Committee or the Kremlin. The Fed keeps in touch and wants to get along."[21]

Some of the more strident cries for reigning in the Fed were blunted in the fall of 1982 when, in a series of decisions, it dropped the discount rate to 8.5 percent, the lowest it had been in four years. These changes were meant to bring down interest rates and help the economy recover, though fears of inflation still kept interest rates artificially high. The Fed then faced again the major dilemma of monetary policy: how can the money supply be expanded enough to expand the economy yet not relight the fires of inflation.

International Economics

The U.S. economy is not an island; it is tied to other countries in a seamless web of mutual obligations. The recovery of the U.S. economy is dependent on the recovery of the world economy, including both industrialized and lesser developed countries, and vice versa. Two major threats faced the world economy in the 1980s: weakness and exposure in the international banking system and the danger of snowballing protectionism.

The threat to the world banking system had its roots in the OPEC decision to increase oil prices in 1973. The great sums of money flowing into the OPEC nations could not be entirely absorbed and were "recycled" to developing countries through the large banks in developed countries. In the rush to get in on the action, many banks overextended themselves and made risky loans, thus "exposing" themselves to large decreases in their own assets if the loans went into default. The loans caused the economies in developing countries to grow and prosper in the later 1970s.

But at the same time the outflow of money from the U.S. to pay for the higher-priced oil and an accommodating monetary policy and expansive fiscal policy caused inflation to grow at unacceptable levels. Then after the second oil shock of 1979 the Fed decided to strictly control the money supply in the U.S., which—along with the expansive fiscal policy of the early 1980s—caused interest rates to rise and the economy to slow down.

The higher interest rates in the U.S. attracted capital from other countries and lowered demand for commodities from Third World countries. The reduced demand and lower prices combined with the higher cost of loans put pressure on the finances of the developing countries, causing them to refinance their loans from the banks of the developed countries. Many of these banks had high percentages of their total equity tied up in these loans, and a default on major international loans might have threatened their viability. Several such defaults could cause a chain reaction and collapse of the world banking system. Banks could not afford to foreclose on the loans or allow the countries (or private institutions within them) to default, and further loans with stretched out repayment schedules were necessary to maintain the system. As John Maynard Keynes observed, "Owe your banker one thousand pounds and you are at his mercy. Owe him one million and the position is reversed."[22]

The political question arose of whether and to what extent the U.S. Treasury should bail out countries likely to default on loans from U.S. banks. Some argued that the banks made the risky loans and ought to bear the cost of their bad judgments. The problem was that any default by a large borrower could significantly reduce the total equity of a bank which could lead to difficulties in meeting its own obligations and to its possible failure. This in turn could cause a chain reaction of bank failures. Those favoring U.S. subsidies said that letting countries default on their loans would be like shooting ourselves in the foot since a run on the banks could trigger a depression as happened in the 1930s.

The only way out of the morass was a recovery of the U.S. and world economies. But recovery was threatened by the specter of world trade protectionism. During periods of recession the sentiment for protectionism is high. When people are out of work and plants are closing, the tendency is to blame foreign imports for the slowdown in domestic sales, and there is resentment of the subsidies that some governments give to their export businesses. In the long run protective tariffs amount to subsidies of some domestic industries by consumers and other businesses, and may remove incentives to modernize and increase efficiency.

But the more dangerous and immediate threat from protectionism is that when tariffs are provided for one industry, it is difficult to rgue that others cannot have the same protection. In response other ountries are likely to impose tariffs of their own. The compounding f such reciprocal actions is difficult to stop once it has begun. The ventual result could be a reduction in world trade leading to the ollapse of the world economy. At a time when unemployment in the Vest is relatively high, politicians must resist the siren call of protec-ionism. If the world is not to be plunged into another great depres-ion, the U.S. and international economies must recover before the negative spiral of protectionism goes too far.

Another threat to the international system stems from the effects of exchange rates. In the early 1980s the U.S. dollar was very strong, nd many argued "overvalued," vis-á-vis the major world currencies. his was due in part to high interest rates in the U.S. that attracted oreign capital and also to economic conditions in other countries.

While a strong U.S. dollar is good for U.S. tourists who can buy oreign goods relatively cheaply, it is bad for export industries be-ause U.S. goods are costly in relation to foreign products. This has he double effect of making U.S. goods less attractive to other coun-ries and making their goods very attractive to U.S. consumers. The onsequence is large trade deficits and fewer jobs for American work-rs. The trade deficit in 1982 was more than $40 billion, one of the argest in U.S. history. Thus the irony of a strong U.S. dollar is that it nurts the economy by cutting jobs dependent on exports and may ndirectly encourage demands for protectionism, which just make natters worse.[23] Unfortunately, there is not much that can be done lirectly to alleviate the situation, though lower interest rates in the J.S. would help.[24]

CONCLUSION

The U.S. economy was in a state of turmoil in the early 1980s. Among he longer-range causes were raging inflation stemming from external il shocks, the expansive fiscal policies of the sixties and seventies, and rapidly growing entitlement expenditures. Among the im-nediate causes of the crisis were the deep recession of 1981–82 and he projected $200 billion deficits due to large tax cuts and sharply ncreased defense expenditures. The underlying political causes were overpromising politicians and voters with unrealistic expectations. In addition there were very real disagreements over economic priorities and conceptual confusion about solutions, even among those in agreement on goals. This chapter has outlined some of the causes and consequences of these economic and political problems.

NOTES

1. William Greider, "The Education of David Stockman," *The Atlantic* (December 1981), p. 43.

2. *Los Angeles Times* (November 16, 1982), Part V, p. 1.

3. See Rudolph G. Penner, "Forecasting Budget Totals: Why Can't We Get it Right?" in Michael J. Boskin and Aaron Wildavsky, eds., *The Federal Budget: Economics and Politics* (San Francisco: Institute for Contemporary Studies, 1982), p. 89.

4. See *Budget of the U.S. Government: Fiscal Year 1982*, pp. 59–60.

5. Greider, p. 32.

6. *The Wall Street Journal* (November 10, 1982), p. 3.

7. *The Wall Street Journal* (December 21, 1982), p. 1.

8. *The New York Times* (November 17, 1982), p. 10.

9. *The New York Times* (November 17, 1982), p. 10.

10. *The New York Times* (January 20, 1983), p. 1.

11. Congressional Budget Office, *Reducing the Deficit: Spending and Revenue Options* (February 1983), p. 230.

12. Congressional Budget Office, February 1985.

13. Congressional Budget Office, *An Analysis of the President's Budgetary Proposals for Fiscal Year 1984* (February 1983), Chapter 1.

14. *An Analysis of the President's Budgetary Proposals, p. 10.*

15. For cost estimates of these proposals, see *Reducing the Deficit: Spending and Revenue Options*, Chapter 3.

16. Steven R. Weisman, "Reaganomics and the President's Men," *The New York Times Magazine* (October 24, 1982), p. 26.

17. Congressional Budget Office, *Reducing the Deficit* (February 10, 1983), p. 28.

18. Greider, p. 40.

19. Joseph A. Pechman, *Setting National Priorities: The 1983 Budget* (Washington, D.C.: The Brookings Institution, 1982), p. 99.

20. See John T. Woolley, *Monetary Politics: The Federal Reserve and the Politics of Monetary Policy* (New York: Cambridge University Press, 1984).

21. *Fortune* (September 6, 1982), p. 39.

22. *The Wall Street Journal* (February 24, 1983), p. 27.

23. See C. Fred Bergsten, "What to Do About the U.S.-Japan Economic Conflict," *Foreign Affairs* (Summer 1982), p. 1059.

24. For an excellent analysis of many of the issues dealt with in the last two sections, see John Odell, *U.S. International Monetary Policy* (Princeton, N.J.: Princeton University Press, 1982).

THE PUBLIC &
ECONOMIC POLICY

2

Elections and Macroeconomic Policy

WILLIAM R. KEECH

Recent work on politics and macroeconomic policy has significantly advanced our understanding of the relationship between electoral incentives and the desirability of public policy, one of the central questions of political science. Specifically, both economists and political scientists have been investigating the possibility that elected officials yield to narrow or short-run political goals in guiding the economy, rather than effectively seeking to enhance the general welfare. These studies also suggest ways to consider the possibility that "politics" may be responsible for the high levels of inflation and unemployment and the low levels of income growth we have experienced in the last decade or so.

Empirical analyses have left most of the relevant questions unresolved, but this literature provides us with a more sophisticated grasp of the issues. The first section of this chapter reviews several rationales for expecting cynical manipulation of the economy according to an electoral cycle, and the second reviews some of the empirical evidence. The third section identifies two ways in which short-run political incentives may lead to adverse long-run trends, and the final section offers concluding observations.

Research for this chapter was supported in part by a grant from the National Science Foundation.

RATIONALES FOR POLITICALLY INDUCED ECONOMIC CYCLES

A central theme in recent studies has been the possibility that economic cycles are created by politicians who used them to enhance their prospects of reelection. This idea is of course in stark contrast to the view that politicians try to smooth out business cycles and to keep the economy on a path of steady growth. There are two basic kinds of rationales for politically induced business cycles. One kind is abstract and theoretical, and the other is more loosely grounded in common sense.

Commonsense Rationales

Probably the most widely discussed rationale for the existence of political manipulation of the economy is that expressed by Edward Tufte. He suggests that "incumbents may seek to determine the location and timing of economic benefits in promoting the fortunes of their party and friends" because they believe that "short-run spurts in economic growth in the months immediately preceding an election" can benefit them, perhaps tipping the balance and deciding a close election in their favor.[1]

Martin Paldam presents other less cynical commonsense rationales for a cyclical pattern of economic activity wherein the cycles follow electoral periods.[2] An expansion in the second year of an electoral term might result from the government's activity in carrying out the promises it made in the preceding electoral campaign, many of which are likely to imply government expenditure and economic stimulus. Alternatively, many kinds of programs designed to deal with economic problems might imply austerity or belt-tightening early in the term, which is designed to bring about better conditions later, and hopefully by election time. Most programs designed to bring down inflation or to increase future consumption by increasing present investment would have this character. They can be defended on general welfare grounds and do not necessarily involve cynical political manipulation. This sort of "things will get worse for a while so they can get better later" philosophy seems to have been part of Prime Minister Margaret Thatcher's policies, and it may be used to defend President Reagan's.

These commonsense views represent a mixed set of plausible reasons for a cyclical pattern in economic variables following electoral periods. Any one of them might take place from time to time without any necessity that they occur all of the time. However, it is difficult to analyze the consequences of such behavior if the rationale is loosely formulated.

A Theoretical Rationale

More rigorous ideas do exist on this topic; the leading example is William Nordhaus's theory of the "political business cycle."[3] The Nordhaus model is based more on assumptions and mathematical argument than on common sense. While it simplifies reality in a way that may be at odds with common sense, its rigor enables us to learn more than common sense can teach us.

Nordhaus assumes that politicians maximize a single goal, their vote in the next election. He assumes further that votes are a function of inflation and unemployment, which are controlled by the incumbent president subject to real world economic constraints. Voters are assumed to make their choices on the basis of a retrospective evaluation of economic performance in the electoral term preceding the election, and they are assumed to have better memories of the recent past than of what happened early in the term. Because of these assumed features of voting behavior, and because of the way the economic constraints limit political control of the economy, the vote-maximizing politician may create a recession early in his term in order to facilitate unsustainably low combinations of unemployment and inflation later in the term. In other words, short-sighted voters are fooled into giving the incumbent more votes than he would deserve on the basis of equal weighting of the entire term.

The Nordhaus theory makes demanding assumptions which we may find a caricature of reality, but it enables us to analyze the consequences of a kind of behavior we may find in the real world. Furthermore, it is so precisely formulated as to facilitate more rigorous thinking about the nature and consequences of political manipulation. For example, Nordhaus presents a precise conceptualization not only of votes, but also of welfare (or public well-being) as functions of unemployment and inflation. He gives us a basis for comparing policies chosen to maximize votes with policies chosen to maximize welfare. In effect he provides a practical definition of "the public interest" in the context of macroeconomic policy, as well as a basis for assessing the costs for public well-being of narrow political motivation.

Furthermore, Nordhaus shows how votes (or welfare) might be maximized subject to real world limitations. Everyone knows that not all economic outcomes are possible, and Nordhaus gives us a specific statement of the nature of the possibilities. Specifically, he takes into account what contemporary macroeconomists agree is the nature of the relationship between unemployment and inflation: while there may be a short-run trade-off between the two, unemployment below a "natural rate" is not sustainable without accelerating inflation (see Table 2-1). Thus Nordhaus gives us a precise way of thinking about real world limitations on the possibilities of maximizing either votes or welfare, and he gives us a precise way of seeing how much political support or welfare is possible under these constraints.

TABLE 2-1.   Political Implications of the Natural Rate of Unemployment Hypothesis

This table is based on the equation $I = 7 - U + E$, where I is inflation, U is unemployment, and E is expected inflation. Expected inflation is defined here simply as last year's inflation. The equation is interpreted below to show that unemployment may be manipulated in the short run, but that doing so has both immediate and lasting consequences for inflation. The only unemployment rate compatible with a sustained absence of inflation is the natural rate, which is 7 percent in this example.

Year	$I = 7 - U + E$	Comment
1	$0 = 7 - 7 + 0$	Both inflation and expected inflation are zero, with unemployment at the natural rate.
2	$1 = 7 - 6 + 0$	A reduction is unemployment below the natural rate brings immediate inflation.
3	$2 = 7 - 6 + 1$	Leaving U below the natural rate makes inflation continue to rise.
4	$4 = 7 - 5 + 2$	A further drop in U brings accelerating inflation.
5	$4 = 7 - 7 + 4$	Returning U to the natural rate merely stops the increase in inflation. It does not end inflation.
6	$4 = 7 - 7 + 4$	
7	$3 = 7 - 8 + 4$	
8	$2 = 7 - 8 + 3$	Sustained unemployment above the natural rate may be necessary to eliminate inflation.
9	$1 = 7 - 8 + 2$	
10	$0 = 7 - 8 + 1$	
11	$-1 = 7 - 8 + 0$	
12	$-2 = 7 - 8 - 1$	
13	$0 = 7 - 5 - 2$	A recession early in an electoral term can make possible unsustainably low combinations of inflation and unemployment just before an election.
ELECTION		
14	$2 = 7 - 5 - 0$	
15	$4 = 7 - 5 + 2$	

Using Theory and Common Sense

In making his theory mathematically tractable, Nordhaus makes some simplifications that we may find hard to accept, such as the assumptions that a president can precisely control the level and timing of unemployment rates, and that he does so in a way that maximizes votes in the next election. Tufte is more realistic in that he recognizes the complex institutional structure through which economic policy decisions are made, that elected officials directly control only policy *instruments* such as transfer payments and tax rates, and that policy *outcomes* such as unemployment are affected indirectly at best. Furthermore, he recognizes that not all politicians necessarily have the same objectives, explicitly arguing that President Eisenhower did not seek the short-run pre-election spurts in economic growth that Tufte attributes to other presidents.

However, while Tufte has an advantage over Nordhaus in describing reality, Nordhaus secures important advantages with his simplified mathematical version of reality. First of all he is able to recognize explicitly the nature of real world economic constraints on politicians' ability to control the variables which influence votes. These constraints are represented in two equations which show exactly how the choices of unemployment affect present and future inflation rates. Since inflation as well as unemployment affects votes, Nordhaus can show how the politician who is interested in maximizing votes can take all of this into account in making his policy choices.

Moreover, the precise mathematical formulation provides the tools for asking further questions regarding issues such as the long-run consequences for welfare and for votes of repeated vote maximizing, and such as the length of the electoral term which would minimize the welfare costs of vote maximizing. While the answers generated may be limited by the assumptions on which the model is built, a theoretical model facilitates asking as well as answering more questions.

EVIDENCE REGARDING POLITICALLY INDUCED ECONOMIC CYCLES

Now that we are informed and guided by both theory and common sense, we can briefly consider some of the evidence regarding political manipulation of the economy, looking first for cyclical patterns in macroeconomic outcomes such as inflation, unemployment and income growth, the variables about which voters are presumed to care. Then we will look for evidence of cyclical patterns in the economic instruments, the variables that politicians directly control.

Outcome Cycles

The evidence regarding the existence of outcome cycles is thoroughly mixed and does not provide a strong basis for making a case that macroeconomic outcomes are systematically manipulated for political purposes. About as many authors find that the evidence does not support cyclical patterns as find that it does.[4] However, we should not expect conclusive evidence about politicians' behavior in the study of economic outcomes, which are influenced by many things besides their political choices, such as droughts and OPEC. Politicians may have tried to manipulate economic outcomes with incomplete success due to these other factors. A more direct way to address the question is to look at the instruments of economic policy which government does directly control, such as monetary and fiscal policy.

Fiscal Instrument Cycles

Tufte argues that the central way in which politicians manipulate real disposable income, an outcome important to voters, is through government control of transfer payments. "The quickest way to produce an acceleration in real disposable income is for the government to mail more people larger checks."[5] He finds that Social Security is the main transfer program subject to such manipulation, while Winters and his coworkers raise questions about such findings.[6]

More statistically sophisticated efforts to identify cycles in the instruments of fiscal policy have also produced mixed results. For example, Frey and Schneider test the hypothesis that when incumbents fear that they will not be re-elected, they increase expenditures as the election draws near.[7] They found support for this hypothesis in non-defense government expenditures, but not in transfer payments or government jobs.

A better indicator of the use of fiscal policy instruments is the full employment surplus, or FES. This is a measure of the part of the government budget surplus (or deficit) which is due to the choices of the government itself, as opposed to other developments in the economy. For example, when the economy goes into a recession, tax revenues decline without any change in tax policy, simply because income declines. At the same time government expenditures will increase because unemployment will rise and the newly unemployed will be automatically eligible for government benefits.

Thus much of the state of the government budget depends on the state of the economy; only part depends on fiscal policy. Therefore, a useful measure of fiscal policy is the size of the federal surplus or deficit *if* the economy were at full capacity. Using the full employment surplus as the indicator of fiscal policy, evidence is again mixed about the existence of electoral cycles. Golden and Poterba find that the FES does not follow an electoral cycle, but Laney and Willet find that it does.[8]

The final word is not in for such quantitative evaluations of the political business cycle hypothesis. However, other knowledge about the political process undermines the hypothesis. One main component of fiscal policy is the tax law, which remains in place until changed by Congress. Changes in this law are major events which receive considerable public debate and attention. Committee recommendations have to be approved on the floor of each house of Congress; differences between the houses must be resolved in conference, and the final bill must be signed by the president or else his veto must be overridden.

Similarly, government expenditures are either automatic, and therefore not subject to political manipulation, or they involve a complex annual appropriations process which demands the agreement and cooperation of at least as many different bodies as a tax law change. It stretches the imagination to conceive of these cumbersome processes being manipulated according to the electoral cycle without the awareness of those who do not stand to gain by it. The press and opposing politicians seem likely to become aware of what is happening and to "blow the whistle."[9]

Monetary Instrument Cycles

Several studies have investigated the possibility of electoral cycles in the instruments of monetary policy. Monetary instruments are not so cumbersome to manipulate as fiscal instruments. And since they are controlled by the Federal Reserve system rather than by elected officials, manipulation might be easier to hide. On the other hand, since the officials of the Federal Reserve are appointed rather than elected, we may expect them to be free of the incentives of electoral politics. Still numerous observers have found that the Fed is sensitive to the desires of the elected officials who select them, but as usual there are mixed and contradictory findings. Tufte has found evidence that money growth accelerates in the two-year periods before elections and decelerates in the periods after.[10] Monroe, on the other hand, raises the same question in a slightly different way and finds little support for the hypothesis of political manipulation;[11] Golden and Poterba likewise found limited support.[12]

Studies of the money supply cannot be conclusive, however, because the Fed does not directly control the money supply, which is a product of private as well as governmental decisions. The money supply is an intermediate target, which the Fed may seek to control with the instruments available to it. The most important of these is open market operations, and the best indicator of Fed intentions is the federal funds rate. Luckett and Potts[13] and Beck[14] have tested models explaining variation in the federal funds rate and find no convincing evidence that it is manipulated according to an electoral cycle.

Another interesting possibility is discussed by Laney and Willett. They find that changes in the money supply are not directly affected by an electoral cycle, but that these changes are influenced by the full employment surplus, which they contend is affected by the electoral calendar. They argue that changes in the money supply do respond both to electorally induced and to residual changes in the full employment surplus, and that the Fed in effect monetizes the political component of the deficit.[15]

While we should be cautious in accepting this finding, since it is based on an argument that is at odds with Golden and Poterba,[16] it does suggest a new possibility. The Federal Reserve might use abstractly defensible decision rules, such as one of accommodating federal deficits with money growth in order not to choke off investment. But if the deficits themselves follow an electoral cycle, then the Fed's rule may lead it to follow an electoral cycle inadvertently. "Partisan politics may affect variables to which the Fed responds in a nonpartisan manner."[17]

LONG-RUN CONSEQUENCES OF POLITICAL MANIPULATION OF THE ECONOMY

Any of the kinds of short-run political manipulation we have reviewed might lead to adverse long-run consequences, but in order to address the question we need a theory that shows how conditions at one time might affect later conditions. As indicated earlier, the Nordhaus model has that feature.

Consequences of Vote Maximizing

Keech and Simon have analyzed the long-run consequences of repeated vote maximizing in the Nordhaus model.[18] They found that such behavior could lead to a variety of trends, depending on a variety of conditions, including the parameters, or coefficients, of the mathematical equations.

Most importantly, they found that the level of inflation when vote maximizing was first used had important effects on the lasting consequences of vote maximizing. If initial conditions involved very high inflation, vote maximizing could make things steadily better. Similarly, if initial conditions involved very low inflation, repeated vote maximizing could make things steadily worse.

But there were limits on how bad repeated vote maximizing could make things become. The worst that could happen in the Nordhaus model is that repeated vote maximizing leads to inflation which steadily increases from term to term, leading to steadily declining welfare or public well-being. However, since votes depend on inflation as well as unemployment, such a pattern means that the electoral reward for maximizing votes in each term would decline term after term. Thus maximizing votes in the present term might ironically make for fewer votes in the future; a bigger vote margin in the upcoming election might be at the expense of a subsequent re-election.

This sort of conclusion is also drawn in an analysis of a model inspired by Nordhaus, but having a more realistic and elaborate representation of the economic constraints on maximizing votes as a function of unemployment and inflation. In this model, Chappell and Keech show that an incumbent president who maximized public well-being rather than votes over three subsequent terms would receive more votes in the third term than a president who maximized votes in each of the three terms.[19]

Both these analyses of the long-term consequences of Nordhaus-type models suggest that term-by-term vote maximizing is likely to be a shortsighted if not misguided goal for politicians. Unless the incumbent president is so insecure as to feel the need of every possible vote in order to avoid defeat, he will be better served in the long run to maximize public welfare rather than votes, even if he cares more about votes than welfare. However, since Chappell and Keech suggest that it may take more than two terms for the welfare-maximizing president to be rewarded with more votes than the vote-maximizing president, they imply that the Twenty-second Amendment, which limits American presidents to two terms, may not be an entirely good idea.

Since the research reviewed above did not establish that political business cycles exist, these models of the long-run consequences of such cycles are useful for making inferences about what *would* happen in a world described by such a model. They should not be taken as descriptive of actual behavior.

Consequences of a Lack of Fiscal Discipline

The literature we have reviewed up until now revolves around ways in which political incentives and motivations may lead to *cyclical* patterns in economic variables, and how such electoral cycles might lead to long-run trends. This final section presents an alternative view developed by James Buchanan and Richard Wagner, which attributes adverse trends in public indebtedness, public sector growth and inflation to the breakdown of fiscal discipline implied by Keynesian economics.[20]

Before Keynes the principle that public budgets should be balanced provided a discipline that enabled public officials to resist the temptation to provide more public benefits than were paid for by taxes. After Keynes provided an argument that intentional government deficits could stimulate an economy out of a depression or recession, the discipline of the "old-time fiscal religion" was lost, and it was never replaced with a comparably clear standard for covering expenditures with revenues.

Without such a standard there was no clear restraint on the temptation for politicians to cater to public desires for more benefits than they paid for with their taxes. The result of this lack of discipline is "a regime of permanent deficits, inflation and an increasing public sector share of national income."[21] Even without a cyclical pattern, political incentives may in this way lead to long-run adverse trends.

There is no doubt that deficits have been the norm for the federal government since the beginning of the Keynesian era, designated as roughly since 1960. The only surplus in that period was a small one in 1969. However, total public debt has been declining throughout that period as a proportion of gross national product, as is normally the case after major wars.[22] Ironically, this trend has reversed under President Reagan's massive deficits, in spite of the fact that he came into office sounding like a more dedicated budget balancer than his predecessors. But with this exception, public indebtedness has grown in absolute size while the economy has grown even faster through most of the Keynesian era. We should consider the possibility that some deficits are a price of short-term prosperity, though excessive public indebtedness can cause reductions in long-term economic growth by crowding out private investment.

While the Reagan administration may seem to bear out Buchanan and Wagner's argument about growing indebtedness, it does not bear out their case about the growing public sector. In spite of budget cuts the public sector has not shrunk as much as President Reagan would like, but the main source of deficits in his administration is clearly the massive tax cuts passed in 1981, rather than growth of public programs. Furthermore, two of the fastest-growing components of the public sector are Social Security and state and local government, both of which are severely limited in their ability to use deficit spending to fund expansion.

William Niskanen provides the most careful empirical test of Buchanan and Wagner's hypotheses about the consequences of the lack of budgetary discipline. He found some preliminary evidence that deficits are associated with increases in federal spending. He did not, however, find evidence to support their hypothesis that deficits cause inflation by virtue of the Federal Reserve's accommodating them by expanding the money supply.[23]

CONCLUSION

Economic conditions have deteriorated in the last two or three decades in terms of the three main target variables of macroeconomic policy—unemployment, inflation and income growth. We have considered some theories and arguments that may help account for such deterioration in terms of the consequences of political motivation, but none of these arguments has received unambiguous support in empirical tests. Yet these arguments have enriched our understanding of the ways in which electoral incentives might affect public policy. With this knowledge, which will surely be enhanced by future research, the public and the press can be more alert to the dangers of narrow political incentives. And politicians can see how political manipulation for short-run electoral gain may be at the expense of their, or their party's, prospects of repeated re-election.

NOTES

1. Edward R. Tufte, *Political Control of the Economy* (Princeton, N.J.: Princeton University Press, 1978), pp. 3–9

2. Martin Paldam, "An Essay on the Rationality of Economic Policy: The Test-case of the Electional Cycle," *Public Choice* 37:2 (1980), pp. 287–305.

3. William D. Nordhaus, "The Political Business Cycle," *Review of Economic Studies* 42 (April 1975), pp. 169–190.

4. Studies that do find evidence of cyclical patterns in outcome variables, in addition to Tufte and Nordhaus, include Kevin J. Maloney and Michael L. Smirlock, "Business Cycles and the Political Process," *Southern Economic Journal* 48 (October 1981), pp. 377–392. Studies that do not find evidence of such cyclical patterns include Bennett McCallum, "The Political Business Cycle: An Empirical Test," *Southern Economic Journal* 44 (January 1978), pp. 504–515; and Nathaniel Beck, "Does There Exist a Political Business Cycle? A Box-Tiao Analysis," *Public Choice* 38:2 (1982), pp. 205–209. See also Martin Paldam, "Is There an Electional Cycle? A Comparative Study of National Accounts," *Scandinavian Journal of Economics* 81:2 (1979), pp. 323–342.

5. Tufte, p. 29.

6. Richard F. Winters et al., "Political Behavior and American Public Policy: The Case of the Political Business Cycle," in Samuel Long, ed., *The Handbook of Political Behavior,* vol. 5 (New York: Plenum, 1981), pp. 66–76.

7. Bruno S. Frey and Friedrich Schneider, "An Empirical Study of Politico-Economic Interaction in the United States," *Review of Economics and Statistics* 60 (May 1978), pp. 174–183.

8. David G. Golden and James M. Poterba, "The Price of Popularity: The Political Business Cycle Reexamined," *American Journal of Political Science* 24 (November 1980), pp. 696–714; and Leroy O. Laney and Thomas D. Willett, "Presidential Politics, Budget Deficits, and Monetary Policy in the United States, 1960–1976," *Public Choice* 40:1 (1983), pp. 53–69.

9. These themes are developed in Winters et al. It is also relevant to note that general historical treatments of fiscal policy generally find no need to mention or take into account such manipulation. See, for example, Herbert Stein, *The Fiscal Revolution in America* (Chicago: University of Chicago Press, 1969); Richard M. Pious, *The American Presidency* (New York: Basic Books, 1979), Chapter 9; and James L. Sundquist, *The Decline and Resurgence of Congress* (Washington, D.C.: The Brookings Institution, 1981), Chapter 4.

10. Tufte, pp. 49–52.

11. Kristen Monroe, "Political Manipulation of the Economy: A Closer Look at Political Business Cycles," *Presidential Studies Quarterly* 13 (Winter 1983), pp. 37–49.

12. Golden and Poterba, "The Price of Popularity."

13. Dudley G. Luckett and Glenn T. Potts, "Monetary Policy and Partisan Politics," *Journal of Credit, Money and Banking* 12 (August 1980), pp. 540–546.

14. Nathaniel Beck, "Presidential Influence on the Federal Reserve in the 1970's," *American Journal of Political Science* 26 (August 1982), pp. 415–445.

15. Laney and Willett, "Presidential Politics."

16. Golden and Poterba, "The Price of Popularity."

17. Laney and Willett, p. 54.

18. William R. Keech and Carl P. Simon, "Electoral and Welfare Consequences of Political Manipulation of the Economy," (unpublished, 1983). In "The Political Business Cycle," Nordhaus presented the following conclusion regarding the long-run properties of his model (p. 178): "under conditions where voting is an appropriate mechanism for social choice, democratic systems will adopt a policy on the long-run trade-off [between inflation and unemployment] that has lower unemployment and higher inflation than is optimal."

19. Henry W. Chappell, Jr., and William R. Keech, "Welfare Consequences of the Six-Year Presidential Term Evaluated in the Context of a Model of the U.S. Economy," *American Political Science Review* 77 (March 1983), pp. 75–91.

20. James M. Buchanan and Richard E. Wagner, *Democracy in Deficit: The Political Legacy of Lord Keynes* (New York: Academic Press, 1977).

21. Buchanan and Wagner, p. 72.

22. See Herbert Stein, "The Decline of the Budget Balancing Doctrine, or How the Good Guys Finally Lost," in James M. Buchanan and Richard E. Wagner, eds., *Fiscal Responsibility in Constitutional Democracy* (Boston: Martinus Nijhoff, 1978), pp. 35–53.

23. William A. Niskanen, "Deficits, Government Spending and Inflation; What Is the Evidence?" *Journal of Monetary Economics* 4 (August 1978), pp. 591–602.

The President and
the Political Business Cycle

M. STEPHEN WEATHERFORD

It has long been a familiar but unexamined piece of folk wisdom that presidents manipulate the economy to win elections. Over the last decade political scientists have produced a technically sophisticated research literature which appears to give support to this simple canard. But the verdict is not entirely convincing on intuitive grounds. (Else why would President Reagan produce a recession as prelude to the 1982 elections?) And in fact the research literature is far from consistent in supporting the notion.

Do the anticipated reactions of the electorate determine macroeconomic policies? The answer is critical to understanding the interplay between politics and the economy. If the demands of electoral politics were the primary driving force behind economic policy decisions, those decisions might be praised as democratically accountable or impugned as unsteady and excessively concerned with the short run. Similarly, politicians might be lauded for their attentiveness to the wishes of the people, or scorned for ignoring the expert advice of economists. From a longer perspective there would be little interest in this issue if all the economic policy options clustered around a steady growth path for the nation's output. But they don't. Several economists and political scientists have shown that by opting for short-term improvement to achieve electoral gains, administrations often produce inconsistent policies which have demonstrably worse long-term outcomes than other courses foregoing short-term stimulation for long-term stabilization.[1] Understanding the role of the electoral constraint in economic policymaking thus is important not only to interpreting public policies, but also to evaluating them.

This chapter summarizes a larger research project which attempts to assess the importance of elections in shaping economic policymaking in America. It briefly reviews the literature underlying the hypothesis that elected officials cause political business cycles. Next it presents an argument against this description of economic policymaking. That argument comprises two central tenets. First, the goals of economic policymakers are reviewed and reformulated in a manner which is broader and more variegated than envisaged in the political business cycle theory. Specifically, it is argued that short-term popular approval is only one of several goals which might be pursued through economic policy tools. Second, the understanding which presidents and their economic advisers have of the "electoral constraint" is likely to be more subtle and complex than corresponding assumptions of the theory. It involves, for instance, not only trying to please a majority of the voting population, but also maintaining the support of major economic interests and campaign organizations, while remaining true to the party's platform and its economic ideology. The chapter's third section takes a brief look at two periods—one preceding the 1958 midterm elections and the other preceding the 1960 presidential contest—which contradict the political business cycle theory but can be explained in terms of the approach presented here. This case study of economic policymaking in the second Eisenhower administration, while not amounting to definitive evidence, shows the theory's explanatory utility as well as illustrating how the approach fits in with alternative interpretations of economic policymaking during this period.

ARE THERE POLITICAL BUSINESS CYCLES?

Let us begin by reviewing briefly recent econometric studies of political-economic interaction. A simple, fundamental assumption motivates the bulk of these studies: politicians are vote maximizers. This supposition underlies a line of research which has given solid statistical support to the notion of a regular political business cycle. Some of the strongest evidence comes from Britain during the period of stop-go cycles in the 1950s and 1960s,[2] but studies of the United States have also found that various economic aggregates tend to shift toward more favorable levels as elections near. In its simplest version the political business cycle hypothesis proposes that the president will inflate the economy just before the election (to lower the unemployment rate and raise per capita income), then suppress the level of activity just after (to reduce the resulting inflation), so that the foundation for another boom can be laid during the inter-election period.[3] More sophisticated versions of the model relating elections to economic cycles propose that the president uses economic policy to serve the interests of his party constituency,[4] or possibly of the opposition's most marginal adherents,[5] unless constrained by some pressing macroeconomic emergency.[6] The bulk of this chapter will be concerned with the simpler version of the political business cycle theory.

In time-series analyses, models of this sort account for an impressive share of the historical variation in election outcomes. The data on which these models are based, however, are limited: they consist essentially of the national vote outcome paired with various indicators of aggregate economic conditions. They give us no direct information either about voters' attitudes or about politicians' intentions. The findings of these studies, therefore, are consistent with a wide range of underlying causal processes.[7] Logically there are two ways to unpack the complexity of this aggregate result: by a micro-level analysis of individual voters or by a detailed examination of the elite-level process of economic policy formation.

The first of these approaches focuses on public opinion and the attitudes that lead voters to choose particular parties and candidates. The question here is: Do voters punish incumbents for bad macroeconomic management and, if so, which components of aggregate economic conditions concern the public most? This research has produced a variety of proposed explanations, but the empirical support for any particular one is distinctly mixed. At this point it seems fair to say that micro-level analyses of public opinion have not produced a convincing explanation of the election-economy linkage. Kramer poses the analytical problem clearly, and other summaries appear in Kiewiet, in Hibbing and Alford, and in Weatherford.[8]

This chapter takes another approach to charting the micro-level events that produce election-economy regularities. Rather than looking at individual voters and asking whether they vote on the basis of personal or national economic conditions, we survey executive branch decision-making on economic policy to see whether presidents appear to seek electoral rewards through short-term manipulation of economic aggregates. In short, do presidents act like short-term political business cycle vote maximizers?

THE PRESIDENT AND
ECONOMIC POLICYMAKING

The assumption that politicians are vote maximizers is generally true but always a dramatic simplification of reality. The question arises: Is this a justified abstraction or does it simplify to the point of misconstruction? Two important simplifications underlie the political business cycle (PBC) model. First, in common with every other model of the accountability linkage between governors and governed, the PBC theory holds that presidents *can* influence the course of the economy. Second, in focusing narrowly on the goal of winning elections, the PBC theory makes a strong assumption of "other things being equal." Let us examine each of these assumptions in more detail.

A strong argument can be made to the effect that the administration does not exercise much control over the economy, and politicians occasionally advance this justification for the poor performance of the economy under their tutelage. The theoretical and empirical knowledge which economists bring to bear on their macroeconomic analysis is voluminous and complex; relationships among economic aggregates are often indirect and tenuous; and the timing of policy action and impact is complicated by various lags and unpredictable events like bad harvests or oil embargoes. All this resoundingly signals the difficulty—perhaps the impossibility—of formulating a national economic policy which could be defended as "optimal" in some absolute sense. But it does not entail that the government's influence on the course of macroeconomic activity is nil.

Another sort of attack on the efficacy of macroeconomic stabilization policy takes its cue from the "rational expectations" literature in economics.[9] The claim of these authors is that major economic actors and common citizens alike will form expectations of the government's behavior, extrapolated from their knowledge of its policy responses in similar past situations. Having thus anticipated the government's policies, they will adjust their own actions so as to insulate themselves from precisely the constraints the policies are intended to exercise on their economic behavior. While the writings of the rational expectations school have garnered a great deal of attention in the theoretical economics literature, they have not influenced policymakers, primarily because they are based on the assumption that economic actors can adjust prices and expenditures instantaneously. As Blinder and others have argued,[10] even if consumers and producers could perfectly anticipate policies, they could not often readily change their behavior to take advantage of that knowledge. Liquidity constraints, limitations on the ability of firms and individuals to borrow, fixed contractural obligations for both prices and wages all work to stabilize economic activity by inhibiting immediate responses to changed conditions.

From the perspective of a study of the political context of economic policymaking, however, it is more important to determine whether elected officials and their economic advisers have enough information to know what social and economic groups are helped or hurt by particular policies than it is to decide whether they could produce a universally optimal policy. A large body of evidence bears on this question of political responsibility. First, politicians and political parties think their policies influence the economy, and they base this supposition on historical experience.[11] Second, politicians take actions once in office which are intended to use government power to guide the pace or the course of economic activity, and they make statements at the time inviting the public to consider their economic policy performance in rating the administration's overall quality.[12] Finally, historical studies of real economic activity show clearly that in virtually every advanced Western country, governments of different partisan or ideological hues implement policies which have clearly distinguishable outcomes for inflation, unemployment and economic growth.[13] Politicians may not exercise perfect control over the economy, but there can be no question that the policies of the state play a critical role in both short-term fluctuations and long-term growth.[14]

The second important simplification of the PBC approach comes by way of the assumption of "other things being equal." This assumption lumps together as if equal a multitude of other factors whose benign "equality" can never be determined without empirical investigation. The anticipated reactions of voters are unquestionably important, but they play a role which is embedded in a context formed by other types of power-holders whose actions and anticipated reactions also constrain the president's policy choices. These include:

1. executive branch actors other than the president (the Council of Economic Advisers, some Cabinet officers, the Chairman of the Federal Reserve, and others);
2. patterned executive-legislative relations (especially strategic Congressional committees and their chairmen and, since 1974, a more fully rationalized Congressional budget process);
3. demands from extragovernmental sources (political parties, interest groups, etc.).

By surveying economic policymaking our research attempts to take into account not only the multiple centers of power and advocacy within the administration, but also the various sources of economic information, diagnosis and policy recommendation within the administration and outside it. The research seeks evidence not only of whether the president tries to control the economy in order to win elections, but, more broadly, of how he perceives the electoral constraint and how he fits it into the matrix of other economic goals he may be pursuing.

These constraints circumscribe but they do not determine the president's economic choices: in any given situation the chief executive is presented with multiple options for policy. Over a full term or more, the cumulation of options implemented and others foregone gives the president a great opportunity to place his stamp on the source of macroeconomic activity in the nation.

Even the most pragmatic president comes to the White House with ideas about the composition of economic activity, the distribution of wealth and income and the role of government in influencing economic outcomes. This economic ideology is as important a decisional component as any of the other sources of influence or constraint listed above. His economic ideology clearly is not independent of his conceptions of the policy course for which voters chose him (and hence of the standards by which they will judge his performance at the next election), nor of the interest groups, Congressional factions, and party coalitions to which he feels closest. But at any given time his ideology is not a proxy for those influences, but rather a tool that allows him to select from their demands, to meld them or to adopt a novel option.

Given his own ideological predilections in economic affairs, along with numerous sources of influence and demands for particular economic policy actions, the president can pursue a "maximizing" strategy by following any of several policy schema. He could, for instance, pursue a political business cycle strategy or strive for a smooth economic growth path.

The important common characteristic of these options is that they leave the determination of allocative and distributive outcomes up to the market. They take the composition of the national product and the distribution of income as given, and specific policies implemented in pursuit of these goals would attempt to avoid placing new, governmentally created advantages or disadvantages into the flow of market transactions. Such neutrality is harder to achieve than to theorize about, but it is just these sorts of policies that commentators have in mind when they refer to the change of government as replacing one "management team" with another, or when we surmise that bipartisan subscription to the Employment Act of 1946 entails that both political parties are pursuing the same economic policy goals.[15] For political science, then, the critical aspect of these three types of economic management strategies is that they could be pursued by either party, with only efficiency considerations distinguishing one party from the other.

Most presidents, however, do not seek a socially or economically neutral role for the state. The typical president would be much more likely to (1) attempt to serve the short-term interests of his partisan or socioeconomic constituency; (2) diminish or increase the share of government as a proportion of aggregate demand; or (3) pursue long-term goals of party or presidential economic ideology (for instance, by using tax and expenditure policy to alter the distribution of income).

The distinguishing feature of these three policy paths is their unmistakable partisan bias. Each would produce predictable changes in the pattern of economic advantages and disadvantages, and the class coalitions of each party would correspondingly favor one side and oppose the other for each alternative.

No administration is allowed the luxury of single-mindedly pursuing its conception of the ideal use for economic policy, whether it be short-term vote maximization or some long-run partisan goal. Balance of payments and foreign exchange considerations, for instance, constrain equally any government's freedom to pursue other macroeconomic targets. Neither price stability nor full employment can be pursued by inducing a dramatic deviation from stable economic growth. And if some exogenous shock threatens prevailing levels of employment or inflation, the administration's primary policy goals may have to be abandoned in order to cope with the crisis. These bounds are neither narrow nor inflexible, however, for they are set by historical experience more than by formal legislation—and an active president intent on a novel course can alter the context within which his actions are evaluated. (President Reagan's first two years provide a good example of such presidential power in use.) The result of formulating economic policy at the vortex of strong external constraints and powerful domestic pressures is a mixed policy in which major partisan themes must be distinguished among ad hoc variations.

This reminder may strike readers as underlining the obvious, but it is worth mentioning that quantitative studies of the covariation between economic aggregates and presidential popularity base their conclusions on the very small quantitative tip of a large, essentially qualitative, iceberg. We will be concerned not only with the time path of the economy, but also with the perceptions, decisions and intentions leading to the policy choices which produced those outcomes. If there were no unexpected shocks to the economy, no pressing crises forcing the administration off its desired macroeconomic course, then it would be a simple task to divine the goals or intentions of policy. The administration displays its policy goals, however, in managing crises as well as in more tranquil times, and the period chosen to illustrate this approach was selected because it exemplifies the way in which the president responds to short-term problems while still attempting to pursue his primary economic goals.

ECONOMIC POLICYMAKING IN THE SECOND EISENHOWER ADMINISTRATION

President Eisenhower entered his second administration with reason to believe that the electorate approved his principled stand on the role of the government in the domestic economy as much as they did his policies with regard to foreign nations. The elections in November 1956 again showed the landslide of affection which the public held for him, and this approval translated into coattails on which enough Republican Congressional candidates rode to assure a small margin for his conservative policies. In the Senate the Republicans had lost only one seat since 1952, and their 47 seats were a virtual stand-off to the Democrat's 49. In the House the GOP had lost their majority in 1954, but they remained close, with 201 seats to the Democrat's 234. The White House could gain a majority on most measures because it could count on a comfortable number of conservative Southern defections from Democratic ranks. The economy was in the midst of a three-year recovery from the 1954 recession, and the president's policies were widely believed responsible both for curtailing the recession and for establishing the foundation for a stable recovery.

By 1956 the economy had resumed a slow but steady growth. Economic conditions were tranquil with inflation virtually nil[16] and employment climbing slowly from the recessionary trough. Observing the president's perception of the economy in these years it is possible to glimpse his continuing concerns, free of the pressure of short-term problems. His reflections on the period reveal that the threat of inflation was a constant preoccupation.

> Critics overlooked the inflationary psychology which prevailed during the mid-fifties and which I thought it necessary to defeat. In 1957, for example, consumer prices were rising at an unacceptably high annual rate of 3.2 percent. Ten years of this could devalue the current dollar more than 30 percent, while if the rate accelerated, we would have an entirely intolerable situation. Even during the 1957–58 recession, prices rose more than 2 percent . . . The administration believed that if wages and prices could *increase* during a recession, we could get into real inflationary trouble in time of prosperity.[17]

Moreover, price stability is explicitly ranked higher than economic growth. (A fundamental difference between Democratic and Republican economic ideologies during this period, the distinction becomes even sharper during the 1958 recession.)

> We do not wish to realize this objective [economic growth] at the price of inflation, which not only creates inequalities but is likely, sooner or later, to be followed by depression.[18]

Finally, the president's view of inflation and its dangers is closely assimilated to his broader political ideology, where the analogy with appeasement is irresistible:

> We believe that one of the most sinister threats to prosperity is inflation. An even worse danger is the attitude that accepts inflation as inevitable or even desirable. Appeasement is just as dangerous in dealing with inflation as in dealing with aggression.[19]

Eisenhower strengthened the conservative bent of his administration just after the 1956 elections, taking the occasion of Arthur Burns' resignation from the CEA to appoint the even more solidly conservative Raymond Saulnier to head the Council.

Some slowdown in the level of economic activity in 1958 was inevitable as, by late 1957, neither the investment boom which had paced the early stages of the recovery nor the subsequent bulge in exports could be sustained for long. The natural tendency for the recovery to lose steam, however, was compounded by a sharp decline in the money supply. The result was a dramatic drop in economic activity, with unemployment rising from about 3 percent in mid-1957 to above 7 percent by the third quarter of 1958. The overall decline in expenditure was virtually the same as in the 1954 recession, but the composition of the shortfall was quite different: in 1954, diminished government spending (at the conclusion of the Korean war) accounted for most of the drop; in 1958, real private final sales and inventory changes absorbed the decline.

The Eisenhower economic team surveyed the 1958 recession and saw little more than a new version of the 1954 episode. Both the success of his patient resistance to government intervention and the unmistakable dictates of personal and party ideology convinced the president and his advisors to resist calls for new expenditures in 1957–58. Asked late in 1957 whether the government would take action if there were a further decline in the leading indicators of plant and equipment expenditures, Treasury Secretary Humphrey responded:

> I don't think so . . . no . . . I will put it this way: we didn't do it last time, did we? Pressure was brought on us to do it. We didn't do it and it worked . . . We didn't cut taxes until we got ready to balance the budget, until we saw it in hand and it came true.[20]

The president's sentiments were similar:

> From the outset of the [1958] recession, my associates and I took the same view as we had in 1954 that we should prepare strong programs to prevent a serious and lengthy decline but should never be swayed from reason by purveyors of gloom. We watched with concern the increase in unemployment, but we refused to take action that would fail to cure unemployment and cause more acute trouble later on.[21]

In contrast to the administration's position that the recession represented a "temporary correction," the Democrats in Congress formulated an alternative diagnosis of the economy's ills and an opposition program which was "bolder, sharper, and more confident than in 1954."[22] The Democrats proposed that two types of programs be used to correct the downward slide of the economy: the first involved public employment and public works projects to restore employment and purchasing power immediately; the second envisaged tax cuts which would have both short-term stimulative and long-term distributive effects. Leadership for the program was slow to emerge in the Congress, due largely to the "gentlemen's agreement" between Majority Leader Johnson and Speaker Rayburn on one side and the administration on the other, an agreement not to make political capital out of the economic issue.[23] As the recession lengthened, however, support—especially for the tax cut—became stronger, with George Meany of the AFL-CIO advocating it in March and the Democratic Advisory Committee coming out for it in April 1958. In the Senate, Paul Douglas actively advocated government intervention along several lines to shore up economic activity, and the Joint Economic Committee under his leadership formulated the Democratic alternative more systematically. Even Arthur Burns, then at the National Bureau of Economic Research but speaking as a private citizen, warned that dangerous public work schemes would be inevitable if the administration did not move toward tax reduction.[24]

The administration meanwhile rejected proposals for public works and public employment, a position consistent with party and presidential philsophy. Their position on several versions of the tax cut proposal, however, was more difficult to explain. Administration economists—Humphrey at the Treasury, Brundage at the Bureau of the Budget, and CEA Chairman Saulnier—expressed inconsistent criteria for justifying tax cuts in general, and they opposed specific tax reduction proposals throughout the recession.

With no counter-recession program of its own and lacking a clear rationale for rejecting the proposals of others, and with business and economic news growing worse each week, the administration found it impossible to resist the piecemeal proposals for increased expenditures coming from Congress and from the executive agencies. Wilfred Lewis summarizes the administration's unenviable position:

> The Eisenhower administration was carried along by the force of events. It accepted, indeed embraced, actions and policies to stimulate the economy which were contrary to its expressed wishes and advance injunctions, and for which its spokesmen later expressed regret. . . . Perhaps the most interesting of all, the President and other administration spokesmen specifically expressed a preference for actions stimulating private activity rather than public, but when the time came accepted a variety of increases in government expenditures and opposed tax cuts.[25]

A variety of Democrat-inspired expenditure increases were implemented during mid-1958, and their stimulative effects worked as predicted. Along with the automatic stabilizers they raised federal spending on goods and services by 6.1 percent between the 1957 peak cyclical third quarter and the fourth quarter of 1958. At least as important to the recovery as these fiscal policy measures, however, was the sharp increase in the rate of growth of the money supply beginning early in 1958. Thus aided by monetary policy and by mildly activist fiscal policy measures pushed by Democrats at several levels of government, the economy emerged from the recession early in 1959.[26]

Unfortunately for Republican prospects in the 1958 midterm Congressional races, however, the trough of the recession (in terms of employment) precisely bracketed the November elections. The Democrats gained 15 seats in the Senate, 49 in the House, and virtually every study of voting in 1958 reads the outcome as a rejection of administration economic policy.[27] This outcome bears on several issues in the relation between economic conditions and election results.

It clearly establishes a link between bad economic conditions and declining shares of votes and seats. But it appears to catch the PBC model in a *reductio ad absurdum:* either the theory is incorrect in predicting that Eisenhower would stimulate economic activity just before the election, or it entails that Eisenhower is not one of the "rational politicians" to whom the theory applies. The president may have been trying to serve his core constituency's interest in price stability, but then the theory must explain the Republican party's failure to gauge the electoral costs of their economic policy (including the dissipation of their legislative power to serve their constituent interests). However simple and powerful these theories of political-economic manipulation seem when applied to quantitative time series, the case of 1958 suggests that further explanations are needed if the theory is to help us understand the rudimentary details of actual situations. We will return to this issue after surveying the final two years of the Eisenhower presidency.

Economic Ideas and Policy in the Late Fifties

By the late 1950s, the Phillips curve had become the prevailing analytical mode for explaining the relationship between inflation and unemployment in the United States.[28] The effect was to sharpen economic goals by forcing policymakers to abandon the rhetoric of optimizing goals and to strive for one among an infinite number of second best points along the Phillips curve. Robert J. Gordon argues that the central economic policy debate for the ensuing decade is over this issue:

> The history of economic policy between 1957 and 1967 can be summarized in the choice during 1957–60 by Republican policy makers of a point relatively far to the southeast along the curve, and the rejection of that point by Democratic policy makers after 1961 in favor of a stimulative "new economics" designed to reach a point further to the northeast.[29]

The contrasting emphasis in these two positions can be seen

nowhere more clearly than in juxtaposing the Economic Report of the President for 1959 and the Joint Economic Committee Staff Report on Employment, Growth, and Price Levels issued during the same year. Eisenhower and his economic advisors, concerned that the dangers of inflation were being seriously underestimated due to an exaggerated concern for economic stabilization, used the Economic Report to press Congress to amend the Employment Act "to make reasonable price stability an explicit goal of federal economic policy, coordinate with the goal of maximizing production, employment, and purchasing power now specified."[30] The Democrats, on the contrary, worried that heightened concern with stabilization or price increases would lead to a stagnant economy which could not productively employ a growing population:

> While the background of the Employment Act explains its emphasis on economic stabilization, emphasis in public policy has turned increasingly toward economic growth over the long run. The objective of achieving and maintaining a high rate of growth has assumed a status of equal importance with the stabilization goals explicitly stated in the act.[31]

In historical perspective both these documents are significant in signaling the shift away from a monistic focus on what Arthur Okun has called the "categorical imperative" of post-Depression political economy—to avoid another Depression. In the process each party began to formulate a distinctive approach to short-run stabilization.

Recovery and Recession

The steadfastness of the Republican administration's stand at the anti-inflation pole is underlined by their macro policy actions as the economy emerged from the 1958 recession and the annual rate of inflation again rose to 2 percent. Concern shifted abruptly from "pump-priming" to the size of the government deficit. In his State of the Union message in January 1960, President Eisenhower strongly emphasized "the continuing threat of inflation together with the persisting tendency toward fiscal irresponsibility." Moreover, the primary tool "by which the federal government can counter inflation and rising prices is to insure that its expenditures are below its revenues" and to use the resulting surplus to retire the national debt.[32] In pledging to balance the budget for 1960, Eisenhower signaled a surprising and abrupt reversal of the $12 billion deficit accumulated during the recession. This had a particularly significant effect because most of the deficit amounted to counter-cyclical transfers triggered by the various automatic stabilizers. Since the tendency of the automatic programs is toward quick reversal as the trough of the cycle gives way to recovery, without some explicit stimulative increment total reliance on these mechanisms often inhibits the economy's upward climb.

As Wilfred Lewis points out, this is exactly what happened:

> After the middle of 1959, the discretionary antirecession actions were not only turned off but sharply reversed. This was powerfully reinforced by the attempt to reduce government expenditures generally— in part a reaction to the deficit produced by the recession itself. The fiscal reaction after the recession was over may have been the worst feature of the fiscal policy response to the 1958 recession; and, significantly, that reaction was a matter of discretionary policy rather than built-in stabilizers.[33]

Lewis H. Kimmel comes to a similar conclusion: "A balanced budget for 1960 meant that the stimulative effects of the automatic stabilizers would be restricted mainly to the fiscal year 1959."[34] The quick reversal of the automatic stabilizers and the wholesale move toward erasing the deficit abruptly curtailed the recovery and ensured that it was a temporary peak rather than a steady plateau.

Combined with this withdrawal of fiscal policy support for the recovery, monetary growth ceased in the first quarter of 1959 and began a steep drop which did not bottom out until 1960's third quarter. The result was that investment spending was especially sluggish in resuming its growth after the 1958 recession, with neither consumer durable expenditures nor business fixed investment regaining their 1955–57 peaks until well into the next administration. Unemployment rose steadily from late 1959 until after the 1960 elections, while inflation fell slowly to around 1 percent by early 1961.

Economic Management in the Second Eisenhower Administration

If the PBC model suggests that it was mistaken timing to induce a recession just prior to the midterm congressional elections in 1958, then repeating the exercise immediately thereafter seems perverse indeed. Moreover, the president and his political advisors were not unaware that only a minority of the electorate favored recessionary conditions, as Nixon apparently reminded the Cabinet.[35] Do these two episodes fail to fit the PBC model only because policy is irrational

or simply mistaken? If we adhere to the notion that the public rewards sustained high levels of capacity utilization, and we admit that
economic policymakers in the second Eisenhower administration
were aware of this, we are forced to conclude either that:

1. the economic policies of the second Eisenhower administration were
   hopelessly bungled attempts to pursue the policy goal of continued
   party control of the government, or
2. the president did not feel constrained by the electoral incentive, or
3. the president regarded the public's preference function as more
   complex and flexible than the PBC model proposes.

Each of these possibilities contains a grain of truth. The first is
clearly exaggerated, but it correctly implies that the administration's
policies were frequently driven by a concern for inflation which was
excessive even at the time. Indeed, even Allen Wallis, the economist
who served as vice chairman of Eisenhower's Cabinet Group on Price
Stability for Economic Growth, reacted in this way to monetary
stringency following the 1958 recession: "The Federal Reserve Board
tightened up the money supply in 1959 overvigorously and over-
promptly as a move against inflation. But the inflation wasn't there."[36]
But Eisenhower did handle the 1954 recession and the 1955–57 expansion with a restrained competence quite consistent with the party's
economic ideology, and it is only from the perspective of two activist
and inflationary decades later that his rather laconic response to the
1958 recession looks to be in error. Even in 1958, the indicators did not
signal the onset of a depression, and the genuine threat to a price
level that had been essentially stable since the Civil War must have
seemed quite pressing.

The second possibility points correctly to Eisenhower's status as
an elder statesman and a lame-duck president, and it is the explanation most favored by economists attached to the PBC theory. Milton
Friedman argues that this conclusion is the key to understanding why
the inflationary process in the United States did not begin immediately following the implementation of the 1946 Act:

> That interruption, I conjecture, is the accident of a nonpolitical Presi-
> dent, Dwight Eisenhower, who was willing to sacrifice his party's and
> his vice president's presidential prospects in order to cut short the
> inflationary process.[37]

This is a strong argument. Against it could be advanced any
number of anecdotes from presidential campaigns in 1952, 1956 or

even 1960, showing Eisenhower's concern for party victory and indeed for his vice-president's prospects. But the fact remains that among recent presidents Eisenhower is uniquely "above politics." A critical test of the argument's validity would depend on assembling more cases, both of "political" and of "nonpolitical" presidents. But one consideration of scientific method holds strongly against this argument, whose import is to avoid theoretical failure by omitting the case from the universe of relevant cases. Given that the PBC theory applies only to the postwar period, omitting the Eisenhower presidency eliminates about a seventh of the presidents and about a fifth of the elections. No worthwhile theory should be forced to surgery that radical in the name of self-preservation.

Adopting the third conclusion would entail giving up the attractive simplicity of a theory which envisions economic policy to be constrained primarily by an electorate with simple and inflexible preferences. This possibility hints at a much older theory of public opinion in which officials are expected to act as educators as often as they serve as errand boys, and in which short-term electoral gains are only one among several considerations which rightfully influence economic policymaking. With regard to the role of inflation in the economy, Eisenhower looks very much like this sort of politician, particularly in his second administration. He did not disagree with Nixon's warning that high unemployment was bad politics. But the president did not view his economic policies as an attempt to increase unemployment: he saw them as painful but unavoidable programs addressing a greater threat to the public's long-term interests—inflation. The president was not simply being quixotically noble, however: the inflation issue had served him well as a campaign standard in 1954 and 1956, and it was only at the trough of the 1958 recession that the Gallup poll's "most important problem" question elicited more references to unemployment than to inflation. He was very much aware that his policies toward inflation ran counter to the simple notion that voters are only interested in policies that enhance their nominal income:

> The anti-inflation battle is never-ending, though I fear that in 1959 the public was apathetic, or at least ill-informed, regarding this issue. This attitude caused me to recall a laconic comment of Winston Churchill when someone asked him during World War II what the allies were fighting for: 'If we stop,' he replied, 'you will find out.'[38]

Several of the best publicized economic activities of his administration's waning days were undertaken with the primary intention of educating the citizenry to the dangers of inflation. In January 1959, Eisenhower established the Cabinet Committee on Price Stability for Economic Growth, chaired by Vice President Nixon. In announcing the Cabinet Committee, the president stated that a primary objective of the committee would be to "strive to build a better public understanding of the problem of inflation and of public and private policies that should be followed if cost and price increases are to be avoided."[39] In November 1959, the White House sponsored a National Conference on Price Stability. Eisenhower used the occasion of his address to the conference to urge the need for a "citizens' campaign against inflation." Craufurd Goodwin summarizes the impact of the conference in these terms:

> The conference did not culminate in any specific organization or policy
> . . . But its main purpose, in the eyes of the administration, was to
> sound the tocsin on the dangers of inflation, which, more than specific
> acts, had become the heart of the administration's anti-inflation policy.[40]

Eisenhower's letter of transmittal of his final State of the Union message caps this strategy with a clear restatement of his faith in a public educated to economic realities:

> A well-informed and vigilant public opinion is essential in our free
> society for helping to achieve the conditions necessary for price stability
> and vigorous economic growth.[41]

The 1960 election results themselves give some evidence that the president's attempts were successful in convincing voters that he and his party were performing competently at a difficult task. The presidency was lost by the narrowest of margins. More importantly, the GOP made a net gain of two seats in the Senate and 21 in the House, defeating 24 Democratic incumbents in the process. There were other issues than the economy in the 1960 election, of course, but macroeconomic management must be numbered among the most important. This is hardly the record of straightforward electoral punishment for bad economic policy. A fair reading of these results might see them rather as a generally favorable verdict on economic policies that the public viewed as capable responses to challenging times.

CONCLUSION

This chapter has presented a schematic view of presidential economic policymaking. Rather than attempting to assess simply whether the political business cycle theory is contradicted or supported by the evidence from elite decision-making, the discussion seeks to place the electoral imperative into a broader context of opportunities and constraints. The empirical evidence summarized here should be viewed as illustrative or heuristic,[42] rather than as definitive. As such, however, it does provide several leads toward a more theoretically well-rounded image of political-economic interaction, and it suggests several summary statements which may be useful in guiding subsequent research.

Explaining economic policy during the second Eisenhower administration requires giving careful consideration to the electoral constraint. From the 1952 presidential contest, in an almost unbroken thread until his retirement from office in 1961, Eisenhower was concerned with the state of the economy and was eager to make it a winning issue for his party. That he was troubled by unemployment and recession is clear from his memoirs and from Cabinet discussions of economic policy. But the willingness of the president and his advisors to take (rather than merely to plan) government action to stimulate the economy was always contingent on a healthy respect for the economically enervating effect of government intervention and for the danger of inflation.

That he was troubled by the prospect of price inflation and declines in the value of the dollar is clear from his administration's policy actions in both his terms of office. The president, his economic advisors and the leaders of his party all viewed inflation as the greatest danger to postwar economic prosperity. For the president and his party, the good economy was one in which there was, above all, a stable price level. If this entailed occasional deflationary cycles, the resulting unemployment was only necessary to reduce the growth of wage costs, and its human dislocation would be cushioned by compensating policies in place since the New Deal. Moreover, they believed—Eisenhower most of all—that the American public could be made to understand that inflation rather than depression was the appropriate focus of government activity in the 1950s. Once voters understood the alternatives and could see the long-term value of price stability, they would support the Republican party's conservative policies.

These officials and party leaders comprehended clearly the definitive power of the electoral mandate, but their strategy for dealing with this constraint on economic policy was quite different from the one suggested by political business cycle theorists. The strategies diverge because they spring from conceptions of the electoral constraint which differ in two important ways. First, actual policymakers in the Eisenhower years construed the electoral constraint as a much more complex and malleable bond than do the simple political business cycle theories. Second, actual policies reacted to, and were conditioned by, the actions of power-holders outside the circle of the administration, while the PBC theory tends to de-emphasize the influence of non-electoral constraints.

The way in which electoral considerations enter Republican party strategy during the period highlights a gulf between the calculations of politicans and the prescriptions of the political business cycle theory. One is repeatedly impressed, in reading through documents on policymaking in the Eisenhower years, with the broad range of considerations which entered into the final decisions. In the context of the times, the vice president's reminders in 1958 and 1960 that the electorate might punish the administration and the party for unemployment must have seemed ineffectual at best. Nixon did, however, show himself to be a more "modern" politician than the president. The unarticulated theories which underlie the modern technology of electoral campaigning are marked by their commitment to taking those issues of greatest concern to the public as fixed points. Once located the modal public attitude is the stand toward which strategically rational parties and politicians are advised to move. The president's interpretation was more old-fashioned, for he believed that his opinion was the correct one, and he felt that his presidential responsibility entailed using the "bully pulpit" of his office to try to convince a majority of the public to support him. Eisenhower pursued the strategy of attacking inflation with economic policy at the same time that he attempted to convince the public of the key importance of the inflation issue.

If the political business cycle theory suggests that using economic policy to maximize votes is less complex than it really is, the theory also implies that economic policymaking is less constrained than in fact it is. The second strand of this chapter's argument has sought to place electoral considerations into a context shared by other intra- and extragovernmental centers of economic policy influence. These include Cabinet officers and economic advisors as well as influential senators and representatives of the president's party. But they also include spokesmen for influential segments of public opinion—for the Republican party, the business and banking communities and some writers in the conservative press—in addition to interest groups, campaign supporters and activists in the party organization. In the 1958 recession, the question of whether the administration would support public works and tax cuts, or would take no corrective action to supplement the automatic stabilizers, led to several months of intensive lobbying across the boundary between the government and the public.

Finally, the notion that economic policymaking is hedged about with constraints and alternative interpretations which make vote maximization only one of several possible goals should not obscure the most important counterpoise to the simple pursuit of electoral victory: the economic ideology of the president and his party. The prevailing economic ideas about the role of the government in short-term stabilization and in allocating the national product underlie the administration's interpretation of the economy's ills, its assessment of the need to act and its choice of policy alternatives. The pursuit of ideological goals through economic policy is hardly unusual for governments,[43] nor unexpected by the electorate.

If the threat of electoral punishment is not the primary source of short-term economic stabilization policies, this does not necessarily undermine democratic control of macroeconomic management. It is in longer historical perspective that popular control of economic policy is to be found. The electorate may throw out the party under whose tutelage the economy enters a recession, but they do not vote the other in on the simple expectation that their family's financial condition will be enhanced. The voters rejected Republican policies in 1958 because economic conditions in that year signaled a clear failure of economic management. But in 1960, the governing party was pursuing very similar policies (in an economic climate more favorable to those policies), and its leaders were working more assiduously to convince the public that those policies were on the right course. It is always difficult to specify the precise role of economic issues in any election outcome, but it would be dubious to argue that the difference between winning and losing the presidency in 1960 was attributable to Eisenhower's economic management. Indeed the dramatically different rates of success by Republican Congressional candidates between 1958 and 1960 (a net loss followed by a net gain) could just as convincingly be read as reflecting approval of the president's regimen of short-term restriction in pursuit of long-term stability.

One case study is hardly adequate ground for generalizing to other administrations, but some tentative hypotheses can be suggested at this point. One inference which can be drawn from this attempt to evaluate the political business cycle theory is for the notion of party control of economic policy. If the PBC scenario is correct, then it matters relatively little which party is in power: both will eventually manipulate economic activity to assure their next election victory. If presidential ideology and long-standing party goals dominate economic policy formation, then party control of the government matters critically, because the differences between parties lead to differences of economic advantage or disadvantage which accrue to social groups, classes and interests. One implication of this chapter, then, is to underline the distinctiveness and historical continuity of the American political parties as alternative governments.

A second implication relates to the way in which political scientists view representation and accountability in the economic policy area. To the extent that the parties are distinguished merely as more or less efficient management teams—both pursuing the same economic goals—the accountability of the government is attenuated when it comes to responsibility for the distribution of costs and benefits in the economy. When public debate and elite attention are focused on broad economic aggregates like unemployment and inflation rates, other important issues—like the distribution of income and wealth or the incidence and economic effects of taxation policies—are omitted from the public agenda. A second implication is thus to shift attention from the short-term fluctuations of economic aggregates and back toward the socioeconomic and ideological foundations of party differences.

NOTES

1. James M. Buchanan and Richard Wagner, *Democracy in Deficit* (New York: Academic Press, 1977); William R. Keech, "Elections and Macroeconomic Policy Optimization," *American Journal of Political Science* 24 (1980), pp. 345–67.

2. C. A. E. Goodhart and R. J. Bhansali, "Political Economy," *Political Studies* 18, 43–106.

3. Gerald Kramer, "Short-term Fluctuations in U.S. Voting Behavior, 1896–1964," *American Political Science Review* 65 (1971), pp. 131–45; William Nordhaus, "The Political Business Cycle," *Review of Economic Studies* 42 (1975), pp. 160–90; C. D. MacRae, "A Political Model of the Business Cycle," *Journal of Political Economy* 85 (1977), pp. 239–63; Ray C. Fair, "The Effect of Economic Events on Votes for President," *Review of Economics and Statistics* 60 (1978), pp. 159–73.

4. Douglas A. Hibbs, Jr., *Political Parties and Macroeconomic Policy* (Cambridge, Mass.: MIT Center for International Studies, 1975).

5. Sam Kernell, "Explaining Presidential Popularity," *American Political Science Review* 72 (1978); Sam Kernell and Douglas A. Hibbs, Jr., "A Critical

Threshold Model of Presidential Popularity," in D. A. Hibb and H. Fass-
bender, eds., *Contemporary Political Economy* (Amsterdam: North-
Holland, 1981), pp. 42–72.

6. Bruno Frey, *Modern Political Economy* (Oxford: Martin Robertson, 1978).

7. Edward R. Tufte, "Determinants of the Outcome of Midterm Congressional Elections," *American Political Science Review* 69 (September 1975),
pp. 812–26; M. Stephen Weatherford, "Economic Conditions and Electoral Outcomes," *American Journal of Political Science* 22 (1978), pp. 917–
38.

8. Gerald H. Kramer, "The Ecological Fallacy Revisited: Aggregate versus
Individual-level Findings on Economics and Elections and Sociotropic
Voting," *American Political Science Review* 77 (1983), pp. 92–111;
Roderick D. Kiewiet, *Macroeconomics and Micropolitics* (Chicago: Univer-
sity of Chicago Press, 1983); John R. Hibbing and John A. Alford, "The
Electoral Impact of Economic Conditions: Who is Held Responsible?"
American Journal of Political Science 25, pp. 423–39; M. Stephen
Weatherford, "Economic Voting and the 'Symbolic Politics' Argument,"
American Political Science Review 77 (1983), pp. 158–74.

9. Thomas J. Sargeant and Neil Wallace, "Rational Expectations, the Optimal Monetary Instrument, and the Optimal Money Supply Rule," *Journal of Political Economy* 83 (1975), pp. 241–57.

10. Alan S. Blinder, *Economic Policy and the Great Stagflation* (New York:
Academic Press, 1979).

11. Gerald M. Pomper, *Elections in America* (New York: Dodd, Mead, 1968).

12. Edward S. Flash, Jr., *Economic Advice and Presidential Leadership* (New
York: Columbia University Press, 1965); Roger B. Porter, *Presidential Decision Making: The Economic Policy Board* (Cambridge, Mass.: Harvard University Press, 1980); Benjamin I. Page, *Choices and Echoes in Presidential
Elections* (Chicago: University Press, 1978); Richard A. Brody, "Public
Evaluations and Expectations and the Future of the Presidency," paper
presented at the Conference on the Future of the Presidency.

13. Douglas A. Hibbs, Jr., "Political Parties and Macroeconomic Policy,"
American Political Science Review 71 (1977), pp. 1467–1487; Edward R.
Tufte, *Political Control of the Economy* (Princeton, N.J.: Princeton Univer-
sity Press, 1978); Nathaniel Beck, "Parties, Administrations, and Ameri-
can Macroeconomic Outcomes," *American Political Science Review* 76
(March 1981), pp. 83–93; David R. Cameron, "The Expansion of the
Public Economy: A Comparative Analysis," *American Political Science Re-
view* 72 (1978), pp. 1243–61.

14. Eric Nordlinger, *The Autonomy of the Democratic State* (Cambridge, Mass.:
Harvard University Press, 1981).

15. George Stigler, "Aggregate Economic Conditions and National Elections," *American Economic Review* 64 (May 1973), pp. 160–67; Herbert

Stein, *The Fiscal Revolution in America* (Chicago: University of Chicago Press, 1969).

16. J. M. Culbertson, *Full Employment or Stagnation?* (New York: McGraw Hill, 1964); Richard Ruggles, "Inflation and Unemployment," in Arthur Okun, ed., *The Battle Against Unemployment* (New York: Norton, 1965).

17. Dwight David Eisenhower, *Waging Peace* (Garden City, N.Y.: Doubleday 1965), pp. 461–2.

18. Council of Economic Advisers, *The Economic Report of the President* (Washington D.C.: U.S. Government Printing Office, 1956), p. 28.

19. Dwight David Eisenhower, *Public Papers of the President* (Washington, D.C.: U.S. Government Printing Office, 1958), p. 115.

20. Wilfred Lewis, Jr., *Federal Fiscal Policy in the Postwar Recessions* (Washington, D.C.: The Brookings Institution, 1962).

21. Eisenhower, *Waging Peace*, p. 304.

22. James L. Sundquist, *Politics and Policy: The Eisenhower, Kennedy, and Johnson Years* (Washington D.C.: The Brookings Institution, 1968), p. 21.

23. Rowland Evans and Robert Novak, *Lyndon B. Johnson: The Exercise of Power* (New York: New American Library, 1966); Ralph K. Huitt and Robert L. Peabody, *Congress: Two Decades of Analysis* (New York: Harper, 1969).

24. Lewis, p. 206.

25. Lewis, p. 214.

26. Robert J. Gordon, "Postwar Macroeconomics: The Evolution of Events and Ideas," in *The American Economy in Transition* (Chicago: University of Chicago Press, 1980), p. 160.

27. Angus Campbell, Philip E. Converse, Warren E. Miller, and Donald E. Stokes, *The American Voter* (New York: Wiley, 1960), chapter 13; Eisenhower, *Waging Peace*, p. 310; Weatherford, "Economic Conditions and Electoral Outcomes"; Kiewiet, *Macroeconomics and Micropolitics*.

28. Paul A. Samuelson and Robert M. Solow, "Analytical Aspects of Anti-inflation Policy," *American Economic Review* 50 (1960), pp. 177–94.

29. Gordon, p. 124.

30. Council of Economic Advisers, *The Economic Report of the President* (Washington, D.C.: U.S. Government Printing Office, 1959), p. 25.

31. *Joint Economic Committee Staff Report* (1959), p. 208.

32. Dwight David Eisenhower, *Public Papers of the President* (Washington, D.C.: U.S. Government Printing Office, 1960), pp. 11–12.

33. Lewis, p. 234.

34. Lewis H. Kimmel, *Federal Budget and Fiscal Policy, 1789–1958* (Washington, D.C.: The Brookings Institution, 1959).

35. Richard M. Nixon, *Six Crises* (Garden City, N.Y.: Doubleday, 1962).

36. *Congressional Record*, v. 108 (April 9, 1962), p. 6137.

37. Milton Friedman, "Financial Markets in the Postwar Period," in *American Economy in Transition* (Chicago: University of Chicago Press, 1980), p. 81.

38. Eisenhower, p. 312.

39. Craufurd D. Goodwin, *Exhortation and Controls* (Washington, D.C.: The Brookings Institution, 1975), p. 123.

40. Goodwin, p. 127.

41. Eisenhower, *Public Papers of the President*, p. 118.

42. Harry Eckstein, *Case Study and Theory in Macropolitics* (Princeton University, Department of Politics, 1971).

43. Hibbs, "Political Parties and Macroeconomic Policy"; Bruno Frey, *Modern Political Economy*; William R. Keech, "Elections and Macroeconomic Policy Optimization."

2

THE PRESIDENT & FISCAL POLICY

Macroeconomic Policy Choices of Postwar Presidents

CHARLES E. JACOB

Since the end of the Second World War, American presidents have been assigned by history, by legislative act and by public expectations to a new role: general overseer of and trustee for the achievement and preservation of national economic stability. In consequence, each of the postwar presidents, from Truman to Reagan, has had to allocate time, thought and energy to the enterprise of planning for economic stability. This has involved, in turn, coming to terms with the imperatives (if not the more arcane rationales) of fiscal, monetary and incomes policies. Finding, choosing and calibrating the various policy options offered has gone on with the aid of multiple advisory institutions, and the development of a stable array of organizational processes, routines and sequences.

The strategy adopted in this chapter for the exploration of developments over the past third of a century is to examine the performance of the presidency (as individual and as institution) in various macroeconomic decision-making settings. Finally, the broader repertoire of presidential roles surrounding the decision process will be addressed, including the management of institutions, the monitoring of implementation and the "selling" of policy choices to the environment.

PRESIDENTIAL DECISION MAKING

The paradox of the American presidency consists in the intertwined relationship between man and institution. The closer we have come to the present time historically, the heavier has been the emphasis on "institutionalization." This suggests a much greater degree of determination of executive activity by a vast paraphernalia of bureaucratic agents. And yet, on the vital questions of the day, one agent must make the final choice and accept the responsibility for decision—the sitting president.

All modern presidents are children of the Enlightenment in that they seek to act rationally in the pursuit of policy objectives. The exhaustive examination of means and methods in order to select those most expeditious to the achievement of sought ends or objectives is a crude description of the behavioral ideal model of all decision makers. This being the case, the discussion to follow will examine variations on the attempt by postwar presidents to achieve economic stability through the administration of correct policies by their governments. Concentration will, of course, be directed to the three major macroeconomic policy packages offered during the past half century: fiscal policies involving aggregate tax and expenditure decisions; monetary policies involving the money supply and interest rates; and incomes policies involving attempts to manipulate private economic behavior by means ranging from exhortation and pressure to formal, legal controls.

Although we tend to associate fiscal policy activism with politicians of the liberal persuasion, and monetary policies with a conservative bent (and correctly so), in fact, in the course of all postwar administrations, macroeconomic policy choices have had some reference to all forms of governmental activity in some measure, most frequently in a mix of policy strategies. Yet emphases are an important source of distinctions, as we shall see. The nature of choice and of mix becomes more crucial, of course, in times of economic maladjustment. Thus the appearance of growing inflation, high unemployment or the slough of recession provokes deeper examination of policy alternatives and a more agonizing process of choice in the knowledge that the consequences will be portentous.

Our examination of several decision settings in times of relative economic crisis will be roughly chronological. This mode was chosen because of the importance of legacy. Each president, in meeting the policy challenge, will be conditioned to some extent by the consequences of his predecessors' choices as well as by the nature of the policy repertoire administered. Beyond the stimulus offered or restraint imposed by past events, a number of other factors conditioning choice will be addressed. These include the personal philosophical dispositions of the president; state of the art questions about available economic intelligence; the organizational imperatives of advisory mechanisms; the impact of exogenous factors such as random, unanticipated shocks; and ominous threats to the political security of the presidency itself.

Dwight Eisenhower and the Quest for Fiscal Orthodoxy

Dwight Eisenhower brought to the presidency in 1953 a traditional, conservative antipathy to high spending, unbalanced budgets and public control of economic life which characterized his political party and not a small fraction of the citizenry. After the election, the heirs-apparent to public responsibility were aghast at the discovery of the outgoing Truman administration's nearly $10 billion planned deficit for fiscal 1954, and at the costs of the administration's ambitious spending forecasts. In his first State of the Union message the president pledged to reduce the planned deficit, balance the budget, stretch out the public debt and fight inflation.[1] In his memoirs Eisenhower discusses his disagreements with the economic beliefs of his predecessors and concludes:

> In initiating a reversal of trends based upon such beliefs—trends which by 1953 were twenty years old—we were setting in motion revolutionary activity. We suffered no delusion that such a revolution would become a reality through the frenzied drama of a first one hundred days, or that it could be the work of improvization, however clever.[2]

In an act that seems almost a preview of Budget Director David Stockman's spending surgery of 1981, the president put an enthusiastic budgeteer, Joseph Dodge, to work in paring programs in fiscal 1954, and Dodge squeezed some $4.5 billion out of the deficit. Even so, Eisenhower was not monomaniacal on the subject of a balanced budget. The notes of Emmet Hughes reveal lively debates between the president and some of his more rigid associates, Humphrey and Dodge. The president was apprehensive about sacrificing defense capability and the structure of the Western alliance on the altar of fiscal purity.[3] Similarly, Eisenhower's decision to remove the wage and price controls of the Korean war era as early as February came only after his assurance that such an early suspension date would not be so sudden a shock to the economy as to be damaging.

In the end, however, Eisenhower remained as true to his economic convictions as could be expected. To be sure there were pragmatic concessions here and there to fiscal stimulus interludes. The *Economic Report* of 1954 would even claim credit for timely action taken to relieve the mild recession of 1953–54.[4] Still the characteristic stance of the administration throughout most of the eight years was modesty in the use of fiscal tools, a consistent drumbeat against the evils of inflation and a willingness to tolerate unemployment levels higher, for a longer time, than liberal critics could accept. And while it may not constitute good economics by some objective standards, the president did manage to produce three budgetary surpluses during his administrations. While this amounts to less than a .500 batting average, perspective is lent by the knowledge that, with a single exception (1969), the president's six successors in office were unable or unwilling to match that feat.[5]

Certainly the clearest test of Eisenhower's determination to hew to a conservative line was in his response to economic recession in 1959–60. While the administration did engage in some anti-recessionary fiscal activity during the 1958 and 1959, this activity mainly involved increased spending for *other* reasons—particularly increased defense spending in the post-Sputnik period.[6] But to the pleas of many of his advisers in favor of a tax cut stimulus in 1959–60, the president turned a deaf ear. Earlier, former Council of Economic Advisers Chairman Arthur Burns had lectured Eisenhower in correspondence:

> It is an oversimplification to assert, as some fine and thoughtful citizens do, that a balanced budget or surplus is necessary to build confidence. The very opposite can be true and in fact has been true at times.[7]

But this president was not a docile student, and in spite of high unemployment levels in 1959 and 1960 that seemed resistant to self-correction, Eisenhower called for a 1960 budget that would produce a surplus. Throughout the spring of 1959, he vetoed a series of spending bills for urban renewal, housing and college aid. In the spring of 1960 he would repeat the same veto strategy.[8] In a letter in response to Burns's advocacy of a $5 billion tax cut, Eisenhower expressed himself as "not getting stubborn in my attitude about logical federal action . . . [but that] precipitate and therefore largely unwise action would be the worse thing."[9] Subsequently, at a cabinet meeting where the president was lobbied by several aides who feared the political fallout of economic stagnation in the 1960 elections, the answer to the tax-cut proposal remained no. Vice President Richard Nixon later confided, in his recounting of the decision: "In supporting Burns's point of view I must admit that I was more sensitive politically than some of the others around the cabinet table."[10]

John F. Kennedy and the New Economic Era

Vice President Nixon's sensitivity was well placed. In the fall presidential campaign of 1960 the economy was in a recessionary trough and candidate Kennedy's domestic theme promised to "get the country moving again."[11] As president, enthusiasm for motion would be reflected in many facets of his approach to economic policy. Kennedy's formal training in economics was meager and undistinguished, and his philosophical orientation was pragmatic. As a result he was eager to learn and willing to entertain a variety of approaches. In consequence the 1960s mark a major turning point in the application of macroeconomic policy.

Although it is argued here that versatility of programmatic applications is the key part of the "new economics," clearly the adoption politically of what had become *professional* economic orthodoxy stands out. The Keynesian idea that compensatory fiscal (and monetary) policy should be addressed to balancing the business cycle found its application in the tax cut proposal which the president would accept by 1963. CEA Chairman Walter Heller instructed Kennedy with the zeal of a missionary in the precepts of the new economics and was gratified by his success:

> Nevertheless, President Kennedy's occasional doubts and concessions to prevailing economic sentiment stand out only as detours on his road to modernism. What was pleasing to his economic advisers, and fortunate for the country, was his responsiveness to *analysis*, the force of economic logic and fact; to *analogy*, the demonstrated success of Keynesian policies abroad; and to *anomaly*, the continued sacrifice of human and material resources on the alter of false concepts of "sound finance."[12]

For a number of reasons, the president did not buy the Heller plan on first offering. There remained for a time the habit of attachment to the commonsense virtue of the balanced budget. Then, too, he had sounded a note of sacrifice to his countrymen in the Inaugural, and the seeming inconsistency of a program to lighten the tax burden nagged. Finally, within the economic advisory subcabinet itself there were differences of opinion. Treasury Secretary Dillon feared the impact of budgetary deficits on foreign bankers who, becoming concerned about the strength of the dollar, might be inclined to take American gold, exacerbating the balance of payments problem.[13] By mid-1962, however, the economy had slackened and with 5.5 million unemployed, the specter of recession haunted the president and his advisors. Thus consensus was reached, and even Dillon "signed on" as a reluctant spokesman for the new tax measure. Designed at the time to put some $11 billion in income tax reductions in consumers' pockets, the fiscal stimulus was announced in the 1963 *Economic Report*.[14]

While the tax measure stands out dramatically, the larger characteristic of "Kennedy-nomics" was movement along other economic frontiers simultaneously. Thus, just as the administration was announcing the fiscal stimulus-demand strategy, it had also engaged in movement on the supply side. We are accustomed to hearing of supply-side economics as an ideology of the eighties. It is instructive to note that stimulus to the supply side as a strategy—if not a full-blown ideology—is a policy practice with a history.[15] Thus, in the same 1963 *Economic Report*, the CEA announced plans for increased and earlier depreciation write-offs for business firms and a new investment tax credit, permitting firms to take tax deductions for new equipment.[16]

An incomes policy variation was yet another piece drawn out of the political economy armory of the Kennedy administration. The homely sobriquet "jawboning" has come to characterize that exercise in persuasion carried on by public leaders to influence discretionary wage and price decisions in the private sector. Under the new title "Guideposts" the Council first announced in the 1962 *Economic Report* sets of general guides it would promote to encourage non-inflationary wage and price behavior. Characterized as "aids to understanding," the Guideposts correlated wage and price increases with increases in productivity and concluded with an acceptable quantitative average increase of 3.2 percent which would constitute the target for several years.[17]

The guidepost mechanism was not a revolutionary innovation in its essence. Presidents before, most recently Eisenhower in the late 1950s, had sought to discourage strikes, encourage moderation in pricing, and appeal to the communitarian instincts of private economic leaders.[18] What was innovative, however, was the attempt to achieve precision with quantitative measures of "good behavior."

Moreover, the very routinization of the process in the *Economic Reports* lent an aspect of permanence to this new "given" in the national economic decision-making environment.[19] In perspective it cannot be said that the guideposts had more than a marginal impact, and they were criticized on many grounds, ranging from equity and due process, to strictures about administrative viability and relevance, to changed economic conditions (for example, in times of high levels of employment).[20] By 1967 the CEA publicly recognized some of the criticisms, discounted the specified numerical guides, and emphasized the voluntarism and flexibility of government guidelines.[21]

The opening sentence in Walter Heller's account of economic policy in the Kennedy era states: "Economics has come of age in the 1960s."[22] Both the optimism and satisfaction implied by this pronouncement characterize macroeconomic policy in the Kennedy (and indeed Johnson) years. The belief was widely shared that experience with the adaptation of Keynesianism to modern America, the beneficent development of computer-aided econometrics and enlightened public leadership all resulted in the capacity truly to manipulate the business cycle in the public interest. "We've finally got it right," they seemed to be saying. And this should not be surprising. The economic indicators suggested that we were on a steady course of stability. By 1965 the Council of Economic Advisers could point to increased investment, GNP growth, stable wages and prices, and declining joblessness as the achievements of the sixties:

> The expansion of economic activity during the past four years has carried virtually every economic indicator to a new record level.[23]

The optimism harbored in reviews of success would be subjected to harsh challenges in the declining years of the decade. A jolt to the macroeconomic environment and a president concerned with political survival would test the limits of economic expertise.

Lyndon Johnson and the Politics of Political Economy

Given the kit of economic tools available to the postwar presidents, it should not be surprising that those policies designed to stimulate certain kinds of economic activity and discourage other kinds should be adjusted to the political advantage of the administration in office. That commonsense notion, reinforced by the experience of some citizens, has now been documented for our examination. Edward Tufte has shown the coincidence between the economic calendar and the political calendar. In brief, during the period examined, 1948 to 1976 the typical pattern is one where the growth of real disposable income per capita accelerates in even-numbered (national election) years and decelerates in odd-numbered years. In addition the pattern reveals declines in the unemployment rate in presidential election years and increases in unemployment usually a year or two after the election.[2] The link between the political and economic correlates is forged by the manipulation of tax payments, transfer payments, and occasional help from the Fed in enhancing the growth of the money supply.[2] The major exception to this general pattern occurred under President Eisenhower, implying, as suggested above, the power of personal ideology.

Lyndon Johnson's stewardship of the macroeconomic trust suggests a slightly different dimension to the nexus between political judgments and economic policy choices. The first year of Johnson's personal, elected presidency gave understandable cause for euphoria. A host of domestic reforms, including aid to education, medical care and civil rights measures, passed into law smoothly, accompanied by applause for the president's political aplomb. In January 1966 Johnson's economic advisers could exult:

> The strength of the advance in 1965 was exceptional and surpassed expectations. The Council's Annual Report of 1965, which contained one of the more optimistic forecasts at that time, estimated a gain of $38 billion in GNP for the year—the midpoint of a $33–44 billion range. In contrast, the actual gain was a record $47 billion.[26]

The new year, however, brought a disturbing turn of events. Wage negotiations in transportation, automobiles and even civil service salaries pushed over the guideposts. But it was defense expenditures associated with the Vietnam war that created the greatest cause for alarm among the economic advisers. Prices were rising sharply toward the end of 1965, and the rises continued into the first three quarters of 1966. In December 1965, CEA Chairman Ackley sent the following memorandum to the president:

> If the budget is $115 billion, there is little question in my mind that a significant tax increase will be needed to prevent an intolerable degree of inflationary pressure. With a budget of $110 billion the question is more difficult. My tentative view now is that a tax increase would probably still be necessary.[27]

In the spring and summer months of 1966 Ackley, strongly supported by Budget Director Charles Schultze, continued to lobby for the tax measure. This campaign included mobilizing a blue-ribbon corps of economists from Harvard that expressed its consensus in favor of deflationary fiscal moves.[28] As the 1966 elections neared, the president became more resolved in his opposition to new taxes. After the elections he decided in favor of a 6 percent tax surcharge and recommended this in the January 1967 *Economic Report*. The administration, however, failed to follow through with a tax message to Congress.

The absorption of productive capacity by the Vietnam war effort created an excess of civilian demand and thus continued to fan the inflationary fires. There seem to have been two reasons for Lyndon Johnson's rejection of the near-unanimous advice of his economic aides. First, ever the legislative strategist and tactician, he judged that he might not be able to persuade Ways and Means Committee Chairman Wilbur Mills and Congress to give him a "peacetime" tax increase. Second, criticism of his foreign policy mounted and his overall popular approval was declining.[29] Adding a tax increase to all the other public vexations would be courting political disaster. Better to finance the Vietnam war with inflation than with taxes.

In the end—and it was the end—the president did accept and maneuver through Congress a 10 percent corporate and individual income tax hike. In late June 1968, the tax surcharge bill passed both Houses, but in a long-term sense it was already too late in the judgment of most economists. In retrospect CEA Chairman Arthur Okun considered some of the imponderables: Might a vigorous presidential advocacy of the tax in 1966 or 1967 have endangered other Great Society programs? Could any *feasible* tax increase in 1966 have offset the defense spending stimulus of the budget?[30] Whatever the case, it seems clear that long-term inflationary pressures were built up as a result of Johnson's decision to pursue the Vietnam mission at all costs and to forestall the direct payment of those costs. The imperatives of presidential priorities transcended the macroeconomic dictates of the Employment Act.

Richard Nixon and the Disposition of a Legacy

The inflationary trend first evident in 1965 continued to grow after the change of administrations in 1968. From the 4.5 percent consumer price increase levels of 1968, the following year brought rises moving from 5 to 7 percent. Presidential confidant Arthur Burns, speaking before the American Bankers Association in the spring of 1970, rehearsed the melancholy tale:

> The mistakes of stabilization policy in 1965 reflected an unwillingness to face up promptly to the urgent need for restrictive actions on the fiscal and monetary front.[31]

As for strategies to meet the wage-price runaway, "jawboning" was excluded from the administration's repertoire. Council Chairman McCracken recorded in the *Economic Report* of 1970:

> The administration's plan of policy for 1969 did not include an attempt to revive wage-price guideposts, such as those existing in 1962–66. The results of our own experience and numerous trials of such policies in other countries over the preceding 20 years did not justify confidence in that such efforts would help solve the inflation problem in 1969.[32]

Nor did the administration respond obligingly to the Democratic congressional suggestion of incomes policy authorizations. Commenting on the economic stabilization legislation of 1970, President Nixon has observed:

> Over my objections Congress sent me sweeping legislation that empowered the president to control prices, wages, and salaries. Since my strong opposition to controls was well known, I viewed the bill as a political ploy on the part of the Democratic Congress aimed at putting the ball publicly in my court. To a certain extent the ploy worked. Although I would not accept a complete move to a mandatory system of wage and price controls, I feared that if I refused to take some action I might exacerbate the general lack of confidence that was itself beginning to harm the economy and hamper its chances of recovery.[33]

What Nixon had come to accept during the first two years of his presidency was a policy of "gradualism." This consisted of tightening up the money supply (with the willing assistance of Fed Chairman Martin); a tighter rein on expenditures (producing that rare bird, a small budgetary surplus, in 1969); and noninterference with wage-price negotiations. For a time the policies seemed to be paying off, with money at nearly a no-growth rate and an early decline in the price index. Shortly, however, it appeared that the monetary brakes had been applied too vigorously and economic growth declined dangerously. At the same time, consumer prices began shooting up.[34]

As a result 1971 brought a budgetary deficit of over $23 billion, consumer price increases of over 5 percent and an unemployment level of 6 percent.[35] It also brought declining public approval ratings to the president.[36]

By June 1971 Richard Nixon regarded the economic situation to be in crisis. One of the measures he had already taken was to appoint a strong figure as his new Treasury Secretary—John Connally. Motives for the appointment were probably mixed. Connally was not only a conservative Texas Democrat, but also a possible future presidential contender.[37] In midsummer the president met with his cabinet and sought recommendations for policy shifts. Secretary Connally responded with a call for the "big play."[38] A top-level meeting was held at Camp David on August 13, 1971. Herbert Stein has noted the drama that surrounded the Camp David deliberations, finding them landmarks in the history of economic policy development.[39]

Nevertheless, the outcome of the Camp David scenario may well have been fixed much earlier, even as Nixon's political instincts of a year before are suggested in the reaction to congressional passage of the Economic Stabilization Act. In any case, on Sunday night, August 15, 1971 (timed to anticipate the stock market's opening bell on Monday morning), the president announced his "New Economic Policy," to begin with a 90-day freeze on wages, prices and rents, and a suspension of the convertibility of the dollar into gold.[40] In subsequent phases of the program, controls were first eased as to comprehensiveness of coverage in November, and then, as prices began to rise again in January 1973, reimposed temporarily.[41] Finally, all mandatory controls were lifted in 1974. We shall consider the implementation of these policies at a later stage. In the meantime, perhaps the fairest epitaph for the experiment was written by the president himself:

When mandatory wage and price controls came to a complete end in 1974, the aftermath was far from pleasant. Energy shortages and high food prices contributed to an increase in inflation and to recession, and the pressures that built up after the period of controls led into the destructive double-digit inflation that plagued the early months of the Ford administration. Three years after controls had been completely ended, both unemployment and inflation hovered around 7 percent, and there was even nostalgia for the "good old days" of 1971 when we had only 4 percent inflation and 6 percent unemployment.[42]

This brief look at the Nixon administration's attempt to forge policies to produce macroeconomic stability provokes three general observations. First, the "dead hand" of past policies shapes and controls future alternatives in a relentless fashion. Second, ideological rigidity cannot be blamed for the president's failures. Unlike Eisenhower, Richard Nixon was prepared to swim in the untested and historically dreaded waters of statist control when the political climate for dramatic action seemed right. Finally, Herbert Stein idealized the Camp David conclave as robust with economic imagination. In fact the decisions were more crucially based on political instincts than on economic expertise. In the group that arrived at the consensus, the political actors, led by John Connally and the White House bureaucratic elite, weighed more heavily than the economists, many of whom opposed the program.

Jimmy Carter and Macroeconomics in Disarray

Analysts speculate about the mix of reasons for Jimmy Carter's resounding defeat in the 1980 presidential election, but none fails to emphasize the state of the American economy as a major factor. Public opinion polls at the time reinforce this conclusion. In August 1980, a national survey conducted by CBS News and the *New York Times* revealed that only 19 percent of the respondents approved of President Carter's "handling of the economy."[43] References to change in the leading economic indicators recorded in the outgoing president's last *Economic Report* document the reality behind public dissatisfactions:

	Changes in GNP	Unemployment Levels	Consumer Prices
1977	5.8%	7%	6.5%
1978	5.3	6	7.7
1979	1.7	5.8	11.3
1980	−0.3	7.1	13.5

The most vexing problem was, of course, inflation. Carter's predecessor, Gerald Ford, had managed to bring down inflation by the time-honored practice of producing recession out of tight money. Thus in 1976, unemployment was regarded as the immediate problem by the new Democratic president. For the next four years, the administration sought to bring about stability through a succession of programs, none of which provided an effective antidote to stagflation.

The reasons for the failure of policy are, as always, complex and not completely clear. Nevertheless, a number of economic pathogens seemed to converge in the late 1970s, and their nature at least helps to explain Jimmy Carter's tribulations. First of all, most economists, including those in the administration, believed that a decade's time had not exhausted the impact of the Johnson era's inflationary thrust. Moreover, the cumulative impact of past public policies, such as the indexing of federal program benefits and the increased size of the "untouchable" commitments in federal budgets, had created built-in upward budgetary pressures. Second, a new random shock from the environment had to be contained. Echoing the experience in 1974, OPEC administered a second major oil price increase in 1979, and between 1979 and 1981 oil prices nearly tripled.[44] Third, the rapid growth of public regulation during the seventies—most of which took place in the area of externalities (such as environmental, consumer, health and job safety rules)—had exacted an inflationary penalty.[45] Finally, although long ignored, the rate of growth of American productivity had been declining since the Johnson years. By 1981 this development had achieved recognition by the president's economic advisers:

> Since the mid-1960s, the growth rate of labor productivity has been declining from its postwar height. In recent years the decline has been so marked as to pose a major challenge to public policy. Because declining productivity growth brings with it prospects for slower improvement in our standard of living and contributes to inflation, a program to stimulate productivity must be a keystone of economic policy.[46]

To understand the nature of problems is a logical necessity. But a democratic society demands solutions to those problems. For many reasons the Carter administration seemed incapable of coping effectively with the problems of instability. It bobbed and weaved in the face of the challenges of stagflation. A tax rebate would be proposed and a few weeks later withdrawn. Incomes strategies would be mandated and then softened. Budgets would be submitted, revised markedly and resubmitted. Economic forecasts, authoritatively announced, would not survive the fiscal quarter intact. Part of this was a reflection of presidential style. Characterized as an "episodic" decision-making style, the lack of a broad context in the president's analysis was criticized by one official:

> You get the impression that things are done in boxes and are not related. . . . The president says, "I'm going to have an urban program. I'm going to have a welfare program. I'm going to keep the farmers

happy. . . . We need to fight inflation." Each issue gets put to the president with options and is dealt with on its own merits, but not in relationship to the others. Inflation is an across-the-board issue, and you have to have an overall strategy to deal with it. That's what we lack now.[47]

When forced to the choice, Carter opted to pay economic policy costs in order to satisfy the demands of politically strategic groups. Thus in overriding the inflation-haunted admonitions of his advisers, the president raised the minimum wage by $1.05 in 1977, approved acreage set-asides for grains, and opted for higher milk price supports and sugar prices.[48] In some instances Carter's own lieutenants publicly criticized his generosity. In November 1978, Barry Bosworth, Director of the Council on Wage and Price Stability, published an "Op-Ed" piece in the *New York Times* containing the following statements:

> First, we have to face the fact that government itself has become a major source of inflationary pressures, particularly in the last decade. . . . For example, this year the increased Social Security tax, the minimum wage increase, and the unemployment insurance tax increase—just those three items together—added three-quarters of a percentage point to the rate of inflation.[49]

At length one is led to the melancholy conclusion that while the experience, administrative style and personality of President Carter did not create most of the challenges to stability, they go a long way to explain a limited capacity to cope with those challenges. After exhaustive examination, Betty Glad judged that the president was afflicted by chronic self-absorption and a need to cultivate a sympathetic image to the detriment of serious engagement with real problems.[50] Many have commented on Carter's intelligence and diligence combined with an inability to think holistically. Thus James Fallows, an aide who became disillusioned with the president, has written:

> I came to think that Carter believes fifty things, but no one thing. He holds explicit, thorough positions on every issue under the sun, but he has no large view of the relations between them. . . . Carter thinks in lists, not arguments; as long as the items are there, their order does not matter, nor does the hierarchy among them.[51]

The Reagan Revolution

Dwight Eisenhower talked about a revolution. Ronald Reagan made one. On coming to office in January 1981, Reagan faithfully moved to implement his campaign pledges and the combination of policies that would soon be dubbed "Reaganomics" was invoked. A simple and fundamental premise lay at the base of the Reagan political-economic view of the world. That was the traditional conservative notion— perhaps believed too literally now—that the chief source of economic instability was government interference with the "free market." In the rhetoric of the campaign, "getting government off the peoples' back" was meant to characterize the act of a benign state in permitting the release of the natural appetites and energies of *homo economicus*. As Lester Thurow has pointed out, this was perfectly consistent with the traditional economic myth, the "price-auction model" (free markets, supply and demand, and income maximization).[52]

The keystone of Reaganomics was "supply side" economics. As noted above, attempts at manipulating the supply side of the system were not new. What was new, as the 1980s began, was the fashioning of an economic ideology which for a time produced an almost cultlike following. The "big idea" of the supply side model consisted in the stimulation of investment and harder work on the part of economic suppliers (both workers and entrepreneurs) through the incentive afforded by lower taxes and thus greater income. If George Gilder was the "high priest" of the supply side, Arthur Laffer, with his "curve" plotting the points at which declining tax rates produce greater revenues, was the chief acolyte.[53] While the president was not a pitchman for the supply side fraternity, he did accept the basic notions that found their way into the Kemp-Roth proposal for massive income tax cuts. It was the president's determined commitment to the supply-side principle that formed the base for the revolutionary structure of his program.

Reaganomics incorporated other components, however, some of which were inconsistent with the basic notion. The first was the (consistent) idea of deregulation, by which the supply side was to be emancipated not only by lower taxes, but also by the removal of costly restrictions on activity which government imposes. (This was not a novel idea; the deregulation movement had made substantial progress in the Carter years.) Yoked to these supply-side elements was a commitment to monetarism as a means of fighting inflation. A fourth element in the program was the shrinking of domestic welfare spending to make up for the revenue shortages resulting from tax cuts. The final feature of the policy constellation was not, strictly speaking, a macroeconomic policy, but it was one that would have weighty consequences for the macroeconomic package. That was the commitment to substantially increased defense spending. A halfhearted attempt was made to suggest that defense spending itself would have growth-stimulating results, but the real motive for the increases was grounded in a foreign policy–national security mindset.

Given the implications of these five elements, commitment to Reaganomics required a prodigious act of faith. The gambles were clear at the outset. Would tax cuts have the requisite stimulative effect on the supply side? In fighting inflation with high interest rates, would excessive monetarism serve to depress investment behavior? How could the costs in tax losses (ultimately reductions of 23 percent over three years) and the increased defense budgets be met by sufficient domestic cuts? This avowedly conservative government also stressed the importance of balanced budgets. (As late as September 1981, the president still projected a balanced budget in fiscal 1984.[54]) Yet Reagan refused to be moved in a fundamental way by such doubts, and a dogged commitment to the view of a world reformed constituted the revolutionary ethic.[55] At bottom macroeconomic policy in the Reagan years has rested not so much on economic theory as on political ideology.

If the president did not panic at exploding deficits and stagnation in the economy, many of his economic specialists did. In 1982, GNP continued to show negative growth, and unemployment was on the rise even as the fires of inflation were dampened.[56] Later the National Bureau of Economic Research would announce that the longest recession since World War II had begun in July 1981, and only reached its trough in November 1982. In the 1982 elections, with unemployment standing at over 10 million and a federal budgetary deficit estimated in excess of $200 billion, the president pleaded with the voters to "stay the course." The results of the election were ambiguous. The loss of 26 House seats and the standoff in the Senate constituted less voter retribution than might have been expected. However, examination of the anatomy of the vote indicates that the Republicans had lost support among groups which had been attracted to Reagan two years earlier: middle of the road independents, blue-collar workers and the older age groups.[57]

By midsummer 1983, the administration could take some comfort in the growing signs of economic upturn. The Commerce Department announced that the annual growth rate during the second quarter was up 8.7 percent, two points higher than the government's forecast a month earlier. The consumer price index had risen only 0.2 percent. Yet unemployment still idled about 10 million workers.[58] Throughout the spring of 1983 the president fought off attempts to cancel the third phase of the tax reduction program and persisted in a no-compromise stance during the congressional budget debates. He remained committed to high defense spending and vowed to veto appropriations measures reaching his desk with domestic spending increases. For a time Reagan was once again on the offensive, and 1984 brought a continued upturn in the major economic indicators. But critics still worried about the potential consequences of clashing fiscal and monetary policies and about the long-term impact of unprecedented budget deficits.

A commitment to public policies that have drastically altered long familiar economic relationships is one basis for asserting that individual, presidential agency has provoked revolutionary change. Moreover the changes should not be viewed in terms of the macroeconomic statistics alone. Ultimately the social impact of Reaganomics may be the greater legacy. On the core issue of equality, the first results of the policies of 1981–82 were unmistakably redistributive—from the top down. Retrenchment in public assistance transfer program expenditures in the 1981 and 1982 budget revisions announced in April 1981 hit hardest at Aid to Families of Dependent Children and the Food Stamps Program. The assault on the troubled Comprehensive Employment and Training Program would transfer many thousands from "make-work" jobs to no jobs. An early study done by the Congressional Budget Office estimated that the administration's tax reduction program would be more than offset by losses in public benefits for the poor. While the average citizen was projected to gain 3.9 percent in income from the new program, those whose income in 1982 was over $80,000 could be expected to gain 7.9 percent in income in 1984, whereas those whose income was below $10,000 in 1982 could be expected to lose 1.2 percent of income.[59]

The "social safety net" which was designed to save the poor from the worst ravages of withdrawal turned out to be less secure than forecast. Thus an Urban Institute study found that the safety net caught mainly Social Security recipients and those who had been out of work for less than 13 weeks. People not supported by the safety net were the long-term unemployed, the typical welfare recipient who had some income other than welfare aid, and recipients of non-cash aid, regardless of income level.[60] The general finding of the Urban Institute in 1982 was that administration programs would

> provide modest income gains (after taxes and transfers) for the average household. However, the gains to families in the upper income brackets are quite large and, on average, low-income families will experience a small net loss. . . . It is clear that the changes introduced thus far make the distribution of incomes less equal and require some sacrifices by low-income families.[61]

PRELUDE AND POSTLUDE TO DECISION

In addition to the range of factors conditioning the immediate choices of presidents, the environment of policies and their realization are influenced by presidential activities of other sorts. On the one hand, since so much of the process is institutionalized, the president's prior managerial activities and personnel selections go a long way toward establishing the agenda for choice. On the other hand, the realization of chosen objectives depends in part on a president's capacity and skill in overseeing processes of implementation and in merchandising his policy wares in a marketplace of potential veto groups.

Institutional Management

The four major institutional participants in economic policymaking—the Department of the Treasury, the Office of Management and Budget, the Council of Economic Advisers and the Federal Reserve Board—came into being not by presidential choice, but by legislative policy determination. In employing these institutional aids, presidents have occasionally applied an organizational hand to shape and direct the flow of policy. Examples include Kennedy's bringing together of the first three economic policy institutions as a routinely consulting "troika" (and later, by incorporating the Fed, a "quadriad") and Nixon's conversion of the Bureau of the Budget into the Office of Management and Budget, with a greater managerial role.[62] But clearly the more important presidential impact has been in setting the tone and establishing policy preferences at the outset by appointments of agents to run those bodies. By and large, presidents have gotten what they wanted. Thus budget directors, CEA chairmen and the other major actors have alternately reflected the ideological preferences of their chiefs. Table 4-1 lists policymakers largely in tune (whether liberal or conservative, Keynesian or monetarist) with presidential predilections.

Administering Complex Routines

After basic direction-setting decisions have been made, the institutional presidency must preside over the stages of implementation. An emergency-spawned policy of novel character must cope with certain special administration obstacles. Thus when Richard Nixon resorted to an incomes policy of alternate wage-price freezes and selective controls, the *implementation* of policy constituted the greatest chal-

TABLE 4-1. Presidential Political-Economic Elite, 1946–83

President	CEA Chairman	BOB/OMB Director	Treasury Secretary	Fed Chairman
Truman 1945–1953	Nourse, 1946 Keyserling, 1949	Webb, 1946 Pace, 1949 Lawton, 1950	Vinson, 1945 Snyder, 1946	McCabe, 1948 Martin, 1951
Eisenhower 1953–1961	Burns, 1953 Saulnier, 1956	Dodge, 1953 Hughes, 1954 Brundage, 1956 Stans, 1958	Humphrey, 1953 Anderson, 1957	Martin
Kennedy 1961–1963	Heller, 1961	Bell, 1961 Gordon, 1962	Dillon, 1961	Martin
Johnson 1963–1969	Ackley, 1964 Okun, 1968	Schultze, 1965 Zwick, 1968	Fowler, 1965 Barr, 1968	Martin
Nixon 1969–1974	McCracken, 1969 Stein, 1971	Mayo, 1969 Shultz, 1971 Weinberger, 1972 Ash, 1973	Kennedy, 1969 Connally, 1971 Shultz, 1972 Simon, 1974	Burns, 1969
Ford 1974–1977	Greenspan, 1974	Lynn, 1975	Simon	Burns
Carter 1977–1981	Schultze, 1977	Lance, 1977 McIntyre, 1978	Blumenthal, 1977 Miller, 1979	Miller, 1978 Volcker, 1979
Reagan 1981–	Weidenbaum, 1981 Feldstein, 1982	Stockman, 1981	Regan, 1981	Volcker, 1983

lenge. From autumn 1971 to spring 1974, government controls wer
administered uncertainly in a series of four phases." Instant in
stitutionalization brought with it the hurried elaboration of a broa
mandate and the frantic formation of staff (initially relying heavily o
detailees from other agencies), followed by a history of chroni
understaffing.[63] The verdict on the administration of controls must b
that demands were made upon the system which it was not ade
quately equippped to handle. While this has been true in other area
as well, the experience of ad hoc institutions of questioned legitimac
exaggerates the pathology.

Legislative Followup

Frequently, the first stage of implementation, after policy has bee
decided at the presidential level, is the campaign for necessary legis
lative support. Advance planning is crucial. Thus planning for th
operationalizing of Reaganomics began at least a month before th
presidential inauguration in January 1981. David Stockman, a
budget director-designate, presided over the assembling of more thar
50 policy papers which collectively recommended the elimination o
some $40 billion in domestic spending in fiscal 1982. The fast and
loose quality of some of the economic calculations has come to light ir
a politically embarassing article in *Atlantic* magazine. As Stockmar
related to journalist William Greider:

> The defense numbers got out of control and we were doing that whole
> budget-cutting exercise so frenetically. In other words, you were jug-
> gling details, pushing people, and going from one session to another,
> trying to cut housing programs here and rural electric there, and we
> were doing it so fast, we didn't know where we were ending up for
> sure. . . . But the pieces were moving on independent tracks—the tax
> program, which was just a bunch of numbers written on a piece of
> paper . . . and it didn't quite mesh. That's what happened. But, you
> see, for about a month and a half we got away with that because of the
> novelty of all these budget reductions.[64]

Nevertheless, by the early spring of 1981, the OMB had presented tc
Congress a 435-page document entitled *Fiscal Year 1982 Revisions*
which detailed budgetary savings in some 83 program categories.[65]
Supplementing the blitzkrieg of technical presentations, the president personally took up his special role of soliciting support for adoption—and therefore implementation.

Policy Salesmanship

The Reagan activity in merchandising policy objectives is suggestive of the general need for public support which presidents must seek to satisfy. Indeed there are at least three separate but overlapping publics which must be targeted. First, the elite, governmental constituencies (primarily Congress and the bureaucracy itself) must be courted. Second, attention must be given to the professional economic sector—those whose business is most directly affected by economic policy and who make it their business to influence application as well as formulation of policy. Finally, the "public" in its broadest conception—the attentive citizenry—must often be implored to voice its support or, at least, its apparent approval of the policy product. These overlapping and overseeing constituencies of interest are exemplified by key congressional committees, private economic entities symbolized by Wall Street and the Business Council, and that *vox populi* which responds to surveys soliciting its opinion of "the president's economic program."

General assessments of the contemporary presidency as national economic overseer are risky at best. Yet, even recognizing the limitations of the state of the economic art, the variability of presidential interests, commitments and skills, and the impact of random and unexpected shocks to the environment, it is still possible to conclude that the broad contours of economic policy (and therefore economic stability) over the past 40 years have indeed reflected presidential agency—for better and for worse.

NOTES

1. National Archives and Record Service, *Public Papers of the Presidents of the United States*, 1953 (1960), p. 12, hereafter cited as *Public Papers* by year. See also Wilfred Lewis, Jr., *Federal Fiscal Policy in the Postwar Recessions* (Washington, D.C.: The Brookings Institution, 1962), pp. 131–133. On the agonies and forebodings of the president and his aides, see Sherman Adams, *Firsthand Report* (New York: Harper & Brothers, 1961), pp. 154–155.

2. Dwight D. Eisenhower, *Mandate for Change, 1953–1956* (Garden City, N.Y.: Doubleday, 1963), p. 87.

3. Emmet J. Hughes, *The Ordeal of Power* (New York: Dell, 1962), pp. 64–65. See also Robert J. Donovan, *Eisenhower: The Inside Story* (New York: Harper & Brothers, 1956), pp. 31–32.

4. *Economic Report of the President, 1954* (Washington, D.C.: U.S. Government Printing Office, 1954), hereafter cited as *Economic Report* by year.

5. Office of Management and Budget, *The U.S. Budget in Brief, Fiscal Year 1984* (Washington, D.C.: U.S. Government Printing Office, 1983), p. 84.

6. Lewis, *Federal Fiscal Policy*, p. 233.

7. Burns to Eisenhower, November 27, 1957. Quoted in Crauford D. Goodwin, ed., *Exhortation and Controls: The Search for a Wage-Price Policy, 1945-1971* (Washington, D.C.: The Brookings Institution, 1975), p. 104.

8. See James L. Sundquist, *Politics and Policy: The Eisenhower, Kennedy and Johnson Years* (Washington, D.C.: The Brookings Institution, 1968), and Dwight Eisenhower, *Waging the Peace* (New York: Doubleday, 1965), pp. 459-465.

9. Quoted in Eisenhower, *Waging the Peace*, p. 309.

10. Richard Nixon, *Six Crises* (Garden City, N.Y.: Doubleday, 1962), p. 310.

11. See Theodore H. White, *The Making of the President, 1960* (New York: Atheneum, 1961), pp. 254-258.

12. Walter Heller, *New Dimensions of Political Economy* (New York: Norton, 1967), p. 35.

13. Theodore Sorensen, *Kennedy* (New York: Harper & Row, 1965), pp. 407-408.

14. *Economic Report* (1963), pp. xiii-xvi. See the detailed account in Edward S. Flash, Jr., *Economic Advice and Presidential Leadership* (New York: Columbia University Press, 1965), Chapter 7. Compare accounts in Arthur M. Schlesinger, Jr., *A Thousand Days* (Boston: Houghton Mifflin, 1965), pp. 648-656, and Sorensen, *Kennedy*, pp. 421-433.

15. See Lester C. Thurow, *Dangerous Currents: The State of Economics* (New York: Random House, 1983), p. 127.

16. *Economic Report* (1963), p. 18.

17. *Economic Report* (1962), pp. 186, 189-190.

18. On the Eisenhower practice of moral persuasion, see H. Scott Gordon, "The Eisenhower Administration and the Doctrine of Shared Responsibility," in Goodwin, *Exhortation*, pp. 215-234.

19. See John Sheahan, *The Wage-Price Guideposts* (Washington, D.C.: The Brookings Institution, 1967), Chapter 2.

20. See George P. Shultz and Robert Z. Aliber. eds., *Guidelines, Informal Controls and the Marketplace* (Chicago: University of Chicago Press, 1966).

21. *Economic Report* (1967), pp. 120-134.

22. Heller, *New Dimensions*, p. 1.

23. *Economic Report* (1965), p. 38.

24. Edward R. Tufte, *Political Control of the Economy* (Princeton, N.J.: Princeton University Press, 1978), p. 27.

25. Tufte, Chapter 2.

26. *Economic Report* (1966), p. 38.

27. Quoted in Lyndon B. Johnson, *The Vantage Point* (New York: Holt, Rinehart & Winston, 1971), p. 440.

28. James L. Cochrane, "The Johnson Administration: Moral Suasion Goes to War," in Goodwin, *Exhortation*, pp. 263–267.

29. George Gallup, *The Gallup Poll: Public Opinion, 1935–1971* (New York: Random House, 1972), Vol. 3.

30. Arthur M. Okun, *The Political Economy of Prosperity* (Washington, D.C.: The Brookings Institution, 1970), pp. 72–73.

31. Arthur Burns, "Inflation: The Fundamental Challenge to Stabilization Policies," in Arthur Burns, ed., *Reflections of an Economic Policy-Maker* (Washington, D.C.: American Enterprise Institute, 1978).

32. *Economic Report* (1970), p. 23. See the president's statement on "jawboning" in *Public Papers* (1970), p. 20.

33. Richard Nixon, *The Memoirs of Richard Nixon* (New York: Grosset & Dunlap, 1978), p. 516.

34. Leonard Silk, *Nixonomics* (New York: Praeger, 1972), pp. 8–11.

35. *Economic Report* (1972), pp. 38, 41, 269.

36. At the end of 1970, Nixon's public approval rating was running close to 60 percent. By summer 1971, it had dropped more than 10 points. In the first poll taken after the freeze (August 29, 1971), 73 percent of respondents approved of the new policy. See Gallup, Vol. 3, pp. 2315 and 2321.

37. Silk, *Nixonomics*, pp. 81–83.

38. Nixon, *Memoirs*, p. 518.

39. Quoted in Nixon, *Memoirs*, p. 519.

40. See *Economic Report* (1972), pp. 19–28.

41. See Weber, *In Pursuit;* Weber and Mitchell, *Pay Board's Progress;* and Robert Lanzillotti, Mary Hamilton and R. Blaine Roberts, *Phase II in Review: The Price Commission Experience* (Washington, D.C.: The Brookings Institution, 1978).

42. Nixon, *Memoirs*, p. 521.

43. Kathleen A. Frankovic, "Public Opinion Trends," in Gerald Pomper, ed., *The Election of 1980* (Chatham, N.J.: Chatham House, 1981).

44. For an analysis of the effect of energy cost increases on overall inflationary growth, see *Economic Report* (1981), pp. 149–152.

45. For a discussion of this phenomenon, see Murray L. Weidenbaum, *The Costs of Government Regulation of Business* (Washington, D.C.: U.S. Government Printing Office, 1978), pp. 13–17.

46. *Economic Report* (1981), p. 68.

47. *New York Times* (March 28, 1978). See also R. J. Samuelson, "Economic Policy: Is the Administration in Control?" *National Journal* (December 2, 1978).

48. *New York Times* (May 10, 1979).

49. *New York Times* (November 15, 1978).

50. Betty Glad, *Jimmy Carter: In Search of the Great White House* (New York: Norton, 1980), p. 504. In his own memoirs it is striking how little attention Carter gives to the economic problems of his administration. That which is given is usually expressed in the context of political opposition, fragmentation of Congress, Ted Kennedy's challenge and the 1980 election campaign. See Jimmy Carter, *Keeping Faith: Memoirs of a President* (New York: Bantam Books, 1983), pp. 74–75, 103–104, 526–530, 539, 563.

51. James Fallows, "The Passionless Presidency: The Trouble with Jimmy Carter's Administration," *Atlantic* (May 1979), p. 42.

52. Thurow, *Dangerous Currents*, p. 131.

53. George Gilder, *Wealth and Poverty* (New York: Bantam Books, 1981). See also Rowland Evans and Robert Novak, *The Reagan Revolution* (New York: E. P. Dutton, 1981), Chapter 5. See also Paul Craig Roberts, *The Supply-Side Revolution* (Cambridge, Mass.: Harvard University Press, 1984).

54. *Public Papers* (1981), p. 800, 810, and 831–832.

55. See Laurence I. Barrett, *Gambling with History: Ronald Reagan in the White House* (Garden City, N.Y.: Doubleday, 1983), pp. 38–40.

56. *Economic Report* (1983), pp. 83, 127, 136.

57. *New York Times* (November 8, 1982).

58. *New York Times* (July 24, 1983).

59. Congressional Budget Office, *Effects of Tax and Benefit Reductions Enacted in 1981 for Households in Different Income Categories* (Washington, D.C.: U.S. Government Printing Office, 1982), Tables 11 and 12. Two years later a second CBO study confirmed these trends (see *New York Times*, April 4, 1984).

60. John L. Palmer and Isabel V. Sawhill, eds., *The Reagan Experiment: An Examination of Economic and Social Policies under the Reagan Administration* (Washington, D.C.: Urban Institute Press, 1982), p. 383.

61. Palmer and Sawhill, p. 483.

62. See Larry Berman, *The Office of Management and Budget and the Presidency, 1921–1979* (Princeton, N.J.: Princeton University Press, 1979), and Lawrence C. Pierce, *The Politics of Fiscal Policy Formation* (Pacific Palisades, Cal.: Goodyear, 1971). On the Nixon reorganization, see Allen Schick,

"The Taking of OMB: The Office of Management and Budget During the Nixon Years," prepared for the Princeton University Conference on Advising the President (Princeton University, October 31, 1975), p. 44.

63. See Weber and Mitchell, *Pay Board's Progress*.

64. Stockman quoted in William Greider, *The Education of David Stockman and Other Americans* (New York: E. P. Dutton, 1982), pp. 37–38.

65. Office of Management and Budget, *Additional Details on Budget Savings* (Washington, D.C.: U.S. Government Printing Office, 1981).

Developing Fiscal Policy

JAMES E. ANDERSON

One of the major tasks of the federal government is that of stabilizing the economy. This involves the use of fiscal, monetary, international economic and perhaps wage-price control policies to achieve the goal of economic stability, which is characterized by economic growth, high or full employment, price stability and equilibrium in the international balance of payments.

Primary responsibility for action in stabilizing the economy rests with the president. As Clinton Rossiter wrote in the 1950s:

> The people of this country are no longer content to let disaster fall upon them unopposed. They now expect their government, under the direct leadership of the President, to prevent a depression or panic and not simply wait until one has developed before putting it to rout. Thus the President has a new function which is still taking shape, that of Manager of Prosperity.[1]

The role of the president as economic manager has fully matured. Presidents are now evaluated on how well, or whether, they succeed in stabilizing the economy or, to put it a different way, whether conditions of economic stability prevail during their administrations. Certainly President Jimmy Carter's difficulty at the polls in 1980 was due in considerable part to the economic problems of his administration, most notably the failure to control inflation, which soared to 13 percent in that year.

This chapter will deal with only one facet of macroeconomic policy, namely fiscal policy. Fiscal policy involves decisions on the aggre-

88

 gate levels of taxes and expenditures to secure budget deficits or surpluses and thereby help stabilize the economy. It is intended to correct imbalances between supply and demand which develop in the private economy. Responsibility for the development of fiscal policy proposals rests with the president and his administration. Their approval, however, rests with Congress through the enactment of legislation on taxes and appropriations. The fiscal policy area, then, is one in which the president proposes while Congress disposes.

In this chapter the focus will be on the development of fiscal policy proposals by the president and not on the substance of these proposals. The process of fiscal policy development involves four distinct but not entirely separate management tasks. First, the president must supply leadership to guide the development of fiscal policy proposals, lest the process be characterized by lack of unity, conflict and drift. This involves making decisions on the basic nature and direction of fiscal policy actions. Second, the president must develop and maintain an information system which will provide adequate and timely information, policy options and advice. This system may involve arrangements that are formal or informal, regularized or ad hoc, or some combination of these. Third, the president must insure that there are coordinative processes to reduce or eliminate conflicts among fiscal, monetary, international economic and wage-price policies. Coordination also involves efforts to harmonize the actions of individuals and agencies involved in these policy areas. Fourth, the president must seek consent for his fiscal policy proposals both from within the executive branch and from the Congress. The necessity for consent, which must be secured primarily through persuasion and bargaining, is an important constraint upon presidential capability in fiscal policy development.

Roger Porter states that in recent decades presidents have usually followed one of three basic strategies in organizing "the pattern of advice they receive from their immediate staff and from executive departments and agencies."[2] These are:

1. *Adhocracy,* "which minimizes regularized and systematic patterns of providing advice and instead relies heavily on the president distributing assignments and selecting whom he listens to and when."
2. *Centralized management,* which places much reliance on the White House and units within the Executive Office of the President. They filter advice and information from the departments and agencies before they go to the president.
3. *Multiple advocacy,* which is an open system intended systematically to expose the president to competing arguments and advice pre-

sented by the advocates themselves. It is "a managed process relying on an honest broker to insure that interested parties are represented and that the debate is structured and balanced." The
Economic Policy Board during the Ford administration is illustrative
of multiple advocacy.

Porter notes that variations on these approaches and other dis
tinct alternatives are possible. There are, in short, several ways in
which the president can handle the management tasks, especially
those involving advice and coordination, involved in fiscal policy
development.

In the next section the experience of the Johnson administration
in developing fiscal policy proposals will be examined in some detail
Then attention will turn to succeeding administrations, which will be
handled in briefer and comparative fashion. In the final section some
conclusions on fiscal policy development will be drawn that relate to
the ideas presented in this introduction.

THE JOHNSON ADMINISTRATION

President Lyndon Johnson was an activist with populist inclinations
who favored the full use of the government's powers to promote
economic growth and stability.[3] Although he possessed neither a
deep grasp of economic theory nor much interest in it, he knew what
he liked and wanted as economic goals: economic growth, high employment, price stability and low interest rates. He sought, obtained
and absorbed large amounts of information on economic issues.
While he drew upon a substantial number of agencies, officials and
private citizens for information, advice and policy alternatives, he
reserved final decision of fiscal policy issues—and macroeconomic
issues generally—for himself. To a considerable extent the coordination of fiscal policies with other macroeconomic policies was effected
through centralized decision-making by the president. This was
clearly Johnson's preference.

The Economic Subpresidency

The president is assisted by an extensive network of aides and advisers in the performance of his many duties. Such persons are drawn
from the Executive Office of the President, the executive branch and
from society generally, especially the Washington community. This

network of advice, as it relates to the development and implementation of macroeconomic policy, we shall call the economic subpresidency. It is part of the presidency and under the control of the president. Its function is to assist the president; it does not have or share his responsibility. How it is used, the extent to which it is used and its very composition depend upon the president's needs, goals and style.

The economic subpresidency is a behavioral rather than a structural concept. People become part of the economic subpresidency when, and to the extent that, they are helping the president in the economic policy area. Some, like the Council of Economic Advisers, will be regularly and deeply involved; others, such as personal friends or the Secretary of Agriculture, will be involved only on an occasional or ad hoc basis. What counts in determining whether one is part of the economic subpresidency is what one does rather than one's title or institutional affiliation. The economic subpresidency is drawn in part from the "institutionalized presidency" but should be distinguished from it.

We turn now to an examination of the components of the economic subpresidency, especially as it is centered upon fiscal policy.

The White House. Of the 300 to 400 persons employed in the White House during the Johnson administration only a few dozen could accurately be described as staff aides to the president. Of these only a couple were much involved with fiscal policy. Responsibility for domestic and economic policy was assigned first to William Moyers and then to Joseph A. Califano, Jr. (The latter served as special assistant to the president from mid-1965 until the end of the administration.) Califano had one assistant who helped him with economic policy matters. In the fiscal policy area Califano acted as a stimulator, coordinator and seeker of agreement among the president's major advisers. He generally was not a major contributor of substantive fiscal policy advice. The Johnson White House staff never included an economist. Califano did make use of economists from other executive office agencies such as the Bureau of the Budget (now the Office of Management and Budget) and the Council of Economic Advisers.

The Council of Economic Advisers. The 1960s were years of great influence for the three-member Council of Economic Advisers (CEA). Under capable, activist leadership, and working for presidents who were quite receptive to its advice, the CEA dominated the economic subpresidency. The Council provided President Johnson with large quantities of information, advice and fiscal policy recommendations. Several factors contributed to the CEA's influence. One was its com-

petence and quickness in providing macroeconomic information and
advice. Moreover, it was able to do this in a concise, readable style
which Johnson liked. Second, the Council lacked any policy biases
stemming from institutional commitments, programmatic responsibilities or clientele pressures. Its sole client was the president and it
shared with the president a strong concern for maintaining stable
prices and high employment under conditions of economic growth.
Third, the Council was willing to become actively involved in presidential politics and policymaking (although it tended to avoid partisan politics) rather than acting simply as a detached provider of economic information. Although they were professional economists, the
members also viewed themselves as assistants to the president and
hence as political economists. Fourth, staffing patterns within the
executive branch also contributed to CEA influence. The executive
departments and agencies lacked the economic support personnel
which would have enabled them to have a greater impact on economic policy formation. A Johnson administration official has explained:

> In the 1960s there were a lot of people who would have liked to get into
> the game but just did not have the staff. They were unsupported, and
> when you weren't supported, you couldn't carry the issue. Nobody
> had a group of economists to evaluate all these issues for them. The
> CEA had a monopoly on it along with a few people at the Treasury. . . .
> Few people understood what the term "multiplier" meant in the 1960s,
> much less were able to argue with the CEA's arguments about a tax
> policy to stimulate the economy. When CEA said the effect of a specific
> tax action on investment was such-and-such there wasn't any other
> agency doing its own empirical work to argue with it. . . .[4]

The CEA well illustrated that knowledge can be power when the
president wants, needs and uses its services.

Bureau of the Budget. The role of the Bureau of the Budget (BOB) in
fiscal policy formation was based on its specific budgetary responsibilities. Because of the budget's importance as an economic stabilization instrument, the BOB director was an important presidential
advisor on expenditures and often on other economic matters. During the Johnson administration BOB directors tended to view themselves, and to be viewed, as special assistants to the president as well
as heads of a staff agency serving the presidency. Johnson's first two
budget directors, Kermit Gordon and Charles Schultze, were very
capable economists, which served to enhance their influence in eco-

nomic policy matters and to facilitate cooperation between BOB and CEA.

The Treasury Department. Its responsibilities for tax collection, currency control, customs control and debt management give the Department of the Treasury much institutional power. It had the best sources of information on tax revenues, tax structure and the behavior of the financial markets. In addition it usually served as the lead agency in the preparation of tax legislation and its presentation to Congress. Henry H. Fowler, who served as Secretary of the Treasury during much of the Johnson administration, had a good personal relationship with Johnson and was a major participant in fiscal policy meetings. While Johnson appeared to value his political judgment and advice, Fowler does not appear to have been especially influential on substantive matters. He was somewhat less activist and expansion-oriented than were some of the president's other advisors. The institutional position of the Secretary of the Treasury and his need to maintain the confidence of the financial community impel him to be somewhat more conservative fiscally.

The Federal Reserve Board. Although the Federal Reserve Board (FRB) is structurally independent of the executive there is considerable cooperation between the two. To be most effective in achieving economic stability, monetary policy (which is handled by the FRB) and fiscal policy require coordination. Fiscal and monetary policymakers each need to know what the other is doing lest they take contradictory actions. Various formal and informal relationships existed between the FRB and the CEA, BOB, and Treasury Department for the exchange of information and policy viewpoints. (The "Quadriad," which was composed of the heads of the four agencies and which met occasionally with the president, was the best known of these arrangements.) Moreover, Johnson sometimes sought the personal advice of FRB chairman William McChesney Martin on fiscal policy issues. For example, in April 1966, following a telephone conversation with the president, Martin sent him a lengthy memorandum analyzing the economic situation and urging a tax hike to impose more restraint on the economy.[5]

Other Cabinet Departments. Johnson did not use the cabinet as a policy formulation or decision-making mechanism, although it was used to build support for presidential actions. Various individual Cabinet members were involved in fiscal policy development, although in the cases of Willard Wirtz (Secretary of Labor) and John T. Connor (Secretary of Commerce) not to the extent they would have preferred. They were more likely to be consulted after fiscal policy proposals had been developed, when their reactions and those of the labor and business communities were sought. Gardner Ackley, a chairman of the CEA during the Johnson years, has provided an explanation for their limited involvement:

> . . . on fiscal or monetary policy, tax policy, [and] size of the budget, Connor and Wirtz didn't really have much to contribute. Their ideas about those subjects were ill-formed; it wasn't that there weren't people in their agencies who were intelligent in respect to these issues, but they were further down [in the departmental hierarchy]; the principals spent most of their time at a big administrative job and couldn't really get into the analysis of these issues. They didn't really represent an independent source of ideas or advice . . . or didn't really have much to contribute, except perhaps prejudices or political notions.[6]

In earlier administrations the Secretaries of Commerce and Labor had had more substantial fiscal policy roles.

Outside Advisers. President Johnson also drew regularly on a number of private citizens, mostly in the Washington area, for advice on fiscal policy issues. Notable here were Clark Clifford, David Ginsberg and Abe Fortas. (The last named continued to be called upon occasionally even after his appointment to the U.S. Supreme Court.) After they left their positions with the CEA and BOB, respectively, Johnson continued to call upon Walter Heller and Kermit Gordon. Before he made major fiscal policy decisions Johnson often consulted business and labor leaders. It is not possible to determine the impact these outside advisers had on the president's decisions and actions. Certainly they were important in that they helped furnish the president with the broad range of economic and political information and insight which he wanted when making fiscal decisions. From some he sought trusted judgments, from others political reactions and insights, from still others good economic information. They also provided him with an independent check on the political and economic feasibility of policy recommendations coming from administration officials.

We can now turn our attention to how the economic subpresidency operated to produce fiscal policy proposals.

Developing Fiscal Policy Proposals

The primary source of fiscal policy proposals for President Johnson was the "Troika." Originated during the Kennedy administration to coordinate economic forecasting and retained by Johnson, the Troika was composed of the CEA chairman, the BOB director and the Secretary of the Treasury. These officials together with their agencies had responsibility for preparing periodic economic forecasts and for developing economic advice and policy proposals for the president. (The tasks of the Troika ranged over macroeconomic matters generally, but here again our focus will be on fiscal policy.)

The division of responsibility among the Troika agencies gave the main responsibility to the Treasury Department for the estimation of revenues, to the BOB for the estimation of expenditures, and to the CEA for overall economic analysis and forecasting. The division of responsibilities was not rigid, however, and the agencies did sometimes question one another's estimates. As BOB Director Charles Zwick described their relationships: "Everybody kibitzed on everybody else. We [BOB] questioned their [CEA] model. We always thought Treasury's estimates were too low or something. So there was always a give and take on all aspects."[7]

The Troika was a three-level as well as a three-agency operation. The bottom or technician level was composed of personnel (all economists) drawn from the three agencies who had the task of collecting statistical data and handling the technical work of preparing forecasts of future economic conditions. Forecasts were prepared on a quarterly basis unless more frequently requested by the Troika principals or the White House. Although the technicians did not entirely shed the policy orientations of their agencies, they placed much emphasis on objective economic analysis and the preparation of accurate economic forecasts. A contemporary account stated: "The Troika gets much of its organizational glue from the technicians who staff its bottom level. They have a strong group identification that at times seems to outweigh the institutional pull of their own agencies."[8]

Designated as the option framers, the middle level of the Troika consisted of a member of the CEA, the associate director of BOB, and the Assistant Secretary of the Treasury for fiscal affairs. Policy considerations entered into the forecasting process at this level. When a forecast prepared by the technicians came to the option framers it was reviewed to determine whether anything was happening in the economy that required attention. If the answer was no, the option framers reported this to the principals and the Troika exercise probably was ended. If, however, the answer was yes, if significant changes in the economy seemed to be occurring, these would be analyzed and their causes sought. Policy options which would correct the problems were then searched for, and a number of forecasts using alternative models of the economy might be made. A report containing a few of the most appropriate optional policy forecasts was prepared for the Troika principals. Sometimes this report would present a particular policy alternative as most desirable.

At the top level of the Troika policy considerations replaced forecasting as the focus of attention. Only the top-level officials had access to the president and were privy to policy considerations which could affect the forecasts. After discussing the forecast and policy recommendations with the option framers, the top level sought to reach a consensus concerning the forecast and the policy actions required to deal with the problems revealed by the forecast. Once a consensus was reached, a Troika report was prepared and sent to the president. (In some instances the Troika also requested a meeting with the president, usually when a major change in policy was indicated.) The Troika report usually included "a short narrative statement giving a central story of the economic situation, a list of the assumptions underlying the forecast and policy recommendations, a discussion of the fiscal policy alternatives open to the president, and likely results and risks of each alternative, and, finally, the troika's recommendation and arguments supporting it."[9]

Through discussion and bargaining, the Troika attempted to develop policy recommendations upon which all of its members could agree. Dissenting statements in Troika reports were rare. (One occurred in 1967 when Schultze objected to expenditure reductions favored by the other Troika members as being programmatically impossible.) Differences were usually resolved by "negotiating the adjectives and adverbs" or by including in the report statements of the risks associated with various alternatives.[10] Ackley has described the strategy of the Troika:

> On the vast majority of issues, the Treasury, the tax people in the Treasury, and the Budget Bureau and the Council saw things essentially the same way; and our strategy was so far as possible not to present the president with disagreements on which we had to give him divided advice. So far as we could, we tried to avoid that—particularly if the divided advice rested on different economic analyses or different forecasts. To ask the president to decide a question on the basis of an interpretation of economic data or argument is really unfair. He's not as well qualified, certainly, as his advisers to make the analysis to interpret the data.[11]

Such agreement was also quite likely to increase the influence of the

Troika. Johnson, of course, preferred agreement or consensus among his advisers and exerted pressure for its achievement.

The Troika was the primary source of fiscal policy proposals in the Johnson administration. However, Johnson did not adopt Troika proposals as his own without consulting other advisers. More often than not, Troika proposals served as the basis for debate and discussion within the administration of what should be done about inflationary pressures, for instance, or the need to provide some stimulus to the economy. To illustrate, the set of proposals agreed to in January 1967 by a number of the president's advisers (Secretary of Defense Robert McNamara, Fowler, Wirtz, Connor, Schultze, Ackley, Califano and Clark Clifford) was not greatly different from that recommended by the Troika in its report a couple of weeks earlier. Included in both were the need for a general tax increase (an income tax surcharge) at midyear, reinstitution of the investment tax credit and continuation of efforts to secure an easier money policy from the FRB.

Johnson frequently used such ad hoc groups of advisers on fiscal and other macroeconomic issues. There was considerable continuity among these groups or committees in that they were mostly drawn from a list of 12 to 15 persons during the five years of his administration. What one encounters here, although it seems a contradiction in terms, is a sort of "regularized adhocracy." These groups were used not so much to develop proposals as to consider and refine recommendations originating with the Troika and to help the president assess their economic and political feasibility.

Finally, it should be stressed that Johnson himself was actively involved in the process of developing fiscal policy proposals, whatever their initial sources. A Troika proposal, which itself might be initiated by a presidential request, was often only the beginning of what might be an extended and loosely structured decision-making process. The case of the 1966 suspension of the investment tax credit is illustrative. In early 1966 Johnson had declined to seek an income tax increase as recommended by his advisers, primarily on the ground that it was not politically feasible. However, all during the spring and summer of 1966 the Troika members kept hammering away at the president on the need for an income tax increase to offset the inflationary pressure created by increased spending for the Vietnam war. Finally in late August the president, after telling them they could not get a general tax increase, acceded to suspension of the investment tax credit. This was agreed to by an ad hoc committee of eight advisers. This, according to CEA Chairman Ackley, was "the best the Troika could get from him."[12] In the summer of 1967 the president finally decided to go for a general tax increase.

A Note on the Johnson Record

Attitudes toward Lyndon Johnson and his administration are still strongly affected by his heavy involvement in the Vietnam war. However, a dispassionate look at the economic record reveals that the administration's performance was fairly good. In March 1961, following a period of recession, the American economy entered an era of expansion that was to last for the remainder of the Kennedy term, to continue throughout the Johnson years and to persist for the first ten months of the Nixon presidency. This period of economic expansion, which lasted in all some 102 months, was the longest continuous period of expansion in the history of the American economy. Between 1964 and 1968, the gross national product expanded from $632 billion to $865 billion, while the annual unemployment rate dropped from 5.2 percent to 3.6 percent. The consumer price index rose from 108.1 in 1964 to 121.2 in 1968.[13] (The CPI arose this much alone in 1980 under the Carter administration.) The Johnson administration did leave a legacy of inflationary pressures for its successors. Some commentators have attributed the inflation which plagued the country in the 1970s and early 1980s to the high government spending of the Johnson era. To do so, however, one has to hold a sort of "original sin" explanation of inflation—that once started it cannot be stopped. This is unsupported both in economic theory and the empirical economic record.

This record of solid economic performance did not just happen. Efforts by the Johnson administration to stimulate the economy and to maintain full employment conditions while seeking to restrain inflation clearly contributed to it. This, of course, involved use of all of the instruments of macroeconomic policy, although fiscal policy did generally contribute positively to the result, at least until 1966. The Johnson administration has been frequently faulted for its failure to seek a general tax increase in early 1966, preferring, as the critics put it, a policy of "guns and butter." Other actions to restrain the economy were taken, however. A "bits and pieces" tax program was proposed and adopted, an expenditure reduction exercise was launched, implementation of wage-price guideposts was intensified, and more reliance was placed on monetary policy.

When the administration did actively seek a 10 percent income tax surcharge in August 1967, following a mild economic slowdown in early 1967, it was not enacted by Congress until June 1968. Various factors contributed to this delay. Some members of Congress believed the economy was in sound condition; others objected to the tax because it was tied to the Vietnam war; still others wanted a reduction in the "butter" of domestic expenditures coupled with the tax increase. Indeed Congress agreed to the tax increase only after the administration acceded to a $6 billion expenditure reduction. The fear then developed in the administration, based on a Troika forecast, that these two actions would impose too much restraint on the economy. This viewpoint was shared by the Federal Reserve Board, which then acted to expand the money supply, thereby offsetting the fiscal restraint. As Arthur Okun, Chairman of the CEA during the first year of the Johnson administration, put it: "This turned out to be wrong policy because it was the right policy for what turned out to be the wrong forecast."[14] Inflation accordingly gained momentum.

FROM NIXON TO REAGAN

Limitations of space and information preclude a thorough treatment of fiscal policy development during the Nixon, Ford, Carter and Reagan administrations. So far as presidential documents are concerned, only those of the Ford administration have recently become available. There is also a paucity of good studies of economic policy-making during these administrations.[15] As a consequence this treatment of fiscal policy development since the Johnson administration will of necessity be somewhat fragmentary and impressionistic. Nevertheless, the major changes in fiscal policy since the Johnson administration can be discussed, together with the most recent fiscal policy developments.

Changes in Fiscal Policy Development

The theoretical agreement on Keynesian economics which guided the process of fiscal policy development in the 1960s has clearly eroded. During the sixties any reasonably capable student of economics could have prescribed on the basis of accepted theory how fiscal policy should be used to stabilize the economy. Tax cuts, expenditure increases and budget deficits would be used to offset economic decline; tax increases, expenditure reductions and budget surpluses would be used to combat inflationary conditions. The goal was to shape aggregate demand for goods and services in the right direction. Although argument might occur on precisely how much stimulus or restraint was required, the basic policy prescriptions of Keynesian economics were widely accepted. Even Milton Friedman, in late 1965, was moved to proclaim, "We are all Keynesians now."

The stagflation which developed in the 1970s presented a puzzle for policymakers and economists. This condition, in which inflation and high unemployment occur together, confounds accepted economic theory. It consequently generated disarray in the economic professions and confusion among policymakers. Doctrinal unity in the sixties eased the task of presidential advisers in reaching agreement on fiscal policy proposals to send to the president. Now conflict may occur among supply-siders, monetarists, Keynesians, fiscal conservatives and others.

The influence of the Council of Economic Advisers in the development of fiscal policy, moreover, has declined. Several factors have contributed to this. Other agencies have added economic policy planning units and otherwise increased their capabilities to handle economic analysis. The CEA consequently no longer has the knowledge advantage that it once did.[16] In addition the leadership of the CEA appears to have been less capable and politically astute than it was during the Johnson years. Since the mid-1970s, the CEA has devoted a growing share of its time to microeconomic issues, such as those involving economic regulatory policies and agricultural price supports. In the Reagan administration overall taxation and expenditure policies were essentially established in 1981 before the CEA members were appointed and the Council became operative. The CEA never did play the influential role that it did in earlier administrations. Indeed, when CEA Chairman Martin Feldstein resigned in the summer of 1984, it was indicated that he would not be replaced until after the presidential election.

The Troika has continued in use as the mechanism for making economic forecasts and as a source of advice to the president. The division of labor among the Troika agencies continues to be much the same as during the Johnson years. In the Reagan administration there has been more conflict among the Troika members, particularly at the option-framing level (or T-2, as it is now called). Thus it is reported that in 1981, when Norman Ture was a member as Undersecretary of the Treasury for tax and economic policy, "the group was rent by ferocious disputes over supply-side theory, monetarism and loyalty to the president's program. The T-2 sessions often wound up in name-calling and finger-pointing that got into the press."[17] In the first two years of the Reagan administration there was evidence that forecasts were being manipulated so as to produce results that were politically congenial to the administration. Reagan's first CEA chairman, Murray Weidenbaum, refused to put his name on one of the forecasts.

President Richard Nixon, who was not especially interested in economic issues and who preferred to focus his efforts on foreign affairs, successively designated Treasury Secretaries John Connally and George Shultz, and Kenneth Rush, a White House official, as his major advisors on economic issues. Connally, who had responsibility for making major decisions, worked through the Troika, which he dominated. Schultz, in comparison, relied on interdepartmental committees which focused on particular problems, while Rush relied upon the assistance of an informal, five-member "Economic Group."[18]

Presidents since Nixon have followed the practice of designating one of their officials, usually the Secretary of the Treasury, as their chief economic policy spokesman. Subsequent spokesmen have not had the extensive authority that Connally and Shultz did during the Nixon administration. Lyndon Johnson, we should note, served as his own economic spokesman. Nor were there any public struggles for dominance among his advisers, such as occurred during the Reagan administration.

Beginning with the Ford administration, efforts have been made to institutionalize the advisory process as it relates to fiscal and other economic policy issues. Soon after he assumed office, President Gerald Ford established an Economic Policy Board. The Carter administration abolished the Board and replaced it with an Economic Policy Group (EPG). Chaired by the Secretary of the Treasury, other members of the EPG, which met weekly, were the Chairman of the CEA, the Director of OMB, the Secretaries of Labor, Commerce, State, and Housing and Urban Development, and the Director of the Domestic Policy Staff. Other officials were also involved from time to time in the meetings of EPG. The Reagan administration in turn abolished the EPG and put in its stead a Cabinet Council for Economic Affairs whose composition is similar to that of EPG. The Cabinet Council operates mainly as a forum for the discussion of issues and policy alternatives. Generally, Presidents Ford and Carter involved more people in the development of fiscal policy than did Johnson. They also relied more heavily on formally structured arrangements. In the Reagan administration fiscal policy formulation was dominated by the White House staff. It was also characterized by quite a bit of public squabbling among administration officials, most notably Feldstein and Treasury Secretary Donald Regan.

Ford's 1975 Tax Proposals

In his January 1975 State of the Union message, President Ford proposed some temporary and permanent tax reductions as part of an anti-recessionary package.[19] Although he consulted with private economists, his Labor-Management Committee and others, most of the work in developing the proposals was handled by the Executive Committee of the Economic Policy Board (EPB).[20] The Executive Committee initially consisted of the Secretary of the Treasury, the Director of OMB, the Chairman of CEA, the Assistant to the President for Economic Affairs, and the Executive Director of the Council on International Economic Policy. Subsequently, the Executive Committee was expanded to include the Secretaries of State, Labor and Commerce.

President Ford's first economic program, presented to Congress in October 1974, was aimed at inflation as "domestic enemy number one" and included a tax increase. However, as the fall wore on it became evident that the economy was in a recession. By the middle of December the president was committed to an alteration in policy to deal with this new condition. Much of the work in developing tax cut proposals to stimulate the economy was handled by the Executive Committee, sometimes meeting by itself, sometimes meeting with the president. Some of the meetings were expanded to include persons other than Executive Committee members. Three meetings attended by the president included 15, 17, and 15 other persons, respectively. Ford preferred this kind of face-to-face group decision-making where he could be exposed to a variety of ideas and points of view. It was the task of the Executive Director of the EPB, acting as an "honest broker," to ensure that this happened.

Reagan's 1981 Tax Proposals

The Reagan administration's 1981 tax reduction proposals represented a substantial shift in public policy, based as they were upon the theory of supply-side economics. Essentially, this theory argued that high marginal income tax rates lessened the incentive of workers to work, save and invest, and consequently reduced the productive capacity of the economy. Substantial tax reductions were thus viewed as necessary to increase economic productivity and thereby reduce inflationary pressures. Supply-side economics thus stood in contrast to traditional Keynesian economics and its concern with shaping aggregate demand for goods and services.

During the 1980 presidential campaign, President Reagan became committed to supply-side economics and the Kemp-Roth tax-cut proposal. Named after two of its leading proponents, Representative Jack Kemp of New York and Delaware Senator William Roth, the Kemp-Roth proposal called for a 30 percent reduction in marginal income tax rates over a three-year period. Once in office the new president moved quickly to present a tax proposal to Congress calling for the Kemp-Roth cuts plus accelerated depreciation credits for business. A companion measure called for $48 billion in cuts in the budget for fiscal year 1982. Most of the work in developing the Reagan program was performed by the Economic Policy Coordinating Committee. Set up during the transition period, it was chaired by David Stockman and included other senior economic officials as they were designated.[21] For such a "radical" program it was based neither on extensive economic analyses, nor on meaningful deliberations.

There were, however, doubts within the administration concerning the economic feasibility of the tax proposal because some of the administration's budget projections indicated the tax cuts would produce sizable budget deficits. No one, however, acted to convey this concern to the president. While the president made a variety of concessions to members of Congress to secure enactment of his tax proposal, most of them involved measures providing for additional tax cuts. The only major change in the basic tax proposal agreed to by the president involved reducing the income tax cut from 10 percent to 5 percent in the first year (for a total reduction of 25 percent). Reagan made it clear that he would not compromise further on the income tax reduction.

The Economic Recovery Tax Act became law in August 1981. Estimates were that it would reduce federal tax revenues by amounts ranging from $39 billion in 1982 to $290 billion in 1987.[22] Strong criticism of the Reagan administration's economic program quickly developed. The tax cut was viewed by many as a mistake. In 1982 the administration came to support the adoption of a three-year $98 billion tax increase to help reduce budget deficits. (Reagan had initially rejected the recommendations of his advisers to seek a tax increase.) Another tax increase was adopted in 1984.

Given that various members of the Reagan administration had reservations concerning the tax-cut proposal, why did they not give voice to them? A *New York Times* reporter provides a plausible explanation:

The unwillingness of the Reagan staff to challenge the president's deeply held beliefs can be explained, in part, by their relationship with the man himself. As a newcomer to Washington and the federal bureaucracy, Mr. Reagan depended heavily on his staff to help translate his themes into political and legislative realities. In return he offered these younger men an usually large share of the limelight. A sign near his desk in the Oval Office reads: "There's no limit to what a man can do or where he can go if he doesn't mind who gets the credit." Moreover, Mr. Reagan, as a man of genuine warmth and generosity, earned his staff's loyalty on a personal level.

At the same time, the president was supremely confident in himself and his ideas. He came to the presidency convinced he had been given a mandate by the voters to carry out his program, and his staff by and large agreed. That was another reason why they hesitated in bringing doubts to him.

"It was not our role to go in there and try to reshape the president's policies," said a senior White House official. To rewrite the Reagan agenda was just not appropriate."[23]

In all this incident reveals the stifling effect that strong, determined presidential leadership can have on the advisory process. The "adequate and timely" advice needed by the president was not forthcoming. While the president essentially got what he wanted in the way of fiscal policy during his first year in office, its consequences for society were not very beneficent. Inflation was significantly reduced, but the economy sunk into a recession and, at the end of 1982, unemployment exceeded the 10 percent level. Recovery brought with it a reduction in unemployment to the 7 percent level in the fall of 1984. Record budget deficits continued to loom, however, and the administration's promise to balance the budget by 1984 was clearly unfulfilled.

CONCLUSION

The advisory system used during the Johnson administration for the development of fiscal policy proposals does not really fit well into any of Porter's categories—adhocracy, centralized management and multiple advocacy. Although Johnson did not utilize more formalized advisory structures, such as Ford's Economic Policy Board or Carter's Economic Policy Group, the Troika constituted a systematic and continuing mechanism for both forecasting and fiscal policy development. The committees used to consider Troika proposals generally drew upon a small set of official and unofficial advisors, thereby providing another element of continuity. It was for these reasons that the Johnson system was earlier referred to as "regularized adhocracy." It also continued elements of centralized management in that it relied primarily on Executive Office agencies. The executive departments were involved primarily as suppliers of data, while department secretaries (excepting the Treasury) were brought into the process only after the initial development of proposals. Overall the Johnson system was characterized by flexible structure and limited participation intended to centralize decision-making by the president—which was what Johnson preferred.

The focus in this chapter has been on the process of fiscal policy development and its management. We have seen that subsequent to the Johnson administration there have been some significant changes in the process of fiscal policy management. Each of the four succeeding presidents has managed the process somewhat differently. Given this, is there one particular style of managing the fiscal policy development process that is more effective than others? There is no ready answer. First, accepted criteria of evaluation are lacking. Should a process such as this be evaluated on the basis of administrative criteria—organization, coordination, smooth operation, etc.—or on the basis of substantive results? Second, the process used in developing fiscal policy proposals is only one factor of several affecting the nature of the proposals developed. Others include the president's values and preferences, political considerations, and the knowledge, skills and ability of the personnel involved to work together. Third, there is no guarantee that a given structural arrangement will produce good policy alternatives, although they can be quite helpful in this regard. So, too, nothing guarantees that the president will decide on effective policy alternatives, even if they are presented to him. Moreover, there is sometimes much difference between the fiscal policy proposals emanating from an administration and what gets enacted into law by Congress.

This leads us to a final point. The president now has the role of economic manager. How he performs in this role will importantly shape public evaluations of presidential performance and affect his chances for re-election, as well as influencing the performance of the nation's economy. However, much of the ultimate control over fiscal policy rests with Congress. Indeed control over most of the other instruments of macroeconomic policy is also lodged in sources apart from the president. The old administrative adage that "authority should be commensurate with responsibility" is clearly breached in the macroeconomic policy area. Consequently, as economic manager, the president must rely heavily upon persuasion and bargaining to get all or at least part of what he wants in the way of fiscal policy.

NOTES

1. Clinton Rossiter, *The American Presidency*, rev. ed. (New York: Harcourt, Brace & World, 1959), pp. 36–37.

2. Roger B. Porter, *Presidential Decision Making: The Economic Policy Board* (New York: Cambridge University Press, 1980), pp. 25–26.

3. This section draws substantially upon James E. Anderson and Jared Hazleton, *Managing Macroeconomic Institutions: The Johnson Presidency* (1985).

4. Quoted in Roger B. Porter, "The President and Economic Policy: Problems, Patterns, and Alternatives," in Hugh Heclo and Lester M. Salamon, eds., *The Illusion of Presidential Government* (Boulder, Col.: Westview Press, 1981), p. 215.

5. Memorandum, William M. Martin to the President, April 28, 1966, (Austin: LBJ Library).

6. Gardner Ackley, interview transcript (Nashville: Institute of Policy Studies, Vanderbilt University), p. 20.

7. Charles Zwick, interview with Brooks Myers (Miami, April 21, 1978).

8. "How Washington Makes Its Forecasts," *Business Week* 30 (December 1967), p. 82.

9. Lawrence C. Pierce, *The Politics of Fiscal Policy Formation* (Pacific Palisades, Cal.: Goodyear, 1971), p. 82. Pierce's study describes the forecasting process in detail and is an invaluable source on its topic.

10. Pierce, p. 82.

11. Ackley interview transcript, pp. 16–17.

12. Personal interview with Gardner Ackley (Ann Arbor, August 15, 1979).

13. *Annual Report of the Council of Economic Advisers, 1970* (Washington, D.C.: Government Printing Office, 1970).

14. Arthur W. Okun, *The Political Economy of Prosperity* (New York: Norton, 1969), pp. 47–48.

15. An important exception is Porter, *Presidential Decision Making*.

16. For a recent discussion of the CEA, see Dom Bonafede, "Reagan's Economic Advisers Share Task of Shaping and Explaining Reaganomics," *National Journal* 14 (February 6, 1982), pp. 245–48.

17. *New York Times* (September 28, 1982), p. 39.

18. Richard A. Watson and Norman C. Thomas, *The Politics of the Presidency* (New York: John Wiley, 1983), p. 386.

19. This discussion draws on Porter, *Presidential Decision Making*, Chapter 4.

20. The executive order creating the Economic Policy Board specified the following officials as members: the Secretaries of Treasury; State; In-

terior; Agriculture; Commerce; Labor; Health, Education and Welfare; and Housing and Urban Development; the Assistant to the President for Economic Affairs; the Director of OMB; the Chairman of CEA; and the Executive Director of the Council on International Economic Policy. Others participated occasionally in meetings of EPB, although they were not formally members.

21. Roger B. Porter, "Economic Advice to the President: From Eisenhower to Reagan," *Political Science Quarterly* 98 (Fall 1983), p. 412.

22. John L. Palmer and Elizabeth V. Sawhill, eds., *The Reagan Experiment* (Washington, D.C.: The Urban Institute, 1982).

23. Stephen R. Weisman, "Reaganomics and the President's Men," *New York Times Magazine* (October 24, 1982), p. 83. See also William Grieder, "The Education of David Stockman," *Atlantic Monthly* (December 1981), pp. 27–54.

The Reagan Budget Juggernaut

JAMES P. PFIFFNER

POLITICS: STRATEGY, TACTICS AND TIMING

The Reagan budget juggernaut rolled over its opposition and enjoyed a resounding victory in its fiscal 1982 budget campaign. Since most previous incoming administrations asserted their budget priorities by making marginal changes in the proposed budget of the outgoing president, how was the Reagan administration able to implement such drastic and unprecedented changes in priorities immediately upon taking office? It used to be considered impossible to do much to a budget proposal that had been a year in the making because of the complexity of the document and because of all of the political bargains that had been struck in arriving at the totals for each program. Yet by March 10, only 49 days after taking office, President Reagan submitted to Congress a complete revision of President Carter's 1982 budget, including large defense increases, large tax cuts, unprecedented reductions in domestic programs, and even reductions in the

---

The Oxford English Dictionary defines Juggernaut as a title of Krishna, an idol of whom was "annually dragged in procession on an enormous car, under the wheels of which many devotees are said to have formerly thrown themselves to be crushed"—behavior not unlike that of members of Congress during votes on President Reagan's 1982 budget proposals.

then current 1981 budget. Even more impressive, within six months he had achieved virtually all of his budgetary, if not economic, goals.

The new Reagan administration was the beneficiary of a generally favorable set of circumstances. There was no major foreign policy crisis that distracted it from its budget priorities. It was helped by the mood of the electorate that had given Ronald Reagan a decisive victory and had elected a Republican Senate for the first time in several decades. The country was also very concerned about the state of the economy and ready to support the new president in his attempt to put it back on track. Potential Democratic opposition to the radical priority shifts and budget cuts was in disarray in the Congress. Machiavelli's *fortuna* was on the side of the president. The political and governmental environment does not always present a new president with such an agreeable situation.

Nevertheless, it was only with consummate political skill that the Reagan administration was able to take advantage of these favorable circumstances. The sharp reversal of political and budgetary priorities was no accident. It was the product of a carefully laid out plan that put political and governmental machinery into high gear immediately upon President Reagan's taking office. In the budgetary arena the administration did indeed "hit the ground running," much more so than with respect to personnel or management. This chapter will examine the political and institutional components of the Reagan budget juggernaut as well as the major shifts in priorities embodied in the FY 1982 budget.

Public Opinion: the Mandate

The main justification for the budget cuts made by the Reagan administration was the "mandate" from the people expressed in the 1980 elections. Indeed, since the tax revolt of the 1970s and especially Proposition 13, politicians have been particularly sensitive to the public's desire for budget restraint.[1] In 1981, responding to a series of polls, one-half to three-fourths of the American public said it supported overall reductions in government spending.[2] Politicians at all levels were elected by promising greater efficiency and reduced spending.

While the Reagan administration made very effective use of its electoral victory in convincing members of Congress to vote for its budget cuts, it is not clear that the election or public opinion called for the Reagan budget and economic package. First of all there is nothing new about public support for reduced government spending; it has been a consistent response on public opinion polls since 1936, when 77 percent of respondents favored overall reduced spending. Ironically, support for reduced government spending was at one of its lowest points in November 1980 (44 percent), the month of Reagan's election.

Second, although the polls show a consistent majority in favor of reduced overall spending, they also show consistent majorities in favor of continued or increased spending in most areas of domestic spending. This inconsistency has been documented by Royce Crocker who has compiled data from polls about government spending in different policy areas since 1973. He has found that from 1973 to 1980 the percentage of people responding that the government spends "too much" was greater than the percentage of those who said "too little" in only three program areas: foreign aid, space exploration and welfare. In seven other areas of domestic spending the percentage saying the U.S. spends "too little" was greater.[3] This pattern was sustained through 1981, during which six different polls showed that a majority favored spending reductions only for food stamps. In 16 other areas the percentage was less than a majority, with Social Security and Medicare at the bottom of the spending cuts list.[4] The striking reversal over this time period was national defense, for which more thought we were spending too much in 1973. The situation had reversed by 1980.[5] These data show that the American public supports spending for most domestic programs, particularly health and education programs.

Another irony is that most of the public supports balancing the budget, and a 1980 poll showed that 67 percent favored a constitutional amendment to require that the U.S. budget be balanced each year. In addition 32 of the 34 states necessary have passed resolutions calling for a Constitutional Convention to consider a balanced budget amendment. Although President Reagan campaigned in support of a balanced budget, he was quite willing to sacrifice it to his other priorities of a large "supply-side" tax cut and greatly increased defense spending. Ironically, his fiscal policies did not stop him from endorsing a proposed constitutional amendment passed by the Senate.

In the first year of his administration the public generally supported Reagan's performance. How can we explain this in light of the fact that the public strongly supported a balanced budget and did not favor cuts in most domestic programs? It seems that the election did not provide a very specific mandate for all of the Reagan economic program, but that the president took the opportunity of his electoral victory to implement his priorities.

How then did the Reagan administration succeed in such drastic budget cuts when other administrations had failed, since general support for reduced spending has always been present? The president's budget priorities prevailed in the context of favorable circumstances, but success resulted from a carefully planned strategy of constant political pressure on the public, the Congress and the executive branch. The personal wills and political skills of Ronald Reagan and David Stockman were essential.

The Groundwork

The Reagan budget victories of 1981 were the result of advance planning, singleness of purpose and speed of execution. Much of the groundwork for the specific budget cuts that the new administration would make was done by David Stockman during his two terms in the House as a representative from Michigan. Immediately after Reagan's victory he, along with Congressman Jack Kemp, wrote an economic plan entitled "Avoiding a GOP Economic Dunkirk" that became known as the "Stockman Manifesto."[6] Stockman impressed President-elect Reagan so much that he selected him to be his Director of the Office of Management and Budget, the youngest person to hold Cabinet rank in 150 years.[7] Stockman's intimate knowledge of the budgetary process, his command of budget figures, and his lobbying abilities with the Congress were crucial to the early Reagan budget victories.

The new administration decided to revise completely the Carter budget proposals for fiscal 1982 and submit its own budget to the Congress. Before the inauguration plans for budget cuts were made by Reagan transition teams that were assigned to each federal agency and who had offices in the agencies and access to internal budget and planning documents. In addition the conservative Heritage Foundation was compiling analyses of federal programs that it felt ought to be cut.[8] The Heritage proposals were taken seriously by the Reagan administration.

After January 20, Stockman was in charge of the entire OMB machinery which he put to work overtime tearing apart the budget they had just put together for President Carter. The overall strategy was to achieve most of the budget objectives as soon as possible so that the opposition would still be confused and would not have the time to galvanize against the Reagan plan. Early victories were necessary in order to cow the opposition and stampede as many members of Congress as possible onto the winning band wagon.[9]

Another part of the strategy was to make it seem as if programs benefiting all segments of society, rich as well as poor, were being cut alike. Stockman maintained that "We are interested in curtailing weak claims rather than weak clients. . . . The fear of the liberal remnant is that we will only attack weak clients. . . . I've got to take something out of Boeing's hide to make this look right. . . ."[10] The vulnerable part of cutting programs is that if some are excepted, others will argue for a similar dispensation, and the whole plan may crumble. If the exceptions can be minimized and "everybody's sacred cows are being cut"[11] it is harder to argue for special exemption for one program. Thus part of the strategy was to present the many different initiatives as a coherent budget package that could not succeed in turning the economy around unless it was swallowed whole by the Congress.

In order to maintain the speed and the unified front necessary for success, the administration had to build up early momentum and maintain constant political pressure on the budgetary front. An early gambit was the calculated leak of the "Stockman Hit List." The "Black Book" was a list of programs that might be cut. For each program listed there was a short explanation of the program, the proposed changes, the probable political reaction and cost projections through 1985. In lobbying for support on the Hill, Stockman gave copies to Republican members, and inevitably Democrats got copies.[12] In an effort to muster opposition to the cuts, the liberal Democratic Study Group distributed copies of the 150-page document which was photo-copied all over Washington.[13] This wide distribution of the hit list served Stockman's purpose of absorbing some of the political flack before the release of the official budget and showing that the administration was serious about deep cuts in social programs.

Immediately upon taking office the administration took actions to implement its budget plans in the executive branch. OMB sent out bulletins to heads of executive departments and agencies freezing civilian hiring, reducing travel expenditures, making reductions in consulting and related services, and placing a moratorium on the procurement of certain equipment.[14] On February 11, President Reagan sent out a memorandum stressing the short time that was available to revise the entire Carter budget and stated that any disagreements with the OMB budget or personnel limits had to be conveyed to the OMB director within 48 hours of the agency's receipt of the budget revisions, a process that normally takes weeks.[15] A freeze was also placed on hiring and made retroactive to the election.

In mid-February OMB began to freeze funds for millions of dollars in programs that the administration planned to cut, including funds for municipal sewage treatment plants, CETA workers, Youth

Conservation Corps and the Economic Development Administration. Although it would seem that such actions were prohibited by the Impoundment provisions (Title X) of the 1974 Budget Act, the administration argued that there had been a practice of stopping funds up to 30 days before a formal rescission request went to Congress for its approval.[16] The issue soon became moot, however, when Congress went along with virtually all of the administration's budget requests. The actions did not develop into an impoundment issue because the key element of congressional opposition to presidential withholding of funds was not present.[17]

A series of televised presidential speeches and official documents began the administration's political budget campaign for fiscal 1982. On February 5, in a televised address, the president warned of an "economic calamity of tremendous proportions" if his program were not passed. On February 18, in a speech to a joint session of Congress, he presented his "Program for Economic Recovery" along with an inch-thick document explaining his approach to fiscal and monetary policy. This was followed on March 10 by another address to Congress and the release of *Fiscal Year 1982 Budget Revisions*, the Reagan budget proposal prepared by the Office of Management and Budget. The following month OMB released *Additional Details on Budget Savings*, a document that specified budget projections for each program being cut along with the rationale for the proposed cuts. During the same time members of the Cabinet and Council of Economic Advisers were actively seeking appearances on TV and before various political, governmental and interest groups in order to promote the administration's budget plans.

The Cabinet

One source of potential opposition to the proposed cuts in domestic programs was the executive branch bureaucracies that were being cut. The administration used several approaches to neutralize this potential opposition: it delayed executive appointments and carefully orchestrated Cabinet-level acceptance of budget cuts. Despite the new administration's intention to hit the ground running (which it did in the budget arena), its executive personnel appointments immediately below the Cabinet level were dragged out due to several factors.[18] While this was frustrating for those concerned with managing the executive branch, it served the budget cutters well. Those appointed to run programs in general want to do a good job and may see budget cuts as limiting the resources they might use to accom-

plish their program goals, not to mention turf considerations. I
budget cuts are made before positions are filled, there will be no one
with any credibility in the new administration to marshall arguments
against drastically cutting back programs. Edwin Meese confirmed
that the lack of new appointees was helpful to budget cutting, and
said "when we do fill the office it will be with someone who is abso
lutely committed to the goals and objectives of the president."[19]

While some argue that the career service—the permanent bu
reaucrats—is a potent force in opposition to cuts, it are a negligible
factor in this set of circumstances. Career executives might have been
able to argue convincingly against program cuts, but no one in the
administration will listen to them, whereas they would at least have
had to listen to a Reagan appointee. In addition career executives,
because of their role perceptions and career interests, tend to be very
responsive to new political appointees and their priorities.[20]

Since the Cabinet secretaries had already been appointed, a dif
ferent tack was necessary with them. During the first few weeks of
the administration, before the newly appointed secretaries were fully
able or willing to defend their organizations, small meetings were
held with Stockman, the president, and several White House aides
present, along with the Cabinet secretary. The new appointee was
confronted with Stockman's proposed cuts and given a chance to
argue against them, but that was difficult because "they're in the
position of having to argue against the group line. And the group line
is cut, cut, cut."[21] Although the new Cabinet strongly supported the
Reagan economic program in general and certain cuts to their pro
grams in particular, they may have felt railroaded to go along with
decisions made by others before they were ready to take an active role
in the process. Stockman admitted "That's a very awkward position
for them, and you make them resentful very fast . . . I have a little
nervousness about the heavy-handedness with which I am being
forced to act."[22] But the Cabinet was a small problem of bringing along
the home team compared with the political challenge that faced the
administration in Congress.

Persuading the Congress

The main obstacle to be overcome in the spring budget fight was the
Congress, since it had to pass the laws that make up the budget. The
Republican capture of the Senate virtually assured support for the
president and allowed the administration to focus its efforts on the
House, in which the Democrats had a 52-seat edge. Despite this edge

he Democrats were very vulnerable, in part because they could not
agree on a unified plan to oppose the president. Some wanted to
present a complete alternative approach, while others wanted to give
he administration enough rope to hang itself by approving the proposals and then blaming the president for a faltering economy and
reduced domestic programs.

The natural target of the White House was the group of Southern
Democrats who felt politically vulnerable since they came from conservative districts that might replace them with Republicans if they
were perceived to be undermining the economy by budget busting.
This group of 47 Democrats became a highly visible swing block of
votes that organized itself into the Conservative Democratic Forum
and was informally known as the "Boll Weevils."[23] Since these Democrats were crucial to passage of the administration's budget program,
they were both wooed by the president and subjected to various
political pressures. Similar tactics were also used on "soft" Republicans.

One of the sources of President Reagan's success with the Congress was his affable personal style. He consciously courted Congress
early in his administration by visiting the leadership of both houses
and inviting many members to the White House. The response from
both sides of the aisle was very positive and was felt by many members to be in sharp contrast to the Carter years. During the battle for
votes on the first concurrent resolution in May 1981, the full range of
the president's personal persuasive powers was put to use. He in-
vited undecided members to the White House for group and private
meetings and picture-taking sessions. He made repeated phone calls
to their offices and their districts. In his first public statement after the
assassination attempt, Reagan called Democratic Representative
Eugene V. Atkinson of Pennsylvania, who was on a radio talk show,
and got his promise to vote for the reconciliation bill.[24] He courted
moderate Republican Representative Matthew J. Rinaldo of New
Jersey in a half-hour session at the White House. He also made a
personal call to him and arranged for calls from the vice president, the
Secretary of Labor and the Governor of Delaware. The Democrats did
not make a strong bid for Rinaldo's vote.[25] There is no doubt that the
president's high level of personal involvement was crucial to the administration's budget success.

Other political pressures from the administration were not quite
so gentle. Before the May 7 vote on the reconciliation bill, the political
assistant to the president coordinated a "Southern Blitz" to pressure
southern Democrats to vote with the administration. Government

officials were sent to home districts of House members to focus media attention on the upcoming vote with the hope that constituents would pressure the incumbents to support the president. Trade associations, corporations and local campaign contributors sympathetic to the president were enlisted to put pressure on the members. Letter-writing campaigns were organized, and corporations were asked to take out ads in magazines and newspapers supporting the administration's budget proposals.

Electoral carrots and sticks were also used. The White House contacted Democratic campaign contributors to ask them not to contribute to the campaigns of those who voted against the president.[26] The president even promised not to campaign against southern Democrats who consistently supported his budget program.[27] It was reported that a Democratic representative from Florida promised his vote if Republicans went along with his plan for Florida redistricting. There was also word that conservative Democrats who supported the administration would have easy battles in the 1982 elections. Paul Weyrich, Director of the Committee for the Survival of a Free Congress, said "there is a sense that if the [conservative Democrats] vote for Reagan in the House, they ought to get a bye in '82."[28]

James MacGregor Burns has argued that the president's favors and concessions to the southern Democrats for short-term political victories may have alienated those who want to rebuild the Republican party in the South.[29] They might see the president as willing to sacrifice long-term GOP party building for short-term budget victories.

In the campaign to get the tax-cut bill through Congress the administration again relied on a series of general appeals to the electorate, threats and favors for specific members of Congress, and electoral levers. A $500,000 radio and television campaign was set up by the Republican National Committee and the Republican Congressional Committee. President Reagan made a televised speech on July 27, asking people to urge their senators and representatives to support his tax-cut plan. The next day corporations made phone banks available to employees to lobby the Congress, and the volume on the Capitol switchboard was twice as great as usual. Reagan also called many members, invited them to the White House and even flew 15 members of Congress to Camp David to win their support. He also used programmatic changes to get votes, promising not to shut down a military base in Pennsylvania and changing his farm bill to continue the peanut price support and acreage allotment system rather than to phase them out as he originally proposed.[30] Electoral levers were also used: The Fund for the Conservative Majority offered not to campaign against 27 Democrats in 1982 if they voted with the president on the tax-cut bill.[31]

All of these pressures reinforced for Conservative Democrats a sense of electoral vulnerability. They believed that the voters wanted the president and Congress to cut spending and that a vote against the administration's formula for making cuts would be punished at the polls. They believed in President Reagan's version of his mandate.

THE BUDGETARY PROCESS: PRESIDENTIAL CONTROL

First Concurrent Resolution

After President Reagan sent his detailed budget revision proposals to the Congress on March 10, Congress had to take the first major step in the congressional budget process by passing a first concurrent budget resolution, setting spending, revenue and deficit targets for fiscal 1982. In February the crucial strategic decision had been made by the administration to use the reconciliation process in conjunction with the first concurrent resolution. Reconciliation was set up in the 1974 Budget Act to enable the House or Senate to require committees to change reported legislation in order to conform with the second concurrent resolution. For fiscal 1981 the procedure was used for the first time in conjunction with the first concurrent resolution to reduce outlays $4.6 billion and increase revenues by $3.6 billion.

The Reagan plan, however, was much more ambitious. It called for budget cuts—$48.6 billion initially—to be made by changes in the laws authorizing programs and extended the cuts over fiscal years 1983 and 1984. The usual budget procedure would call for a first concurrent resolution to set spending targets and then a second resolution in September to make the ceilings final. In the interim the appropriations committee would pass spending bills within the targets of the first resolution, and if any individual bill violated the final totals of the second resolution, a reconciliation bill could instruct the committees to report out a revised bill to conform with the second resolution. The Republicans, however, felt that the only way to get Congress to go along with the largest budget cuts in U.S. history was to put them all in one bill and pass it as soon as possible.

The crucial votes came in the House on May 7, when it passed the first concurrent resolution, and on June 26, when it passed the reconciliation package, including changes in existing legislation. In April the House Budget Committee reported out a Democrat-backed budget resolution calling for more spending but a smaller deficit than the administration proposal. On May 7 after several weeks of intense lobbying, 63 Democrats defected and passed the administration-backed "Gramm-Latta" package by a vote of 253 to 176. This vote was crucial because it showed that President Reagan could control the Democratic House and get his unprecedented budget changes through the Congress. On May 14, the House and Senate conference committees agreed to the first concurrent resolution including reconciliation instructions requiring authorizing committees to come up with the changes in law that would provide the $36 billion in budget cuts wanted by President Reagan.

Reconciliation

Over the next few weeks authorizing committees in both houses struggled to make the cuts required of them in the reconciliation instructions. The cuts were calculated from a baseline established by the Congressional Budget Office and determined by current levels of spending adjusted for inflation for each program. Although the authorizing committees were not instructed exactly where to make the cuts, they generally went along with those the administration wanted and the Budget Committees recommended. The cuts required changes in long-established domestic spending programs. "We have to tramp on hallowed ground—kick old friends in the teeth to achieve some of these cuts," liberal Representative Morris K. Udall remarked.[32] As each committee made its changes, the separate bills were referred back to the Budget Committees to compile them in a package and bring them to the floor for a vote. In mid-June each Budget Committee reported out the budget-cut packages.

As in the May vote on the first concurrent resolution, the crucial test came in the House. The House Budget Committee reported a bill compiled from the recommendations of 15 committees that provided $37.7 billion in savings and claimed the bill included 85 percent of the cuts wanted by Reagan. Republicans and conservative Democrats, however, claimed that entitlements were not cut enough and that too few programs were put into block grants.[33] They proposed a substitute called Gramm-Latta II that conformed very closely with what the administration wanted.

The administration again pulled out its heavy guns in lobbying for the Gramm-Latta substitute. The president himself telephoned or telegraphed each of the 63 Democrats who had voted with the administration on the first budget resolution. Compromises and concessions in the final package were made in order to win votes, some of them departures from the administration's earlier proposals. For example, David Stockman promised that the administration would not oppose the revival of sugar subsidies. He later said, "In economic principle it's kind of a rotten idea," but "they don't care, over in the White House, they want to win."[34]

The deciding vote came when the House defeated (210 to 217) a motion that would have allowed the Democrats to force votes on the separate pieces of the reconciliation substitute package rather than voting yes or no on the whole package as the Republicans wanted. The Gramm-Latta reconciliation substitute itself passed 232 to 193 on June 26. The Senate had already passed a very similar bill on June 25 by a vote of 80 to 15. The omnibus reconciliation package cut a total of $35.1 billion from the baseline established by CBO for 1982 with a total savings of $130.6 billion for fiscal years 1982 to 1984.[35]

Implications for Congressional Power of the Purse

The 1982 reconciliation bill was historic in that it was a major reversal of the spending priorities of the past several decades. House Budget Committee Chairman James Jones called it "clearly the most monumental and historic turnaround in fiscal policy that has ever occurred."[36] It provided the largest spending cut in U.S. history, affecting hundreds of programs, and encompassed some of the greatest changes ever made in a single bill by the Congress. The conference committee consisted of 250 House and Senate members who met in 58 subconferences. The process was criticized by Democrats because there was very little information on the exact content of the bill until immediately before the vote. The bill itself was printed with handwritten changes and misnumbered pages.

The power of the Budget Committees was enhanced because the spending cuts were coordinated through them, and they wrote the guidelines that committees compiled with, though technically they were nonbinding. The appropriations committees were by-passed by making the cuts through changed authorizations rather than reduced appropriations. Alan Schick has argued that this has led the appropriations committee in the House to change its role from one of guardian

of the purse to that of spending advocate.[37] The use of the reconciliation process also centralized power in Congress by putting teeth in
the concurrent resolution early in the budget schedule.

The 1974 Budget Act enhanced the power of Congress in the
budgetary process by enabling it to formulate and vote upon a budget
package different from that of the president, a power that it exercised
to a greater or lesser degree in the latter half of the 1970s.[38] Congress
had temporarily recaptured the power of the purse. Then came the
election of 1980, the claimed mandate and the Reagan budget juggernaut.

In 1981 the reconciliation process was skillfully used to enhance
the power of the president in the budget arena. Because of the Republican Senate and conservative Democrats in the House, Congress did
not tear apart the president's proposed budget and deal with it
piecemeal, nor did it present an alternative budget of its own. But
presidential power is only increased in that there exists the reconciliation tool that allows Congress to centralize its own decision-making
and deal with the budget as a package. That tool is only effective,
however, when the political muscle or will exists to overcome the
traditional fragmenting forces within Congress. In 1981 that political
muscle came from a popular president who invested vast political
resources (to the exclusion of other priorities) to fight the long budget
campaign. The electoral insecurity of Congress and the feeling that
since nothing else had worked, the president's economic program
ought to be given a chance, made Congress willing to go along.

Although the reconciliation process may be used in the future, it
is doubtful that it will be used again by a president to achieve the
depth and scope of changes that its use achieved for fiscal 1982.
Congress clearly felt that the circumstances were special: the state of
the economy was so poor that drastic action was necessary. The level
of conflict was raised to an extremely high pitch since so many programs were being cut at the same time with so little opportunity for
the slow deliberation that Congress traditionally prefers. There was a
feeling on the part of Republicans as well as Democrats that the
administration bills were railroaded through the recently developed
legislative process without due deliberation and that members were
stampeded into going along without sufficient opportunity to have
some input in the final product. Democratic Representative Leon
Panetta, chairman of the Budget Committee's reconciliation task
force, said that reconciliation was "a tool that's been terribly abused,"
and that it was used "as a Christmas tree."[39] But such procedures
were necessary in order to get the drastic changes enacted, and all of

the considerable political powers of the presidency were necessary to achieve the budget victory. The favorable circumstances of 1980–81 which allowed this to happen are unlikely to recur in the foreseeable future.

THE REAGAN BUDGET: SHIFTING PRIORITIES

Tax Cut and the Deficit

The Reagan administration tax policy originated in the 1980 campaign when candidate Reagan endorsed the Kemp-Roth tax-cut proposal that had been introduced in Congress in 1977. He argued that decreasing taxes would actually increase revenues by spurring productivity in the private sector. The administration's original proposal of February 1981 called for a 10 percent cut in individual income taxes for three successive years and tax incentives for business investment. The 1982 loss to the Treasury would be $53.9 billion.[40] In early June the administration reduced the 1982 impact to $37 billion by changing the first year income tax cut to 5 percent beginning in October 1981. At the same time lobbyists began to push hard for tax breaks for the groups they represented.

The Democrats were also writing a tax bill as an alternative to the administration's and included tax breaks for special interests in order to gain their support. The administration wanted to assure victory for its version and began to outbid the Democrats in the tax breaks it offered as "ornaments" on the tax "Christmas tree" bill. As David Stockman, who wanted to limit the tax cut in order to minimize the deficit, explained, "The basic strategy was to match or exceed the Democrats, and we did."

In late July, as the time neared for the congressional vote on the bill, more "sweeteners" and "ornaments" were added to assure victory on a vote that was then too close to call. Tax breaks for oil producers were added to gain support from southern Democrats. Real estate and further business loopholes were added. Stockman, though he did some of the bargaining, was critical of the form of the tax cut as well as its size: "Do you realize the greed that came to the forefront? . . . the hogs were really feeding. The greed level, the level of opportunism, just got out of control."[41]

After another massive lobbying effort by the administration, in-

cluding a televised presidential address that helped create public
pressure on Congress, 48 House Democrats defected to vote for the
administration's tax-cut bill. In the Senate 37 of 47 Democrats voted
for it. The bill provided a tax cut of $37.6 billion in 1982 that would
increase to $267.6 billion in 1986. The total five-year loss to the Trea-
sury would amount to $750 billion.[42]

The major provisions included an individual tax cut of 5 percent
on marginal rates on October 1, 1981, followed by a 10 percent cut on
July 1 of 1982 and 1983. Business would be able to depreciate assets at
an accelerated rate of ten years for buildings, five years for machinery
and equipment, and three years for automobiles. The top rate on
investment income was reduced from 70 percent to 50 percent, and
the capital gains tax was reduced from 28 percent to 20 percent. In
addition, beginning in 1985, individual income tax brackets will be
indexed to the consumer price index. Treasury Secretary Regan said
that the administration got 95 percent of what it wanted in the tax
bill.[43]

The justification for such a large tax cut at the same time that
defense spending was being raised was the "supply-side" economic
theory that high levels of taxation were stifling economic productivity. Economists such as Arthur Laffer and Paul Craig Roberts argued that the large tax cut would provide such a stimulus to productivity that tax revenues would actually increase and allow the budget
to be balanced in 1984 despite unprecedented levels of defense
spending and growth in entitlement outlays. In addition to a sudden
increase in economic growth, inflation rates would fall, bringing interest rates down as well, because the expectations of investors would
be changed. Money saved from the tax breaks would not be con-
sumed by taxpayers, but would be saved and invested in productive
activities. "We anticipate that savings rates will increase, perhaps to
historically high levels."[44]

Conventional economists of the right and left were skeptical
about the new supply-side approach and were particularly leery
about the potentially huge deficits if the economy did not turn around
quickly, as predicted by the supply-siders. Some argued that the tax
cut was not targeted well enough to ensure that increased disposable
income would go to savings rather than consumptions. They also
argued that the the decrease in capital gains taxes might encourage
speculative, rather than productive investments.[45] Others argued that
the tax cut was inequitable, with most breaks going to large corporations and individuals with high incomes. They also said that supply-
side economics was merely a new face on the traditional Republican

"trickle-down" approach that holds that increased wealth for the rich will stimulate economic growth that will eventually benefit everyone in the society. This criticism took on more weight when William Greider's interview with David Stockman was made public. Stockman was quoted as saying:

> The hard part of the supply-side tax cut is dropping the top rate from 70 to 50 percent—the rest of it is a secondary matter . . . in order to make this palatable as a political matter, you had to bring down all the brackets. But, I mean, Kemp-Roth was always a Trojan horse to bring down the top rate. It's kind of hard to sell 'trickle-down' . . . so the supply-side formula was the only way to get a tax policy that was really 'trickle-down.' Supply-side is 'trickle-down' theory.[46]

The Economic Recovery Tax Act of 1981 also allowed businesses that qualified for a tax break but were not able to use it because profits were down to sell tax breaks to more profitable companies to reduce their tax liabilities. The selling company would receive some cash and the buying company would pay lower taxes. Only the U.S. Treasury would lose out, by possibly $27 billion over five years.[47]

According to the Reagan administration's March budget estimates, the FY 1982 deficit would be $45 billion, and the budget would be balanced by 1984. Despite the passage of nearly all of its economic package, when the economy did not perform as it had predicted, the administration was forced to make changes in its budget projections. In July 1981, in the mid-year review, it increased 1982 outlay estimates by about $10 billion to cover higher interest rates, but predicted the deficit would be $42.5 billion, and still promised a balanced budget by 1984.[48]

During the summer of 1981 it became clear that more cuts had to be made if defense spending and the social safety net were left intact and the deficit held to administration estimates, so in September the president proposed $13 billion in additional cuts and $3 billion in tax increases. The cuts were to be achieved by an across-the-board 12 percent reduction in non-defense appropriations and changes in welfare entitlements. The new proposals were not met with enthusiasm in Congress, which was still bruised from the $35 billion in reconciliation cuts. Even moderate Republicans were unwilling to cut more and accused OMB Director Stockman of reneging on deals he had negotiated in June when he was lobbying for the reconciliation bill.[49] In December Congress agreed to $4 billion of the $13 billion in cuts that Reagan had asked for in September.

In fall of 1981, the U.S. economy began to unravel the optimistic projections of the Reagan supply-side budget. Although inflation was falling, economic growth was also falling and unemployment was rising. As a result of budget policy and economic factors, the OMB revised its predictions and estimated a deficit greater than $100 billion in fiscal 1982 and greater than $160 billion in 1984.[50] Along with the greater deficit projections came a reversal of the administration's evaluation of deficit spending. In his February 5 speech the president said, "We know now that inflation results from all that deficit spending." But in late 1981 administration spokesmen were echoing previous Democratic administrations in claiming that deficit spending does not necessarily cause inflation. On December 17 President Reagan said that a balanced budget was a "goal, not a promise" and that "this is not a case of a broken promise, but is a case of circumstances beyond our control. . . ." He said he would not balance the budget "by robbing the people, by imposing a punitive tax system on the people. . . ."[51]

After the probable size of the 1982 deficit had increased to the $100 billion range in fall of 1981, the House was unwilling to pass a second concurrent resolution anticipating such an amount. The House Budget Committee thus reported out a resolution that merely restated the May first concurrent resolution despite the changes in economic conditions that would force a much higher deficit than the $37.65 billion then anticipated. This action was similar to passage of the first concurrent resolution for 1981, when President Carter and the Congress had hammered out a balanced budget that economic circumstances had made obsolete before the time had come to vote on it. Congress passed it anyway. In December 1981, the Senate passed the *pro forma* second concurrent resolution by a one vote margin, but added "sense of the Senate" language calling for a revised concurrent resolution that would balance the budget by 1984.[52] The actual deficit for FY 1982 was $110.7 billion.

The Defense Buildup

Even though President Carter was increasing the defense budget, candidate Reagan called for a much greater buildup, including yearly increases of 7 percent in real terms. American public opinion was firmly behind increased defense spending, particularly after the Soviet invasion of Afghanistan and the Iranian hostage crisis. In the March 10 Budget Revisions the president asked for an increase of $6.8 billion for 1981 and $26 billion for 1982 over the budget authority requested in President Carter's January budget.[53] Projected authority for fiscal years 1983 to 1986 was increased over Carter projections by a total of $161 billion with budget authority for 1986 projected at $374.3 billion.[54] Military spending authority for the next five years would approach $1.5 trillion and constitute more than 35 percent of total outlays.[55]

On December 15, 1981, Congress passed the largest peacetime defense appropriation bill ever passed, totaling $199.7 billion.[56] Even so the outyear implications were even more striking. According to Senator John Stennis, "The groundwork here is laid . . . for the need to appropriate great sums of money that are going to start coming due in a big way the second year, the third year, and the fourth year."[57] Senator Ted Stevens also predicted a substantial "funding crisis" in 1983, 1984 and 1985. Although the appropriation was not as great as the administration had originally asked for, part of the shortfall was due to the decision to shift the military pay raise to a future supplemental appropriation and changing some assumptions about the effects of inflation and the economy.

Critics of the Reagan defense proposals hit at two main issues: that the spending was not targeted well and that the huge increases would have harmful inflationary effects on the U.S. economy. Except for funds to develop a new bomber, Reagan's increases mainly added more money on to the Carter defense plans. The increases in funds was so much so fast that defense planners enhanced already existing "wish lists" that did not "represent a well thought-out plan."[58]

When OMB was putting together the massive budget cuts in the spring, not much careful analysis was given to the defense proposals. David Stockman characterized the defense budget as "just a bunch of numbers written on a piece of paper."[59] Throughout the budget campaign Stockman, who was much more interested in balancing the budget than most supply-siders, tried to convince other administration officials to cut the defense budget which contained "blatant inefficiency," "poor deployment of manpower," "contracting idiocy" and a "swamp of waste of $10 to $30 billion."[60] But he was unable to win his battle because conservative southern Democrats might not have supported the rest of the administration's budget program, and because he could not change the president's mind on defense spending. As a result the Pentagon "got a blank check."[61] As Finance Committee Chairman Robert Dole remarked, "Perhaps it is unfair to say that we have exempted the Pentagon from all budget scrutiny, but there is that feeling and that perception by some of us."[62]

James Fallows has argued that President Reagan's approach to defense is a continuation of the debate of the past few decades in which conservatives have urged "strength" through more defense spending and liberals have argued for "restraint" through less spending. Fallows argues that both sides accept the fallacy that what really matters is the *size* of the defense budget, rather than the weapons, management and strategic systems that comprise our defense establishment. The main thrust of his book, *National Defense*, is that debate over defense spending should revolve around *how* the money is spent rather than *how much* is spent.[63] He also points out that though annual defense spending since 1953 has been about the same in constant dollars, it has fallen as a percentage of GNP. But with entitlements and fixed costs approaching 60 percent of the budget, the 25 percent devoted to defense cannot be raised too much without seriously limiting other governmental functions.

In 1981, Deputy Secretary of Defense Carlucci commented on the future spending implications of the administration's defense plans: "there is a substantial tail on the 1982 programs which is going to complicate our life in the outyears: 1983, 1984 and 1985."[64] But even more imposing than the expected "tail" of outyear spending was the probability of cost overruns. Some have argued that projected defense expenditures over the years have been systematically underestimated because of unrealistic initial estimates and changes in design. These charges were made by liberals and conservatives as well as by internal Pentagon studies. Even the conservative Heritage Foundation came to the same conclusion. The consensus was that future costs would be higher than predicted by as much as 30 percent, since the majority of the defense buildup was planned to go to procurement rather than training and personnel.[65] If Congress reacts to cost overruns by holding the lid at the previously projected spending levels, procurement may be cut back, making each unit more expensive, whether planes, ships or missiles. Alternatively, if operations, maintenance and training are cut to reduce cost overruns in procurement, the readiness of U.S. forces may be impaired.

By 1983 there were calls for reduced defense spending from across the political spectrum. A statement signed by McGeorge Bundy, Robert S. McNamara, Cyrus B. Vance and Elmo R. Zumwalt, Jr. argued that due to the Reagan administration military spending policies, "the economic foundations of our national security, which are every bit as important as the defense component, have been undermined." They concluded that the defense budget for fiscal years 1982–84 "can be reduced substantially without endangering the nation's security." They suggested canceling the B-1 bomber and the

MX missile as part of a plan to hold defense increases to 5 percent per year rather than the 10 percent real increase that was proposed by the administration.[66]

In March and April 1983, the "Bipartisan Budget Appeal" took out full-page ads in the *New York Times* to urge restraint in defense spending. Their statement argued that the health of the U.S. economy depended on reducing projected deficits, and that necessarily included scaling back defense spending. They said that the 1983 defense budget was "$96 billion larger than the one three years earlier and represented a 34 percent increase in real defense dollars." They argued that projected increases by 1986 of another $118 billion was "not sustainable—economically or politically—with current federal revenues." They urged the president and Congress to commit the nation "to a more gradual, but significant and sustained increase in the defense budget for the next several years." The statement was signed by five former Secretaries of the Treasury—W. Michael Blumenthal (1977–79), John B. Connally (1971–72), C. Douglas Dillon (1961–65), Henry H. Fowler (1965–68) and William E. Simon (1974–76)—and by Peter G. Peterson, former Secretary of Commerce (1972–73).[67] Such statements were striking because of the willingness of advocates of a strong U.S. defense capability to break publicly with the president and criticize the Reagan administration for going too far in defense spending increases.

Domestic Spending Cuts

In order to get an overview of the scope of the change intended by the Reagan reversal of fiscal policy priorities, it is useful to consider broad budget trends over the past few decades and the Reagan administration's projections for future years. Defense spending, which constituted 44 percent of budget outlays in 1962, slipped to 24 percent in 1981. The proposed increases would in fact raise defense's share to 32 percent. Safety net programs, largely uncontrollable entitlements, grew from 25 percent in 1962 to 37 percent in 1981, and are projected to grow to 41 percent of total outlays. Given interest payments on the national debt of 9 percent, the "all other" category has to shrink from 29 percent of outlays in 1981 to 18 percent. The proposed spending cuts of about $130 billion from 1982 to 1984, including about $30 billion appeared in 1982, from the "all other" category were primarily cuts in human resource programs: education, employment, training, health, income-assistance and social services. Many of these programs are run through state and local governments so that about one-third of the budget cuts would come from grants to state and local governments.

The president proposed the drastic budget cuts in domestic programs in order to deal with "the second great economic crisis of this century." But in doing so he assured Americans that those who were truly needy would be provided for. He thus exempted from cuts certain programs that he designated as the nation's permanent social safety net whose commitments "now transcend differences of ideology, partisanship, and fiscal priorities."[68] The social safety net includes Social Security, Medicare and veterans programs which constitute the bulk of safety net spending. Also included are Project Head Start, some nutrition programs for children and the elderly, and the summer youth employment program. Including the three major programs in the social safety net was a wise political judgment since the beneficiaries of these programs are numerous and politically powerful. This was demonstrated by the forced reversal of the initial decision to eliminate the minimum Social Security monthly payment of $122, and by the president's repudiation of early administration proposals to reform the Social Security system.

Critics argued that the Reagan plan ensured continuation of subsidies for the middle class, since most beneficiaries of the three main safety net programs have incomes above the poverty line, and even those who are affluent can receive benefits from the three programs. On the other hand, they argued, those programs intended for the very poor, such as food stamps, AFDC, Medicaid and rent subsidies, were the targets of administration budget cuts. They also argued that cuts in job training, compensatory education and child care could actually increase welfare expenditures by keeping people on welfare rolls.

Two-thirds of the budget cuts came from the human services area. Food stamps eligibility was tightened, reducing the rolls by about one million people. Subsidies for school lunches were cut, and 300,000 CETA jobs were eliminated, saving $3.9 billion. Additional unemployment benefits triggered by national rates were eliminated, and trade adjustment aid to workers was cut. AFDC payments were cut for those who work. Housing subsidies were cut by decreasing the projected units constructed and raising the percentage of rent poor tenants must pay. Eligibility for student college loans was tightened. Medicaid grants to states were reduced. The Community Services Administration (from the War on Poverty) was abolished. The remaining one-third of the budget cuts came from transportation, subsidies for mass transit and highways, and research and development subsidies for new forms of energy.

Block Grants

State and local governments had long been pressing for the relaxing of federal requirements attached to most federal aid in categorical grants. President Reagan's budget proposals began significant moves in that direction by replacing some categorical grants with block grants. The original proposal was to consolidate 85 categorical grants, which accounted for $16.5 billion in 1981 spending, into seven block grants. The final outcome was nine block grants that amounted to $7.5 billion in spending.[69] The president wanted to accomplish several purposes with this consolidation: he wanted to limit control and power in the federal government, he wanted decision-making about programs to be at local levels where they are implemented, and he wanted to reduce the cost of federal administrative overhead.

While cities and states were pleased with the reduction in federal requirements associated with the block grant approach, they were not pleased with the overall cuts in aid included in the president's economic program. State and local governments claimed that they absorbed two-thirds of the first round of the 1982 budget cuts. By 1986 federal aid is intended to be cut to 50 percent of its 1980 level after adjusting for inflation.[70] Thus state and local governments have to absorb significant cuts in aid at the same time they are benefiting from the reduction of federal requirements.

Although Congress did not pass all of the block grant proposals of the Reagan administration, it did make a significant retreat from the categorical approach to federal aid. The reconciliation bill set up four block grants in the health area that combined 19 federal programs and shifted responsibility to state and local governments. At the same time there was a 25 percent cut in funds from the 1981 level adjusted for inflation.[71] The four areas of health block grants include preventive health services; alcohol, and drug abuse and mental health; primary health care; and maternal and child health.

Although the president wanted to combine 44 separate education grants into two grants for school programs and special needs, Congress decided to retain the two core educational aid programs: aid for the education of the disadvantaged and aid for handicapped children. Several other educational grant programs were combined into one block grant. The social services program, which was already a block grant, was expanded and an energy assistance block grant was

created to help the poor. Federal controls over Community Development Block Grants were eased, and Congress decided to fund
the Urban Development Action Grants (UDAG), though the administration proposed to end them.

After the full extent of the cuts in federal aid proposed by Reagan
became clear, representatives of state and local governments became
more critical. They began to perceive the block grant program as
primarily a means to cut the federal budget. New York Mayor Edward
Koch called the New Federalism of President Reagan a "mask for a
systematic campaign of abandonment," and Governor Richard Snell-
ing of Vermont, a conservative Republican, described Reagan's program as "an economic Bay of Pigs."[72] Critics also claimed that the
president was not sensitive to the problems caused by differentials in
wealth and expensive social problems between the energy-rich states
with huge tax resources and states with older industries and decaying
cities. That feeling was exacerbated when the president in an interview said that such problems could be dealt with by "the right of a
citizen to vote with his feet."[73]

CONCLUSION

President Reagan's first budget defied the predictions of scholars and
old Washington hands alike. Very few would have predicted that he
could have made such drastic shifts in priorities so suddenly. His
budget campaign will be a model for future presidential transitions.
He proved that with careful planning the budget could be completely
revised in a few months and Congress persuaded to approve it. He
demonstrated how an electoral victory could be translated into a mandate for his policies with the single-minded pursuit of his budget
priorities. Not even the assassination attempt derailed him for long.
Fortuna did play a role: other crises, domestic or foreign, did not
intervene to distract him from his budget plan. And he did pay the
price of neglecting other political priorities he might have pursued.
He was also criticized for trading off future electoral gains for some
Democratic votes in Congress on his budget package.

During the 1982 budget cycle the pendulum of the power of the
purse swung toward the president. The reconciliation process was
skillfully used to force Congress to vote on the president's budget as a
package. The feeling on the Hill, especially among Democrats, was
that Congress was stampeded and steamrollered into passing the
budget without the careful deliberation that ought to be given to the

national budget. Even Republicans became more skeptical when they saw the $200 billion deficit that was implied in their previous votes on the budget. Such sweeping presidential victories will be less likely in the future.

A number of proposals for reform of the budgetary process have been made as a result of the 1982 budget campaign. Some of them undoubtedly have merit, but it must be remembered that the root cause of budgetary stalemate is the lack of consensus on budgetary priorities. Changes in procedural arrangements, whether constitutional or in the budgetary process, cannot make up for a lack of political consensus. The experience of the battle of the budget in 1982 has shown that a strong president can bring Congress along, despite its fragmentation. What is needed for a coherent fiscal policy is either a political consensus on economic priorities or the political power that is able to forge that consensus. Neither is possible without the other.

NOTES

1. See James P. Pfiffner, "Inflexible Budgets, Fiscal Stress, and the Tax Revolt," in Alberta M. Sbragia, ed., *The Municipal Money Chase* (Boulder, Col.: Westview, 1983).

2. Royce Crocker, "Federal Government Spending and Public Opinion," *Public Budgeting and Finance* 1:3 (Autumn 1981), p. 25.

3. Crocker, p. 30.

4. Crocker, p. 28.

5. Crocker, pp. 30–31.

6. See *The Washington Post* (December 14, 1980) Sec. C. p. 1.

7. Walter Shapiro, "The Stockman Express," *Washington Post Magazine* (February 8, 1981), p. 8.

8. Eugene J. McAllister, ed., *Agenda for Progress: Examining Federal Spending* (Washington, D.C.: Heritage Foundation, 1981); see also Charles L. Heatherly, *Mandate for Leadership.*

9. Elizabeth Drew, "A Reporter in Washington" *The New Yorker* (June 8, 1981), p. 138.

10. William Greider, "The Education of David Stockman," *The Atlantic* (December 1981), pp. 30–32.

11. Greider, p. 36.

12. See *Congressional Quarterly Weekly Report* (February 14, 1981), p. 311.

13. Democratic Study Group Special Report No. 97-2 (February 7, 1981).

14. *OMB Bulletin* 81-6 (January 24, 1981); 81-7 (January 24, 1981); 81-8 (January 24, 1981); and 81-9 (January 30, 1981). See also *OMB Bulletin* 81-11 (February 11, 1981).

15. Memorandum for Heads of Non-Cabinet Agencies, "Revisions of the 1982 Budget" (February 7, 1981).

16. *Washington Post* (March 5, 1981), p. 1; *Wall Street Journal* (March 6, 1981).

17. For an analysis of the development of the impoundment issue, see James P. Pfiffner, *The President, the Budget, and Congress* (Boulder, Col.: Westview, 1979).

18. See William Safire, "Of Meese and Men," *New York Times* (February 2, 1981).

19. *CQ Weekly Report* (February 21, 1981), p. 333.

20. See James P. Pfiffner, "The Challenge of Federal Management in the 1980s," *Public Administration Quarterly* 7:2 (Summer 1983), p. 162.

21. Stockman quoted in *The Atlantic* (December 1981), p. 33.

22. Greider, p. 33.

23. See *CQ Weekly Report* (June 13, 1980), p. 1023; *Washington Post* (April 26, 1981), p. 1.

24. *CQ Weekly Report* (April 25, 1981), p. 705.

25. Martin Tolchin "It's Reagan's Strong Suit Against the House Odds," *New York Times* (May 3, 1981), Sec. 4, p. 1.

26. *CQ Weekly Report* (June 13, 1981), p. 1023.

27. *CQ Weekly Report* (June 13, 1981), p. 1025.

28. *Washington Post* (April 26, 1981), p. A10.

29. *Los Angeles Times* (January 19, 1982), part IV, p. 1.

30. *CQ Weekly Report* (July 25, 1981), p. 1373.

31. *CQ Weekly Report* (July 25, 1981), p. 1325.

32. *CQ Weekly Report* (May 23, 1981), p. 890.

33. *CQ Weekly Report* (July 4, 1981), p. 1167.

34. Greider, p. 50.

35. *CQ Weekly Report* (August 1, 1981), p. 1377.

36. *CQ Weekly Report* (August 1, 1981), p. 1371.

37. Alan Schick, "The Problem of Presidential Budgeting," in Hugh Heclo and Lester M. Salamon, eds., *The Illusion of Presidential Government* (Boulder, Col.: Westview, 1981).

38. See James Sundquist, *The Decline and Resurgence of Congress* (Washington: The Brookings Institution, 1981), Chapter 8.

39. *CQ Weekly Report* (August 1, 1981), p. 1378.

40. *CQ Weekly Report* (August 8, 1981), p. 1431.

41. Greider, p. 51.

42. *CQ Weekly Report* (August 8, 1981), p. 1435.

43. *CQ Weekly Report* (August 8, 1981), p. 1431.

44. Murray L. Weidenbaum, *Washington Star* (March 10, 1981), p. A13. See also Arthur Laffer, "Supply-Side Economics," *Financial Analysts Journal* (September/October 1981), p. 29; and George Gilder, *Wealth and Poverty* (New York: Basic Books, 1981), Chapter 4.

45. For some criticisms of supply-side economics, see Lester Thurow, "Undamming the American Economy," *New York Times Magazine* (May 3, 1981), p. 38; and "How to Wreck the Economy," *New York Review of Books* (May 14, 1981), p. 3. See also Robert L. Heilbroner, "The Demand for the Supply Side," *New York Review of Books* (June 11, 1981), p. 37; and James Tobin, "Reaganomics and Economics," *New York Review of Books* (December 31, 1981), p. 11.

46. Greider, pp. 46–47.

47. See William J. Quirk, "The Great Tax Benefit Sale," *The New Republic* (December 30, 1981), p. 18; and Robert J. Samuelson, "Fun and Games With Taxes," *Los Angeles Times* (January 5, 1982), Part II, p. 9.

48. *CQ Weekly Report* (July 18, 1981), p. 1308.

49. Greider, p. 50.

50. *CQ Weekly Report* (January 23, 1982), p. 116.

51. *CQ Weekly Report* (December 26, 1981), p. 2606.

52. *CQ Weekly Report* (November 21, 1981), p. 2271; and (December 19, 1981), pp. 2510–11.

53. Office of Management and Budget, *Fiscal Year 1982 Budget Revisions* (March 1981), p. 34.

54. *Budget Revisions*, p. 99.

55. *Budget Revisions*, pp. 34, 99. See also Joseph Pechman et al., *Setting National Priorities: the 1982 Budget* (Washington: The Brookings Institution, 1981), Chapter 4.

56. *CQ Weekly Report* (December 19, 1981), p. 2506.

57. *CQ Weekly Report* (December 19, 1981), p. 2533.

58. Drew, p. 141.

59. Greider, p. 40.

60. Greider, p. 35.

61. Greider, p. 43.

62. *CQ Weekly Report* (December 5, 1981), p. 2397.

63. James Fallows, *National Defense* (New York: Random House, 1981).

64. *Washington Post* (July 12, 1981).

65. See *Time* (March 7, 1983), p. 12.

66. *New York Times* (April 3, 1983), p. 27. McGeorge Bundy was Special Assistant for National Security Affairs to Presidents John F. Kennedy and Lyndon B. Johnson. Robert S. McNamara was Kennedy's Secretary of Defense. Cyrus R. Vance was Secretary of State under President Jimmy Carter. Elmo R. Zumwalt, Jr., a retired admiral, was Chief of Naval Operations and a member of the Joint Chiefs of Staff under President Richard M. Nixon.

67. *New York Times* (April 6, 1983), p. 8.

68. *A Program for Economic Recovery* (February 18, 1981), Part IV, p. 13.

69. See Richard Nathan, "The Nationalization of Proposition 13," *PS* 14:4 (Fall 1981), p. 752.

70. *CQ Weekly Report* (October 24, 1981), p. 2050.

71. *CQ Weekly Report* (August 15, 1981), p. 1501.

72. Neal Pierce, "Cities, States Oppose New Federalism," *PA Times* (December 15, 1981), p. 2.

73. Neal Pierce, "The States can Sink or Swim," *Los Angeles Times* (November 22, 1981), Part IV, p. 5.

7

Presidents, Pensions and Fiscal Policy

GARY FREEMAN

No American president since Franklin Roosevelt has played a decisive role in the development of the Social Security system. Throughout most of its history policymaking for Social Security has been characterized by what may be called "subsystem autonomy." Decisions about the program have been taken within a relatively small and closed circle of program administrators and relevant members of Congress. The ability of this group to make policy with little outside interference, either from other public officials or private interests, was facilitated for many years by the existence of a bipartisan consensus within the political elite over the program and a generally receptive but passive public opinion. Presidents had little incentive or capacity to challenge the bureaucrats and lawmakers who had continuing proprietary interests in the program.

There are numerous pressures working to push the presidency more directly into Social Security policymaking. The consensus on Social Security has been shattered by the trust fund deficits that have been periodically forecast since 1973. The once quiescent public has been fragmented into groups of passionately interested clients jealously guarding their benefits and angry taxpayers and younger workers who fear that they will be the victims of Social Security's demise. The policymaking subsystem has broken down so that it no longer constitutes an effective challenge to presidential leadership. The sheer size of the program, its cost, the weight of its taxes, its impact on millions of beneficiaries and their families, the escalating financial crisis and the program's growing politicization make managing the program's growth central to the realization of two key presidential policy goals: budgetary and economic stability. No chief executive can any longer afford to be excluded from full participation in decision-making for the nation's most important domestic program.

For a number of reasons, however, presidents find it difficult to make much of a mark on Social Security policy. If the old policymaking subsystem has disintegrated, it has nonetheless left behind a legacy of program structures and public attitudes that constrains innovative policies. The politics of Social Security are much more broad-based and loosely coordinated than in the past, but this enhanced pluralism means that no particular institutional actor or set of actors can dominate discussion and that no coherent majority within either political party or across them is behind a clear set of policy alternatives. The president must compete with various members of Congress for control of Social Security reform, and he must do so in an extremely volatile partisan environment in which identification with an opposition stance can spell political disaster.

Beyond these impediments to presidential action, the policy options on Social Security are limited by the interdependence between various alternatives and other important presidential goals. Although the program is enormously complex and controversial, there are solutions to its problems unless one accepts the most extreme prognoses. Unlike the frustrating dilemmas that policymakers face when they try to manage economic fluctuations that are not well understood, the difficulties of Social Security are clear-cut. Promised outlays are greater than revenues for several easily identifiable reasons. The financial crisis can be approached by higher payroll taxes, an infusion of cash from some other source, or reduced expenditures. The severity of the Social Security crisis arises not out of the absence of remedies, but from the interaction of particular remedies with other pressing governmental problems, especially in the budgetary and economic policy spheres. From the point of view of the president, the Social Security crisis is a matter of choosing among a set of politically painful and highly interdependent options.

This chapter analyzes the presidential role in Social Security policymaking. What incentives do presidents have to become involved with the issue and what resources can they bring to bear on it? How do the structure and process of Social Security politics constrain presidential effectiveness? What is the most useful analytical approach to an understanding of Social Security policymaking? We will begin by laying out three alternative models of Social Security politics: one that stresses popular electoral preferences, one that stresses bureaucratic interests and strategies, and one that focuses on the role of the state and its central executive officials. The next sections describe the evolution of the Social Security program, the nature of the financial crisis, and the relationship of the program to federal budgetary politics and the performance of the national economy. We will turn then to a direct assessment of the utility of the three models through case studies of the administrations of Presidents Ford, Carter and Reagan. The evidence shows that each model is helpful in understanding particular aspects or historical episodes in Social Security's development. This chapter argues that even though the state-centered model is less powerful than the others for accounting for policy outcomes, it is the most useful for understanding strictly *presidential* motives and strategies and for interpreting changes in the politics of Social Security since 1972.

EXPLAINING SOCIAL SECURITY POLITICS

One frequent explanation for the reluctance of both Congress and the president to deal definitively with the Social Security crisis is that the popularity of the program, the potency of the elderly lobby and the resistance of the middle class to higher payroll taxes make it too hot to handle, a veritable "Middle East of American politics." We might refer to this as the *democratic politics* model of Social Security politics. It is part of a more general perspective which sees public policies as the outcome or reflection of popular, electoral pressures. Public officials, in this view, are often little more than pawns in a competitive struggle, possessing little relative autonomy with respect to the "private interests" in society.[1]

As we shall see, there is evidence to support such a view. Certainly, Social Security is an explosive issue that can have serious consequences for the politician who mishandles it. The fact that Social Security benefits are widely distributed increases the salience of the program to the public. But conflict over Social Security is not simply a drama of vulnerable and ineffective politicians trying to defuse a social policy time bomb while the public stands on the sidelines, alternately shouting encouragement and threats.

For most of its history the Social Security program has had a substantial autonomy in the sense that it has been relatively insulated from societal pressures and relatively immune from presidential and congressional interference. Its emergence and growth reflect not so much the specific demands of the electorate, nor even the electioneering and coalition-building of the president and Congress, as the ability of an activist bureaucracy to realize its long-run objectives. It is not an exaggeration to say that the goals and activities of the administrators who played leading roles in setting up and running the Social Security program were the main engine of its expansion and that they exploited their considerable freedom, especially in the program's formative years, to create and maintain broad public support for their policies. These facts support a *bureaucratic politics* model that suggests that within the very broad constraints of a public opinion decisively influenced by the bureaucrats themselves, and in the absence of a significant challenge from Congress or the president, program administrators enjoyed what may fairly be called subsystem autonomy.[2]

Program administrators were able to play a dominant role in Social Security policymaking because they had a set of coherent long-range goals, because they exercised a near monopoly over technical analysis of the program and projections of its finances, and because several of their leading personalities enjoyed long tenure with the Social Security Administration and executed their responsibilities with uncommon talent and energy. Working closely with the members of the relevant congressional committees and with their allies in organized labor, program bureaucrats were able to control the Social Security agenda and realize their goals in a piecemeal but consistent fashion. Though it has decreased sharply in recent years as the financial crisis has deepened, the legacy of this autonomy is still strong enough to impede reforms incompatible with basic bureaucratic goals.

All the same there are several reasons that a simple bureaucratic politics explanation is almost as inadequate as the democratic politics model. The politics of Social Security has entered a new phase since 1972 (the last legislative session in which the old subsystem politics held sway). For one thing public opinion does limit the options of policymakers, in large part because of the success of the bureaucrat's support-generating efforts over the years. But the popular electoral arena provides only the context of Social Security politics. The core is an intrastate contest between program bureaucrats (now largely defeated), the Congress (disorganized and essentially leaderless in the wake of the collapse of the old policymaking subsystem), and the president and other central executive officials. Each of these groups has different interests and powers relative to Social Security. The basic distinction is between the narrow, program-specific interests of the agency officials and the proprietary congressional committees, on the one hand, and the generalist concerns of the president and those with responsibility for overall economic and fiscal policy, on the other.

Until recently the president was not normally involved directly in Social Security policymaking. But as the financial crisis has loomed larger, and as the impact of the system on the federal budget and the national economy has become more obvious, presidents beginning with Gerald Ford have waded into the battle. The broad popular support of the program and the great danger involved in seeming to attack it have made these men reluctant to get out front with fundamental reforms, especially those that entail benefit reductions. But their obligations with respect to the budget and the economy have pushed them ineluctably toward more and more ambitious proposals for cutting program costs. Drawing on counsel from those agencies with responsibility for guiding overall national policy—the Office of Management and Budget, the Council of Economic Advisers and the Treasury, primarily—the chief executive is the public official most likely to articulate demands for Social Security reform on the basis of long-run national goals. One can interpret events since 1972 as attempts by succeeding presidents to assert the autonomy of the federal government as a whole against the claims of the beneficiary groups and of the bureaucratic advocates of Social Security.[3]

The democratic politics model implies that the state has little or no autonomy in relation to a mobilized public opinion vigorously guarding its Social Security entitlements. The bureaucratic politics model is more sophisticated because it recognizes the crucial role public officials have themselves played in molding and interpreting popular attitudes toward the retirement system and in manipulating national policy through control of the legislative agenda. In various combinations these two models are helpful tools in an explication of Social Security development throughout much of its history. In its later phases, however, there has been a new element in the politics of Social Security policy. This chapter will argue that a *state-centered* model is helpful in interpreting events since 1972.

After tracing the evolution of the Social Security financial crisis and linking it to the federal budgetary process, we will turn to a more explicit investigation of the utility of these three models for explaining recent Social Security politics. Our primary concern is to determine what, if any, autonomy the president enjoys in Social Security policymaking with respect to the electorate, the Social Security bureaucracy and the Congress. Three specific questions are posed:

1. Has the president proposed policies for Social Security consistent with general national interests, as he defines them, that threaten the particularistic program or electoral interests of the administrators and the Congress?
2. Can the president make and implement Social Security policies in the national interest, as he defines it, over the opposition of the bureaucracy, the Congress or the public?
3. Can the president build majority coalitions around some (less than optimal) policy? That is, unable to have his way, is he nonetheless able to put together a politically acceptable package?

The evidence from the cases supports a modestly positive response to question 1, a distinctly negative response on all particulars except the bureaucracy for question 2, and a modestly positive response to question 3.

THE FINANCING CRISIS

Social Security is an unfunded pension program. Receipts from payroll taxes are for the most part distributed immediately to the retired population rather than being accumulated in a fund to earn interest. This makes Social Security a direct form of intergenerational transfer from the working to the nonworking population. The trust fund contains only enough reserves to ensure the system's ability to pay each month's benefits in a timely manner.[4] All the present financial problems of the program are related to its underlying "pay as you go" structure. The four most important sources of the crisis can be found in the natural maturation process of an unfunded pension system, in deliberate legislative decisions improving coverage and benefits, in short- and long-term trends in the economy and in long-term changes in the age structure of the society.

One major reason that Social Security is experiencing increased financial pressure is that it is approaching maturity. This means that most of the workforce is covered (federal workers and some state and local employees are the most important exceptions), that the majority of retirees have been in covered employment all their working lives and are entitled to full pension benefits, and that average benefits themselves have grown until they replace a substantial amount of previous income. An individual retiring in 1983, for example, might have been making contributions for as long as 46 years if he entered the workforce at age 19 in 1937, the first year in which taxes were levied. And he would likely receive a substantial pension, at least a measured against previous income. The replacement rate (one's pension as a proportion of previous income) for persons with average wages in manufacturing was 44 percent in 1980 for single workers and 66 percent for aged couples.[5] By itself maturity increases the cost of a pension system, but with proper planning it ought not spell disaster. The extreme difficulties of the American pension system are due to the conjuncture of maturity with adverse political, economic and demographic conditions.

Congress has repeatedly expanded coverage and improved benefit levels since 1935, and this process has been accelerated in recent years. There is, for example, a wide range of benefits payable to covered workers in addition to basic retirement income: the lump-sum death benefit (now partly eliminated), dependents' and survivors' benefits, disability, student benefits (being phased out), hospital insurance, among others. All of these make Social Security much more than a simple retirement annuity and add to the program's costs. In addition the benefit formula was decisively shifted in favor of low-income workers in 1939, and a special minimum benefit (now being phased out) was instituted at the same time. Congress has sharply raised basic benefit levels as well. Average monthly benefits paid to retired workers went up from $63 per month in 1956 to $263 per month in 1978.[6] For many years Congress relied on ad hoc adjustment of benefits to keep them in line with increases in the cost of living. Congress decided in 1972 to link future benefit increases automatically to the consumer price index.[7]

This relative generosity on the part of the legislature must be understood in terms of the economic conditions under which it developed and the particular characteristics of a not yet mature pension system. Extension of Social Security coverage to new occupational groups was especially attractive since the newly covered workers began to pay taxes immediately but would not be eligible for benefits for a number of years. Coverage extension was a means to create a short-term infusion of cash into the system—cash which was used to finance benefit improvements or to delay increases in the payroll tax rate. More importantly, economic growth and rising real wages consistently produced trust fund surpluses during the fifties and sixties. Bureaucrats in the Social Security Administration (SSA) fully understood that these "bonuses" were temporary, but they exploited them to push benefits up while it was politically feasible. The appearance of fiscal propriety was maintained by legislating at the same time future increases in the payroll tax to keep the program actuarially sound in the long run. But this procedure was rooted in what were, as it turns out, exceedingly optimistic assumptions about future economic conditions.[8]

The pattern of incremental expansion reached its peak in 1972 when Congress approved an across the board 20 percent boost in benefit levels. By the next year the first official warnings of long-term deficits in the trust funds were published, and shortly thereafter short-term cash flow problems were on the horizon as well. The causes of the short-term problem were for the most part economic. If growth had provided the means for repeated improvements in the retirement program, stagnation had devastating consequences for its finances. Rising productivity and production meant that each new cohort of workers was better off in real terms than those that preceded it. Constant payroll tax rates generated more revenues because the economic base against which they were assessed was growing. Faltering growth and productivity in the seventies meant that the costs of supporting the nation's elderly became much more onerous very quickly. Cyclical fluctuations in unemployment and inflation also had immediate effects on the solvency of the unfunded system. Unemployment reduces the size of the workforce and pushes some older workers into early retirement. This diminishes payroll tax revenues and drives up expenditures. Inflation might have no net effect on trust fund balances if prices and wages kept pace with one another. In fact prices outpaced wages after 1972, and because Social Security benefits were indexed, they rose dramatically. In addition a technical error in the indexing formula by which benefits were inflation-proofed produced for certain workers increases in expected benefits far in excess of inflation.[9]

The long-range problems of Social Security are intimately connected to the fact that the American population is getting older. The problem will make itself most fully felt beginning in 2010 when the first of the postwar baby-boom generation reaches retirement age, but the more general phenomenon is a gradually worsening ratio between the retired and working populations. By one estimate this ratio will rise from .19 in 1980 to .35 in 2055, an increase of nearly 80 percent.[10] Such a shift implies an enormous increase in the tax burden imposed on the working population to support retirement benefits for the rest.

The combination of program maturation, political expansionism, demographic pressure and economic dislocation has driven Social Security expenditures and taxes on an upward spiral. Total monthly benefits paid in 1980 for old age, survivors' and disability pensions

(OASDI) equaled $105 million. This was distributed to 35,618,840 beneficiaries.[11] Social welfare expenditures, which had been only 3.9 percent of GNP in 1929, and had increased to only 10.5 percent in 1960, skyrocketed to 20 percent in 1975 before falling back slightly to 18.5 percent in 1979. Of this social insurance expenditures account for fully 8.4 percent. Social insurance spending equaled 12.5 percent of personal income in 1979.[12] The Congressional Budget Office predicts that OASDI outlays will be 5.05 percent of GNP in 1985.[13] To pay for this the payroll tax has jumped from 4.8 percent, assessed against the first $7800 of income for both employers and employees in 1970, to 6.70 percent on $35,700 in 1983. The combined employer-employee tax is scheduled to reach 7.65 percent in 1990, and the wage base is now automatically tied to inflation. These changes mean that the payroll tax is levied against well over 90 percent of payroll and that it produces about 30 percent of all government revenues. The maximum contribution a worker could make to Social Security in 1937, when the program was launched, was 1 percent of $3000, or $30. In 1981, on the other hand, a worker earning at least $25,000 paid $975, a 66-fold increase.

Despite the fact that in 1977 Congress approved enormous increases in the payroll tax, the financial problems of the program were not resolved. Continuing high rates of inflation and unemployment, coupled with inadequate growth and productivity, produced new and staggering projections of long-run deficits and fears of short-term cash flow problems. OASDI trust fund balances fell from $45.9 billion in 1975 to $24.5 billion at the start of 1982. Only interfund borrowing authorized by Congress in December 1981 kept the old age and survivors' program solvent through 1982. The exact size of the long-run problem was the subject of much debate. Projections are strongly dependent on the economic assumptions employed. Moreover, the wisdom of acting immediately to forestall problems in the distant future that may not actually materialize has become a highly contentious issue. Nevertheless, all sides agreed that the program was in deep trouble. According to the estimates of the bipartisan Commission on Social Security Reform set up by President Reagan, about $200 billion in additional revenues had to be found just through 1989 to meet commitments under the 1982 legislation. The Congressional Budget Office estimated that the old age and survivors' trust fund would go into the red by $18.4 billion in 1984. After that the annual deficits would grow each year until they reached $184.3 billion in 1991. Even a renewal of the provision for interfund borrowing (which expired in December 1982) would not be sufficient in 1989 when the combined OASDHI trust funds would fall $14.9 billion behind projected outlays.[14]

SOCIAL SECURITY AND THE BUDGET

Considered solely in its own context, the Social Security crisis poses a formidable challenge to national policymakers. But it is much worse than this because responses to the deficits cannot be taken in isolation from their effects on the federal budget and the economy. Social Security constitutes a major constraint on national policy responses to the budget crisis, especially efforts to reduce the huge national deficits. Likewise, the continuing economic downturn and chronic budget red ink seriously limit the available responses to the Social Security dilemma.

Outlays on income security programs made up 37 percent of all federal government expenditures in 1980. Of this total (some $216 billion), Social Security accounted for $117 billion, or roughly one-half.[15] It is estimated that expenditures for non-need-related individual benefits, of which Social Security is again the primary example, will rise by 153 percent between 1980 and 1985, faster even than projected defense increases.[16] At constant legislation, spending for OASDI will double between 1982 and 1991, rising from $156.7 to $320 billion.[17] Left untouched, Social Security threatens to consume ever larger shares of the national wealth. Moreover, recent massive increases in the payroll tax have virtually wiped out the effects of income tax rate reductions for many classes of taxpayers. Some observers are beginning to believe that no real progress can be made toward controlling the federal deficit, reducing the upward trend in public expenditure or easing the overall tax burden unless some cuts are made in the rate of growth of Social Security benefits. If the nation's defense spending is to be maintained or enhanced, these social benefit cuts may need to be relatively deep.

Whether the government can meet the contradictory demands of the Social Security financial crisis is a matter of profound importance not only for the contributors and beneficiaries of the public retirement system, but also for the economy as a whole. Former Secretary of Commerce Peter G. Peterson was engaging in a fashionable flight of of apocalyptic hyperbole when he claimed that "if the [Social Security] system crashes, so almost certainly will civic harmony and the economy itself." But he was probably right to make the more limited point that "the prospects for Social Security and for general prosperity are now inseparable."[18]

Peterson might have meant one of several things. Without economic recovery it is inconceivable that the Social Security system can be maintained at its present level indefinitely.[19] Some critics of the program go much further than this, however. They argue that the program itself has undermined national savings, investment and capital formation. In this view the giant unfunded state pension system is a structural cause of long-term economic decline because it takes away individual incentives and capacity to save for retirement without putting public savings in its place. Heavy payroll taxes to foot the bill of escalating benefits, moreover, add to the cost of labor and depress employment.[20]

The evidence to support the most thoroughgoing statements of Social Security's adverse economic effects is subject to intense controversy, and the most extreme attacks have surely been overstated. Nonetheless, there is a growing appreciation of the manner in which the system's financial structure affects economic performance, and it is those public officials around the president who are most likely to be persuaded of the validity of such ideas. Their ability to influence events is diminished by the way in which Social Security is situated in the federal budget process.

Social Security expenditures are conventionally called "uncontrollable." This is technically accurate in that once benefit and tax schedules are in place, and eligibility criteria are set, the actual revenues and outlays depend on the number of people claiming benefits and paying taxes and the amounts involved. Social Security spending rises inexorably with no further legislative action by Congress. But Social Security is uncontrollable in only the most formal sense. The numbers eligible and the size of the benefits they claim are not matters of chance. Careful forecasts are made and taxes are set by law to ensure sufficient revenues to cover outlays. Congress does not decide to spend X amount on Social Security in a given fiscal year, but it does estimate how much will be spent, and this can be taken into account when making more explicit appropriation decisions. If outlays for Social Security promise to be too large, it is fully within the power of the legislature to take steps to reduce them. Benefit schedules, eligibility criteria and other program rules are laid down by Congress, and very minor changes in them can generate substantial savings.

The real uncontrollability of Social Security spending arises from the programmatic and procedural characteristics of the system that prevent Congress from making these changes. The two most important are the autonomy of the program within the general budget process and the strength of the idea that Social Security pays benefits to which individuals are entitled because they have contributed to the system.

The men and women who founded the Social Security system in 1935 were convinced that they were dealing with a program that was fundamentally different from other government activities. The provision of retirement income, they argued, had to be carefully planned over many years so that future beneficiaries could make their financial plans well in advance of retirement. Promises, once undertaken, must be delivered without fail. The social insurance program had to be insulated from the normal political process to keep some disgruntled and shortsighted Congress from imprudently slashing benefits or refusing to raise necessary payroll taxes.[21] Perhaps the most significant feature of the program in this respect was that it would be patterned, to the extent possible, after private insurance. Individuals would make contributions during their working lives and would be entitled to benefits when they reached retirement age. Rather than being a gift from the government, something that might be seen as welfare, Social Security pensions were to be earned by the workers themselves. Everyone involved in the drafting of the legislation understood that this analogy was not very strong—that contributions implied no legal right to benefits, for example, and that the linkage between the amount of contributions paid in and benefits received by particular individuals would be extremely tenuous. But the rhetoric of social insurance was freely employed, and the myth that Social Security was similar to private insurance was deliberately propagated by the program's administrators and supporters, long after major amendments had carried the act even further from the private insurance model.[22]

Two characteristics of the program that reinforced the insurance myth were the ideas of self-financing and actuarial balance. When Roosevelt's Committee on Economic Security drew up the Social Security bill, they planned for the system to run a deficit by the 1960s to be met by a general revenue appropriation. The president, however, objected to this when he learned of it and insisted that payroll tax increases be scheduled to make the system self-financing and to keep it in balance for the foreseeable future. Self-financing complemented the idea that Social Security was designed according to actuarial principles. Relying on the projections of the actuaries at the Social Security Administration, decision-making for Social Security became argely a technical exercise, or more accurately, the basic political decisions that underlay Social Security policy were masked by the technical language employed by policymakers. Actuarial balance consisted in assurances from the experts that, given a large number of assumptions about economic performance and demographic change, the trust funds would remain solvent for at least 75 years.

Self-financing and actuarial soundness allowed Social Security to avoid the regular budget process through which ordinary programs passed. The logic of a sound social insurance system precluded an annual discussion of how much the nation should spend for retirement income. Indeed such a rational approach to Social Security spending has never been undertaken. The size of the Social Security budget was estimated but not directly chosen. SSA officials had a working notion of what constituted "adequate" benefits. They also were very sensitive to politically acceptable rates for the payroll tax. Decisions about these were constrained by the necessity of projecting the long-range costs of immediate benefit improvements. But in the early years of the program this was not a very serious problem since dependency ratios were favorable and one could legitimately adopt positive economic assumptions when making projections. Total Social Security expenditures were thus the outcome of the interaction of policy choices about levels of benefits and taxes with social and economic aggregates such as the level of employment and labor force participation rates. These expenditures might be very large without evoking much concern because the program "paid for itself" and was in any case a real bargain for most taxpayers.[23]

Because Social Security was paid for by an earmarked tax, jurisdiction over the program lay with the two congressional revenue committees—Senate Finance and the House Committee on Ways and Means. This arrangement could have imposed considerable restraint on the growth of the program since any changes in coverage or benefit levels had to emerge from the same committees that raised the taxes to pay for them. Over the years, however, the two committees developed strong proprietary attitudes toward the system and worked in tandem with program bureaucrats on legislation to expand it. Perhaps most importantly, the congressmen came to accept fully the arguments about actuarial balance. During the long chairmanship of Wilbur D. Mills, Ways and Means earned a reputation for expertise and fiscal responsibility in matters dealing with the retirement system. Measures approved by Mills almost never lost on the floor. Having won the enthusiastic support of the leadership of the revenue committees, Social Security Administration officials were spared the necessity of dealing with separate appropriations and revenue stages of the budget cycle.[24]

The autonomy of Social Security in budget politics is reflected by the fact that the program was not part of the unified budget (which is to say its financial operations did not figure in calculations of federal deficits or surpluses) until fiscal year 1969. President Johnson placed it in the unified budget at that time so that the trust funds' huge surpluses could offset his military expenditures. At the time this seemed a trifling move, and it is in fact only an accounting measure, but its symbolic significance has come home with force because the program's recent difficulties exacerbate federal budget deficits that are a major political issue. In 1983 Congress voted to take Social Security out of the unified budget by 1993, a move intended to insulate the program from unrelated budget decisions.

If Social Security has been outside the normal budget process, it has been even further removed from short-term economic policy. This statement may at first seem strange since Congress enacted the program at the height of the Great Depression. Moreover, the amendments that were adopted in 1939, especially the decisions to move the date for the initial payment of benefits up from 1942 to 1940, to "blanket-in" large numbers of persons at or near retirement who had made insufficient contributions to qualify and to avoid accumulating a mammoth trust fund were clearly geared to short-run economic conditions.[25] In addition recent scholarship has suggested that decisions regarding Social Security taxes and benefits follow, at least roughly, an electoral business cycle and are designed to enhance re-election prospects by improving the economic position of voters.[26] Nonetheless, the ideology of the program administrators and congressmen who have constituted the core of the Social Security policy-making subsystem has been starkly resistant to the notion that the program might properly be manipulated with an eye to the economic barometer.[27] The stricture against lowering the benefits of the currently retired and the absence of a general revenue contribution to the program severely limit its flexibility as a fiscal policy tool. The fact that Social Security policy was not really in the hands of the president, or even the party leadership in Congress, but was instead confined to a smaller subsystem made policy directed toward economic ends even more unlikely.

The following sections analyze the efforts of three presidents to come to grips with the Social Security crisis. Each succeeding chief executive, under the pressure of a growing public restiveness and in the midst of a deepening economic downturn, developed more forceful and thoroughgoing proposals. The cases will show, nevertheless, that the obstacles to presidential effectiveness on the Social Security issue are still very great. Pressures from the public, especially organized client groups, resistance from Congress and the lingering influence of retired Social Security administrators largely checked presidential attempts in this period to trim the growth rate of benefits and otherwise impose economies on the program.

THE FORD AND CARTER YEARS

The Ford and Carter administrations are important not so much for what they accomplished—no radical departures from existing policies were approved—but for what they either shrank from proposing or failed to enact. Both presidents attempted to confront the Social Security dilemma in two ways: by modest efforts to reduce costs and by more substantial efforts to raise revenues. The record of their administrations illustrates the great dangers involved in proposing cuts of any type in existing benefits, either for current or future retirees. The Carter term also indicates that the upper limits of the payroll tax rate have been reached. The Ford-Carter years saw the final demise of the autonomous, bureaucratically dominated subsystem, but also the failure of any new policymaking arrangement to take its place. Congress replaced the bureaucracy as the primary defender of the sanctity of the system. Presumed or real electoral volatility on the issue seriously hemmed in the range of options. The few remaining relatively easy means to deal with the financial crisis were fully exploited, but little headway was made toward lasting solutions, and the serious conflicts between program needs and budgetary and economic priorities were not satisfactorily addressed. A brief survey of the major proposals and decisions of each administration will demonstrate the difficulties posed by the growing Social Security crisis.

Both Presidents Ford and Carter supported the most expansive alternative among those seriously considered to correct the error in the inflation adjustment index adopted in 1972. The two major proposals were price indexing (recommended by two special panels that had studied the matter and by key figures in the Ford administration) and wage indexing (the technique favored by Robert Ball, former Social Security administrator and adviser to Jimmy Carter during his election campaign). The technical properties of the two indexing methods cannot be discussed here, but the basic differences between them were the following. Price indexing promised only to maintain the purchasing power of retirees' income, since pensions would be adjusted upward in response only to increases in the cost of living. A wage indexing procedure would not only guarantee protection against inflation, but would allow pensioners to share in the enhanced living standards of each succeeding generation of workers. Carter's wage indexing proposal was adopted in 1977.[28] This episode clearly demonstrates the continuing dominance of the bureaucratic subsystem insofar as it defeated a Treasury-based effort on behalf of price indexing during President Ford's term and successfully framed the issue for candidate Carter in 1976.

Neither man was able to persuade Congress to adopt even limited measures intended to reduce benefit outlays. Ford proposed that a 5 percent cap be placed on the June 1975 automatic inflation adjustment.[29] Carter suggested a series of other steps affecting spouses' benefits, educational benefits and the disability program.[30] None of these proposals ever saw the light of day.

In 1976 President Ford asked for very modest increases in the payroll tax to take effect after the presidential election. Congress failed to act. Jimmy Carter than brought forward an ambitious plan to inject general revenues into the system in periods of high unemployment and also asked that the wage base for employees and employers be hiked to avoid an increase in the tax rate. Congress rejected his plan and instead passed the 1977 Amendments to the Social Security Act that included pushing up the tax to 7.65 percent for workers and their employers by 1990. The impossibility of further wholesale elevations of payroll tax rates was demonstrated when the Ways and Means Committee first voted to roll back the increases, only to reverse itself several days later.[31] Both President Ford's pusillanimous initiative and Congress' waffling indicate that electoral constraints were perceived to be extreme. These constraints were most severe with respect to cutting present or future benefits, or even the rate at which they were growing. Increasingly, however, the public seemed also to be registering concern over escalating payroll taxes.

By the end of the Ford-Carter years, the limits of bureaucratic autonomy seemed to have been reached. To the extent anyone controlled Social Security policy it was Congress, but its leadership on the issue was weak and fragmented. Its response to the crisis had been consistent: in every case it voted to protect benefit levels and raise taxes. Whether Congress could develop a more flexible policy or would bow to presidential leadership was an open question on the eve of the inauguration of Ronald Reagan.

REAGANOMICS AND SOCIAL SECURITY

Ronald Reagan assumed office under circumstances that both made it likely that he would be motivated to take on the Social Security issue and that created for him especially sharp constraints on his options. Reagan was committed to major cuts in public expenditures, federal taxes and the federal deficit. To achieve these goals, while at the same time sharply increasing defense spending, Reagan had little choice but to seek significant reductions in Social Security outlays and to hold the line or reduce Social Security taxes. But in his campaign for the presidency he had vowed not to cut the program. Reagan's ambivalent statements on Social Security were mirrored by his policies in the first two years of his administration. He moved boldly to propose benefit cuts but ultimately retreated to buy more time.

The process by which the 1982 budget was fashioned was marked by a number of innovations, the most important of which was the use to which the president put the reconciliation process. The implication of this procedure for Social Security was that for the first time the program was thrust directly into the budget battle, its projected costs having to be balanced against overall budget goals. OMB, for example, presented Ways and Means and Senate Finance with spending reduction targets of $8.2 and $9.2 billion, respectively. If this did not come out of Social Security, it would have to be found in other programs under their jurisdiction.

The president himself proposed a range of reforms that would have saved $.1 billion in 1981 and an additional $25.6 billion through 1986. These changes went beyond anything Ford or Carter had advocated and were a disavowal of the president's campaign rhetoric. The most important items were the elimination of the minimum benefits and the gradual elimination of student benefits. But these turned out not to be enough as projections by OMB convinced the president that his goal of a balanced budget would require even more severe steps. By May the administration proposed a series of additional cuts to save $46.4 billion between 1982 and 1986. The principal change in this package was the reduction of benefits for persons choosing early retirement at age 62 after October 1981.[32]

The final budget act signed by the president in August contained some, but not all of his proposals. Substantial savings were achieved through the phasing out of student benefits and other administrative modifications in the calculation and payment of benefits. In all the reforms would reduce the long-range deficit from 2.32 to 1.65 percent of taxable payroll. This would cut expenditure by $22.3 billion between 1982 and 1986, which was only $2.3 billion less than the president had requested.[33]

On the other hand, the budget battle seems to have taught the president some important lessons. When the administration announced in May its intention to slash early retirement benefits, the Republican Senate quickly passed by a vote of 96-0 a resolution disavowing the idea. Moreover, on the same day the House approved the Omnibus Reconciliation Act (the budget), it also passed (404-20) a bill restoring minimum benefits. President Reagan found himself calling for the restoration of those benefits on September 24, and in December he signed into law amendments to the budget act to that effect. In his September speech the president also established a national commission headed by economist Alan Greenspan to study the Social Security financing crisis and to report by December 31, 1982. Cynics argued that the purpose of the body was to defer action on Social Security until after the mid-term elections in November. This was certainly part of its mandate. Just as important, however, was its role in seeking a cross-party consensus on measures to bail the system out of its financial troubles. Having been burned by Congress when he had proposed significant cuts in benefits, refusing to preside over further increases in payroll taxes and being adamantly opposed to the use of general revenues (a step made more and more unlikely by looming budget deficits), Reagan hoped to forge a bipartisan consensus on painful but necessary cuts. That Congress must play the major role in this was recognized by the appointment of key legislative leaders from both parties to the study panel.

The appointment of the commission placed Social Security reform on hold. The short-term cash flow problem in the old age and survivors' program was dealt with through interfund borrowing that Congress had authorized in December 1981. The president's 1983 budget requests included no cuts in Social Security at all as he awaited the advice of his commission. The proposed budget assumed that under existing law spending for Social Security would rise from $173.5 billion in 1983 to $232 billion in 1987.[34]

For a time it looked as if Congress would act on its own to reduce the costs of the program. Several plans were floated to freeze or reduce the cost of living adjustment in 1983. A one-time freeze on all entitlement programs would have saved $60 billion in 1985. But President Reagan backed an alternative proposal approved by the Senate Budget Committee to save $40 billion through a combination of unspecified spending cuts or tax increases. At the last minute, however, several Republican Senators balked, fearing an electoral backlash the next November. The president then backed away and the plan died.[35] As the election approached it became less and less likely that any action on Social Security would be taken. Even when the lame duck Congress convened at the president's insistence after polling day, no one took the initiative to move on the issue. News reports on the proceedings of the Greenspan Commission indicated that it might fail to agree on a bail-out plan and would instead give the president two or three different sets of proposals and let him choose. At the last minute, however, chairman Greenspan put together a package that secured the signatures of all but three staunch conservatives on the panel. The president promptly endorsed the agreement.[36]

What followed was a unique episode in the history of the social security program. The Greenspan Commission proposals were introduced into Congress on January 26. Just three months later, on April 20, President Reagan signed into law the Social Security Amendments of 1983, hailing them as "a monument to the spirit of compassion and commitment that unites us as a people."[37] The amendments differed only marginally from the Commission's recommendations, calling for both tax increases and benefit reductions. Some of the major provisions of the law were coverage of federal employees, including members of Congress and the president and vice-president; a delay of the 1983 cost of living adjustment; modification of the formula by which automatic cost of living adjustments are made when trust fund balances are low; acceleration of scheduled payroll tax increases; taxation of 50 percent of the benefits of higher-income recipients and the gradual increase of the retirement age to 67 in 2027. Under middle-range economic assumptions, the combined effect of these revenue and benefit changes is expected to produce an additional $166.2 billion for the system through 1989 and to put the system in long-run actuarial balance.[38]

CONCLUSION

This discussion of Social Security politics since 1972 supports a number of generalizations. Though presidents have not typically dominated Social Security policymaking, the evolution of the program's finances and its vital impact on government fiscal and economic policy ensure that chief executives will either seek to manage the program's growth or bear heavy political consequences. The emergence of the Social Security financial crisis, especially in the context of the economic and budgetary dislocations of the seventies, creates a set of strong incentives for presidents to act. This chapter has shown that with growing energy they have done so. The chief analytical question posed here is whether presidents can exercise a degree of autonomy in the Social Security arena with respect to the electorate, the Social Security bureaucracy or Congress. Clearly, the evidence is very mixed.

Electoral considerations have undeniably limited the range of alternatives presidents have been willing to entertain publicly and have scuttled many of those proposals they have endorsed. President Ford sought to duck the issue of a payroll tax increase until after the 1976 election. Jimmy Carter moved more adventurously in the early years of his term, but the Congress mauled his program and exhibited extreme sensitivity both to benefit reductions and taxpayer resistance. Even budget-cutter Ronald Reagan was compelled to campaign for office on a platform that promised to leave pensions untouched. When he could no longer ignore fiscal reality after he entered the White House, he repudiated his campaign rhetoric and called for significant cuts, but his success was much more limited than he had hoped. The decision to name a bipartisan commission is the best evidence one could have that the political heat on the Social Security issue was too intense for Reagan. Electoral constraints, then, have been severe since 1972, as one would expect in a period of fluidity and bare-knuckled partisan conflict. It is too early to know whether the Greenspan Commission's report and the subsequent reforms enacted by Congress will form the basis for the reconstruction of a consensus. Until such a consensus is established, or a partisan majority forms around a coherent Social Security policy, popular pressures will continue to limit the autonomy of the president in this important policy arena.

One may fairly conclude that by the administration of Ronald Reagan the power of the Social Security bureaucracy was effectively on the wane. Dismissals and retirements of key figures, loss of prestige because of the growing sense that the program is flawed, the proliferation of independent analysis and forecasting, and the breakdown of fraternal relations with congressional committees, all contributed to the decline of bureaucratic power. President Reagan demonstrated the new subordination of the administrators by appointing as chief of the SSA his former welfare director from California, a strong critic of the excessive growth of the Social Security system. Nevertheless, even after they had departed from the official scene (and former Commissioner Robert Ball sat on the Greenspan panel), the legacy of the program administrators stayed behind. The deeply engrained ideology of contributory insurance with its earned rights to benefits made it difficult to contemplate expenditure reductions in precisely the way the program's architects had hoped it would.

It is Congress that represents the greatest challenge to the president. This is especially obvious when Republicans are in the White House, but the sad fate of Jimmy Carter's Social Security proposals demonstrates that the conflict is as much institutional as partisan. Ronald Reagan tried and failed to push a cluster of wide-ranging benefit reductions through Congress. His next tactic was to force representatives of the two parties to agree to a package that contained elements that both sides found distasteful but that they could accept. In other words, unable to achieve the policy he preferred, Reagan had to try to enact some program to forestall the system's insolvency. This he achieved. But it was a limited victory for a president convinced that Social Security taxes and expenditures stand between him and his most prized fiscal and economic goals.

The evidence of the three cases indicates that the autonomy of the president is seriously limited in the Social Security policy arena. Efforts to assert presidential autonomy, though growing in number and intensity, have normally failed. For this reason a model of Social Security politics that gives primary emphasis to the state and its central executive decision-makers is not able to predict or explain policy outcomes better than models that stress electoral or bureaucratic-congressional subsystem politics. Such a perspective is useful, nonetheless, for understanding presidential behavior, which is the particular interest of this chapter. Presidential initiatives in the Social Security arena are not easily accommodated to either the democratic or bureaucratic politics models. All three presidents examined here proposed changes in the program that involved considerable political risk, and all three clashed with the bureaucratic subsystem, though this was much less true of Democrat Carter than the others. The tendency of chief executives to propose more and more ambitious reforms of the retirement system and the obvious origins of these proposals in their concern for budgetary and economic policy suggest a linkage between presidents and Social Security policymaking that transcends simple electoral calculations and ought not be interpreted as a new species of interagency competition.

Looking over the entire history of Social Security one sees that presidents have become key figures in policymaking for the program under two sets of circumstances: periods of severe economic dislocation, as set the context for Roosevelt's role in the founding of the system, and periods that involved major changes in the program, as occurred under Eisenhower, when the disability program was added in 1956, and under Johnson, when Medicare was created in 1965. This episodic participation is likely a thing of the past. It is not only the enduring budget crisis that compels presidents to intervene in Social Security decision-making, but also the enormous size and complexity of the fully mature program. With all the easy options already exhausted and the happy consensus on the program broken, the president's ability to manage Social Security policy is fast becoming synonymous with his ability to control national domestic policy as a whole.

NOTES

1. For a more detailed discussion of the models of Social Security policy-making, see Gary Freeman, "Social Security in an Efficient Economy," paper presented to the American Political Science Association, 1979. There is a broad literature on the role of the state and the concept of relative autonomy. See, for example, Peter Katzenstein, ed., *Between Power and Plenty: Foreign Economic Policies of Advanced Industrial States* (Madison: University of Wisconsin Press, 1978); Stephen D. Krasner, *Defending the National Interest: Raw Materials Investments and U.S. Foreign Policy* (Princeton, N.J.: Princeton University Press, 1978); and Ralph Miliband, *The State in Capitalist Society* (New York: Basic Books, 1969). For a general review and an extended discussion of societal versus state-centered models of public policy, see Eric Nordlinger, *On the Autonomy of the Democratic State* (Cambridge, Mass.: Harvard University Press, 1981).

2. The most forceful advocates of this point of view, though from very different analytical perspectives, are Martha Derthick, *Policymaking for Social Security* (Washington, D.C.: The Brookings Institution, 1979); Carolyn Weaver, *The Crisis in Social Security* (Durham, N.C.: Duke University Press, 1982); and Jerry R. Cates, *Insuring Inequality: Administrative Leadership in Social Security, 1935–54* (Ann Arbor: University of Michigan Press, 1983).

3. Gary Freeman and Paul Adams, "The Politics of Social Security: Expansion, Retrenchment, and Rationalization," in A. Stone and E. Harphum, eds., *The Political Economy of Public Policy* (Beverly Hills, Cal.: Sage Publications, 1982). How one responds to this effort in normative terms is not at issue here. Some observers like Derthick (*Policymaking for Social Security*) tend to see the generalist decision-makers of the executive branch as spokesmen for the interest of society as a whole. In another context Krasner has argued that a "statist" approach must proceed from the assumption of a national interest, operationalized as the preferences of American central decision-makers that "relate to general societal goals,

persist over time, and have a consistent ranking of importance" (*Defending the National Interest*, p. 13). Arguing for a state-centered approach does not necessarily imply that presidential policies are preferable to those of other actors, but simply that the role and responsibilities of the president are such as to encourage him to take a more general and long-range view than lesser elected officials or those with particularistic program commitments.

4. It is not commonly understood that even a fully funded system requires intergenerational transfers. See Bruno Stein, "Funding Social Security: The Reorientation of 1939" (unpublished paper, 1981). There are, in fact, three funds: Old Age and Survivors (OASI), Disability (DI), and Hospital Insurance (HI). A good overview of the system is Bruno Stein, *Social Security and Pensions in Transition* (New York: Free Press, 1980).

5. *Social Security Bulletin* (November, 1982), p. 5.

6. *Social Security Bulletin*, Annual Statistical Supplement (1980), p. 156.

7. For an excellent description of the various motives for this reform, see Derthick, pp. 349–358.

8. Derthick, pp. 277–278.

9. On the indexing error and the controversy over its correction, see Robert S. Kaplan, *Indexing Social Security* (Washington, D.C.: American Enterprise Institute, 1977); Colin D. Campbell, *Over-indexed Benefits* (Washington, D.C.: American Enterprise Institute, 1977); and Rudolph G. Penner, *Social Security Financing Proposals* (Washington, D.C.: American Enterprise Institute, 1977).

10. *Reports of the 1979 Advisory Council on Social Security* (1979), p. 309.

11. *Annual Statistical Supplement* (1980), pp. 105, 107.

12. *Annual Statistical Supplement* (1980), pp. 56–57.

13. *Financing Social Security: Issues and Options for the Long Run* (Congressional Budget Office, November 1982), p. 8.

14. *Financing Social Security* (1982), pp. 104–105.

15. James R. Storey, "Income Security," in J. Palmer and I. Sawhill, eds., *The Reagan Experiment* (Washington, D.C.: The Urban Institute, 1982), pp. 363–365.

16. Peter G. Peterson, "Social Security: The Coming Crash," *New York Review of Books* (December 2, 1982), p. 35.

17. *Financing Social Security* (1982), pp. 104–105.

18. Peterson, p. 34.

19. It is the impact of cyclical economic fluctuations on system finances, and the means to protect the program from them, that has preoccupied policymakers until very recently.

20. The most provocative research has been produced by Martin Feldstein,

Reagan's former Chairman of the Council of Economic Advisers. See "Social Security, Induced Retirement, and Aggregate Capital Accumulation," *Journal of Political Economy* 82 (September–October 1974), pp. 905–926. Very comprehensive reviews of the literature on the economic effacts of Social Security can be found in Sheldon Danziger et al., "How Income Transfer Programs Affect Work, Savings, and Income Distribution: A Critical Review," *Journal of Economic Literature* 19 (September 1981), pp. 975–1028; and in Henry Aaron, *Economic Effects of Social Security*, (Washington, D.C.: The Brookings Institution, 1982).

21. The most comprehensive statement of the philosophy of the founders is Arthur Altmeyer, *The Formative Years of Social Security* (Madison: University of Wisconsin Press, 1968). See also Robert J. Myers, *Expansionism in Social Insurance* (London: Institute of Economic Affairs, 1970).

22. The most important changes in this regard occurred in 1939 when dependents' and survivors' benefits were created, the minimum benefit was installed and the benefit schedule was tilted sharply in favor of low-income workers.

23. Donald O. Parsons and Douglas R. Munro, "Intergenerational Transfers in Social Security," in Michael Boskin, ed., *The Crisis in Social Security* (San Francisco: Institute of Contemporary Studies, 1977), pp. 65–86.

24. Good discussions of the congressional process and Social Security policy may be found in Derthick, *Policymaking for Social Security;* Weaver, *The Crisis in Social Security;* and John Manley, *The Politics of Finance: The House Committee on Ways and Means* (Boston: Little, Brown, 1970), pp. 339–342.

25. See Bruno Stein, "Funding Social Security: The Reorientation of 1939"; Alanson Willcox, "The Old Age Reserve Account: A Problem in Government Finance," *Quarterly Journal of Economics* (May 1939), pp. 444–468; and Altmeyer, *The Formative Years of Social Security*, pp. 99–117.

26. Edward F. Tufte, *Political Control of the Economy* (Princeton, N.J.: Princeton University Press, 1978).

27. See, for example, the discussion of this matter in Altmeyer, pp. 107–110.

28. Colin D. Campbell, *The 1977 Amendments to the Social Security Act* (Washington, D.C.: American Enterprise Institute, 1978).

29. *Financing the Social Security System*, hearings before the Subcommittee on Social Security, House Committee on Ways and Means, 94th Congress, 1st Session (Washington, D.C.: Government Printing Office, 1975), p. 7.

30. John Snee and Mary Ross, "Social Security Amendments of 1977: Legislative History and Summary of Provisions," *Social Security Bulletin* (March 1978), pp. 3–20.

31. For a discussion of this episode, see Freeman and Adams, "The Politics of Social Security," pp. 250–252.

32. John A. Graham, "Omnibus Reconciliation Act of 1981: Legislative His-

tory and Summary of OASDI and Medicare Provisions," *Social Security Bulletin* (October 1981), p. 7.

33. Graham, p. 7.

34. *National Journal* (February 13, 1982).

35. *National Journal* (May 29, 1982), pp. 945–946.

36. The plan involved a combination of expenditure reductions and accelerated payroll tax increases designed to reduce the system's projected deficit by $169 billion. See *Report of National Commission on Social Security Reform* (Washington, D.C.: Government Printing Office, 1983).

37. John A. Svahn and Mary Ross, "Social Security Amendments of 1983: Legislative History and Summary of Provisions," *Social Security Bulletin* July 1983), p. 3.

38. Svahn and Ross, pp. 42–43.

3

FINANCE & FEDERAL TAX POLICY

The President vs. Congress on Tax Policy

JOHN F. WITTE

At the simplest level income tax politics is characterized by two important traits: there is alot of it, and it is very complicated. Given these characteristics it is curious that the history of the income tax can be described by several persistent trends that have weighed heavily in the politics and development of the modern tax code. One of the functions of this chapter is to describe these trends and the principal factors that have affected the development of the income tax. Another purpose is to analyze the relative roles of Congress and the president in the creation of tax legislation. One of the arguments presented here is that it is easier to describe the general historical trends in the structure of policy outcomes than it is to decipher clear patterns of influence between Congress and the president in the field of taxation. Specifically it will be argued that it is difficult to generalize across administrations concerning presidential tax initiatives, strategies and successes. The usual variables used to predict such actions, such as the party of the president or the partisan makeup of Congress, are unimpressive indicators of what administrations attempt or how well they succeed. Rather the tax initiatives of presidents appear to be more a matter of idiosyncratic beliefs and emphasis, while the successes depend on how well presidential proposals fit the long-term policy patterns and the short-term mood of Congress. While the gen-

Research for this chapter was supported by grants from the National Science Foundation and the Russell Sage Foundation.

eral role of the president has expanded in modern times, tax politics continues to be dominated by Congress and by the seemingly indomitable forces that have shaped the expansion of the tax system over its 70-year history. This chapter explores these relationships in three sections. The first sketches the most important historical trends and factors in income tax policy; the second describes the relative roles and successes of presidential administrations and Congress in initiating and passing tax legislation; and the third provides a summary with explanations and conclusions.

HISTORICAL TRENDS IN INCOME TAX POLICY

The Beginning

The birth of the federal income tax followed a long period of labor which resulted in an initially modest offspring. The individual income tax was first enacted during the Civil War as a consequence of the revenue emergency faced by the North. The first peacetime income tax was passed in 1894, following two years of legislative battles. A combination of a depression and the resulting lag in revenues, sectional rivalries which pitted the wealthy Northeast against the rest of the country, and an upsurge in the Populist party were the primary forces that led to enactment of the tax. That bill was ruled unconstitutional in 1895, even before it took effect. Following the Supreme Court ruling the issue lay relatively dormant for a decade as the Populist movement waned. However, by 1909, the Progressive movement was in full stride, and the solid, conservative Republican rule in the Senate, which had prevailed for the previous decade, began to break as liberal, "Insurgent Republicans" began to press for an income tax despite the earlier court ruling. To avoid a potential constitutional crisis, President Taft suggested a compromise that created a modest, 4 percent corporate "excise" tax and allowed for a constitutional amendment to authorize an individual income tax. Both were accepted (although the corporate tax was cut back to 1 percent), and the ratification process began immediately, with Alabama being first to ratify the amendment.

Massachusetts was the 36th state to ratify on February 13, 1913. The timing was appropriate and coincided with a major shift in the balance of power in both houses of Congress and the presidency. Enactment of an income tax, which was a central plank of Woodrow

Wilson's campaign, was a foregone conclusion. The significant political battles had been fought earlier in Congress and over the previous four years in the state legislatures. The legislation created much less controversy than the tariff legislation to which it was attached as an amendment. The legislation was drafted by Democratic Representative Cordell Hull of Tennessee, working with a subcommittee of the House Ways and Means Committee. Both the bill and the debate drew on the original income tax passed in 1894, the income taxes passed in several states, and particularly on the British income tax that had been recently enacted. The debate lasted only two days in the House. Although several amendments were offered, and defeated, no separate vote was ever taken on the income tax sections.

As with the corporate bill passed before it, the provisions of the original income tax were modest. The rates ranged from 1 to 4 percent, and an exemption of $4000 was allowed. The latter effectively restricted the tax to the very wealthy and resembled the "pillage of a class" that Eastern Republicans had been charging from the very beginning.[1] However, its modest form and class character were not to last, as revisions began almost immediately and have continued ever since, encompassing close to 40 major tax bills since 1913. The revisions grew from the original 11-page amendment to include thousands of pages of complicated legal provisions. However, this complicated legislative history is characterized by three persistent factors and trends, which stand out as the primary forces that not only shape tax politics in general, but also the relationship between Congress and the president in this critical policy field. These factors are: (1) the radical effect of wars, (2) the persistent pressure for tax reduction, and (3) continuous expansion of the "tax expenditure" system.

The Radical Effect of Wars

Wars have accounted for nearly all legislated income tax increases; for expansion of the income tax from an elite tax which had little revenue effect to a mass tax that currently accounts for the majority of federal revenues; and for whatever progressivity exists in the tax system. In other words, no other factor approaches the importance of wars in determining federal tax policy. The first important shift in income tax policy followed the onset of World War I and the revenue demands created by American aid to its European allies. However, the dramatic changes came with the entry of the United States into the war in 1917. Both individual and corporate taxes as a percentage of GNP increased sharply during the war, although the steepest rise was in the corporate tax. This was the result of higher corporate rates and a lower exemption, but also resulted from the adoption of a temporary excess profits tax which was added onto the permanent income tax. Corporate taxes increased from less than 0.5 percent to over 4 percent of GNP. Taxes paid by individuals grew from an initially infinitesimal amount to approximately 1.5 percent of GNP. This was accomplished by cutting the exemption in half and raising rates from a scale of 1 to 4 percent to a wartime high of 7 to 77 percent. Progressivity thus followed in the wake of war.

The war also had a permanent impact on the aggregate revenue structure. Prior to World War I and for our entire history preceding 1880 (with the brief exception of the Civil War), federal revenue was dependent almost exclusively on customs duties and excise taxes. The First World War created an understanding and appreciation of the power of income taxes as revenue sources. Even with successive declines in tax rates and revenues during the Republican years of the 1920s, income taxes were never relegated to their prewar status. For example, in 1915, excises and customs accounted for approximately 85 percent of federal revenue, while in 1930 they accounted for less than 30 percent, and income taxes more than 50 percent.

World War II provided another shock to the revenue system, but of a much larger magnitude. Government expenditures during the peak of World War I rose to 22 percent of GNP, falling back to approximately 5 percent in the 1920s and rising to 10 percent during the 1930s (primarily due to declining GNP). By 1945 government expenditures were almost 45 percent of GNP. Government receipts, which previously had reached a maximum of 8 percent of GNP, were at 25 percent by the end of the war (the difference from expenditures being debt). And, as in World War I, most of this increase was made up by increasing the level of the income taxes. However, this time it was not the corporate tax which provided the greatest increase. It alone would not have generated the necessary revenue. Instead, for the first time, the majority of American workers were subjected to the income tax— a result accomplished quickly and easily by four successive reductions in the personal exemption.[2] The effect was to increase those paying taxes from approximately 7 percent prior to the war to close to 70 percent by the war's end.

Rates were also increased throughout the bracket ranges, with the top individual rates rising to 94 percent for income over $2,000,000.[3] Once again a war was necessary to stimulate a shift toward progressive taxation. Table 8-1, which is based on computed

TABLE 8-1. Computed Effective Tax Rates as a Percentage of Net Income*

	Net Income				
Year	$3,000	$5,000	$10,000	$50,000	$100,000
1918	1.2%	3.1	7.8	22.0	35.0
1929	0	0	.4	8.3	14.8
1932	0	1.4	4.2	17.1	30.0
1944	9.2	15.1	22.5	53.7	69.6
1954	4.0	10.4	15.9	37.8	51.9
1965	2.8	11.7	13.0	31.7	43.7
1970	2.3	9.5	13.2	32.4	44.8
1977	− 10.0	− 6.0	4.4	27.2	41.3
1983	− 10.1	− 10.0	3.0	20.8	32.3

*Entries are the percentage of net income paid in taxes for a married couple with two children. Net income does not include deductions so that these calculations only account for rate and exemption changes.

effective rates because historical statistics based on actual return data are inconsistent over time, provides an estimate of changing progressivity. The years in the table reflect the results of important tax bills. Peak progressivity was reached during World War II, and subsequent tax bills have successively reduced that progressivity. Although the distribution of income is of course much different, the rate and exemption structure enacted in the 1981 tax bill will, when all its provisions take effect, produce a result very similar to the tax rates in effect in 1932.

What might have been a predictable shift toward lower and less progressive taxes following World War II was abruptly halted after tax reductions in 1945 and 1948 by the onset of the Korean war in 1950. Congressional response to this new war was simply to reenact the World War II tax system with an automatic repeal date of December 1953. Of more interest and more importance is that when the Republicans returned to power in 1952, the only major tax bill they supported was a slight tax reduction relative to the large wartime buildup in tax revenues. And following that bill, enacted in 1954, the Eisenhower administration was able to resist further tax reduction, even in the face of a major recession in 1957–58. By the time the Democrats returned to power and political resistance against tax cutting had worn thin, the size of the budget had grown to the point where a return to the prewar tax structure was unthinkable. This fact, however, has not reduced the continuous pressure for tax reduction.

The Persistent Pressure for Tax Reduction

The fact that income tax revenues have continued to increase as a percentage of GNP in the postwar period masks the political and legislative intent of postwar tax legislation. Increases in the income tax are not due to legislative changes, which on the contrary have in peacetime attempted to offset the natural growth in revenues generated by real and inflationary income growth. The progressive rate structure, put in place in World War II and essentially left in place during the Eisenhower years, guaranteed such expansion. The political reaction in the 1960s and 1970s, which mirrored the legislation of the 1920s, was to enact ever increasing tax reduction bills. In all only two peacetime income tax bills have produced clear-cut increases in revenues: the 1932 tax bill, which was motivated by a bipartisan consensus that balancing the budget was necessary to end the depression; and the 1982 revenue act, which was only a slight corrective relative to the massive tax reductions of 1981. The 1969 Tax Reform Act, enacted during the Vietnam war, was estimated to increase revenue in the first year, although the impact in subsequent years was tax reduction.

The magnitude and form of these tax reductions are depicted in Table 8-2 for the major tax bills since the Korean war. The revenue effects of the legislative changes are broken down into structural changes (exclusions of income, deduction, credits and specialized rates) and changes in the basic rate system (bracket definitions, nominal rates and exemptions). As is apparent, the largest tax reductions have resulted from rate changes, although in recent years the proportion of reductions derived from increasing the benefits of structural provisions has grown significantly. Even those tax bills which bore the name "tax reform" (1964, 1969 and 1976) produced overall tax reductions, with the exception of the first year following the 1969 legislation. In all three cases the net increases from structural changes were offset by major reductions in standard deductions and the basic rate structure.

Expansion of Tax Expenditures

Table 8-2 verifies the accelerated tax reduction of the 1970s under the combined pressures of inflation, "tax revolt" and the drive to increase capital investment. Structural changes accounted for an increasing proportion of these changes and reached the almost unbelievable figure of $29 billion due to the provisions of the 1981 bill. This trend

TABLE 8-2. Estimated Revenue Changes in Major Postwar Revenue Acts ($ billions)

Revenue Act	1950*	1954	1964		1969‡		1975‡		1976		1978		1981	
Fiscal Year Effect	1952	1955	1964	1965	1970	1971	1974	1975	1977	1978	1979	1980	1982	1983
Structural Gains†	+.4	0	+.9	+1.1	+4.2	+5.0	0	+2.0	+3.0	+3.5	+1.2	+5.4	+2.4	+4.3
Structural Losses	0	−1.4	−.6	−.7	−.5	−.6	0	−4.0	−2.7	−4.7	−1.7	−8.0	−14.0	−29.0
Standard Deduction	0	0	−.3	−.3	0	−1.2	0	−2.6	−4.1	−4.5	§	§	0	0
Individual Rates	+2.7	0	−6.0	−9.2	+2.0	−3.7	−8.1	−6.7	−10.1	−4.8	−15.6	−27.5	−25.8	−65.7
Corporate Rates	+2.3	+1.2	−1.3	−2.2	0	0	0	−1.5	−1.7	−1.2	−3.2	−7.4	−.1	−.4
Total Revenue Change	+5.4	−.2	−7.3	−11.3	+5.7	−.5	−8.1	−12.8	−15.7	−11.7	−19.3	−37.5	−37.5	−90.8

Source: Estimates of the Joint Committee on Taxation following passage of final bills. Estimates include extensions and making permanent prior temporary provisions.

*Does not include excess profits tax bill of 1950.

†"Rates" include rate schedule and bracket changes, general credits and surcharges, exemptions, low income allowances and earned income credits. "Structural" includes everything else except changes in the standard deduction.

‡Calendar year estimates only.

§Not available as a separate estimate; included in rate changes.

can also be documented by analyzing changes over time in specific structural provisions, which in keeping with current usage we will term "tax expenditures."[4] In order to analyze the development of these structural provisions systematically, a set of tax expenditure provisions was constructed from official lists reported in annual budget documents from 1974 to 1982. Although these lists vary somewhat from year to year, 91 provisions which were mentioned in one or more years were selected for analysis. The historical development of each provision was then reconstructed, mapping all major changes accompanied by a set of descriptive variables (date of action, type of action, institutional origin, party originating the action, votes, etc.).[5]

Based on this data set, the institutional origins and modifications of provisions have been displayed over time in Table 8-3. For current purposes it is only necessary to note the summary rows that are in brackets. The tabulations in these rows indicate substantial expansion and modification of tax expenditures in the postwar period. Although a number of tax expenditures originated in the initial income tax legislation in 1909 and 1913, the number of tax expenditures has increased steadily since, and has accelerated in the 1970s and 1980s. This expansion has only been offset by a scattering of provisions that have been repealed, thus the net result has been a clear increase in the number of tax reduction provisions written into the tax code. The volume of modifications and the ratio of expanded benefits to reduced benefits are further evidence of the frantic pace of tax legislation and the pressure for tax reduction that has typified the last decade. The vast majority of modifications have been made since the war, although the balance between changes that reduced benefits and those that increase them was much closer during the first 25 years of this period than in the last decade.

Increases in both the number of tax expenditures and in modifications means that the tax code has enormously increased in complexity since World War II. Although complaints concerning complexity have been voiced since the very beginning of the income tax, with the current discussion of a simplified flat tax, the cries seem somewhat more intense. Although already dated, an interesting historical comparison, presented on the Senate floor near the close of debate on the 1976 Tax Reform Bill by Democratic Senator Gary Hart of Colorado, exemplifies the increase in complexity. Making a 50-year comparison, Hart noted that the 1926 tax code was 136 pages long, while in 1975 the index alone was 125 pages. He also remarked that in 1926 the standard 1040 form was 2 pages long, while in 1975 it was 13

TABLE 8-3. **Institutional Sources of the Origin and Modification of Tax Expenditures Over Time**

	1909–1919	1920–1945	1946–1969	1970–1981	Total
Origin of Provisions	[24]	[19]	[25]	[22]	[90]
Administration	2	1	10	5	18
House	11	8	12	4	35
Senate	2	4	2	10	18
Other	9	6	1	3	19
Modifications	[5]	[33]	[113]	[164]	[315]
Expanded Benefits:	(3)	(21)	(55)	(105)	(184)
Administration	0	0	16	19	35
House	1	18	21	35	75
Senate	1	3	18	49	72
Other	0	0	0	2	2
Reduced Benefits:	(2)	(11)	(53)	(43)	(109)
Administration	0	2	20	8	30
House	1	4	24	27	56
Senate	1	3	8	5	17
Other	0	2	1	3	6

pages with 40 pages of explanation. The Senate was moved by these comparisons to the extent that it unanimously resolved to establish a "Commission on Tax Simplification and Modernization."[6]

The data in Table 8-3, depicting discrete changes in the law, are also consistent with the estimated revenue loss of the total tax expenditure system, which has been computed as far back as 1967. Using the more reliable estimates from 1972 to 1982, the Congressional Budget Office has estimated that tax expenditures have grown from 24.7 percent of all federal revenues and 40.7 percent of income tax receipts in 1972, to 40 percent of federal revenues and 73.5 percent of income taxes in 1982.[7] The latter figure means that for every income tax dollar collected, 73 cents is exempted, excluded or deducted through tax expenditure devices. Barring further legislative changes these figures are projected to increase precipitously by 1986. Thus the historical expansion in the tax expenditure system runs parallel to and is logically consistent with, the longer-term trends toward tax reduction. These patterns, interrupted only by periods of national crisis and brief flirtations with tax reform efforts (designed to reduce tax expenditures), are crucial for interpreting the varying tax initiatives and successes of administrations.

CONGRESS AND THE PRESIDENT ON TAX POLICY

Taxation has always been treated specially in our constitutional framework. Early in the Constitutional Convention of 1787 it was decided that at least one branch of Congress would be directly selected by popular vote apportioned between the states on the basis of population. It was also agreed, without much controversy, that all revenue-raising measures were to originate in that body. The provision establishing that change (Article I, Section 7) makes the first substantive policy reference (and one of the few) in the Constitution. The intent of the founders was clear—tax policy was to be vested in the most representative body of the new government.

For the first 130 years of our history, revenue policy revolved around congressional struggles over tariff and excise taxes. These battles, the details of which rarely involved the president, divided the Congress, and at times the nation, along regionally defined economic lines. In addition to conflicts over specific regional products, there was the general cleavage between the manufacturing Northeast, which sought protective tariffs for their products, and the export- and consumption-oriented South and West. It was the latter regions that led the fight for the income tax, which as previously mentioned began as a minor amendment to a major tariff bill. That early legislation was almost wholly conceived in its detail by Congress, and specifically by a House subcommittee of the Ways and Means Committee. As in other matters, the role of the president in tax politics has expanded in the twentieth century.[8] However, that expansion has not gone as far as some argue has happened in other policy arenas.

Initiation of Income Tax Legislation

Research and analysis of the institutional origin of policy legislation have produced contradictory conclusions which seem to be based on little systematic evidence and a great deal of repetitive speculation. This is not so much a fault of the scholarship as it is a problem of generalization. The number and range of policy decisions made in any administration are enormous, thus any generalizations over time are difficult to sustain. The classic systematic study across policy areas is the now dated work by Lawrence Chamberlain which analyzed the origins of 90 major pieces of legislation from 1890 to 1940.

He found a very mixed pattern that demonstrated that Congress and the president shared influence, with Congress as the leading partner.[9] Since that work additional conclusions have been reached, based on case studies of specific legislative issues or on impressionistic summaries of a number of such studies. Although both the resilience and the relative decline of Congress have been stressed by different authors, the weight of summary speculations seems to favor the conclusion that presidential power now eclipses that of Congress in most policy areas.[10] One small lesson from tax politics is that such generalizations are hardly more than speculations and that such propositions camouflage a much more complex relationship.

The historical mapping of specific tax provisions described in the last section provides a systematic basis for determining the institutional origin of a large portion of income tax legislation. It does not, however, incorporate basic rate changes which have been extremely important in tax history (particularly in times of war), and which are much more difficult to pin down in terms of origin. Putting this limitation aside, Table 8-3 displays the institutional origin of both initial tax expenditure legislation and the more numerous modifications that have followed. Since the bulk of tax politics is highly incremental, with many provisions beginning modestly but later expanding,[11] the accumulated results of such modifications constitute important policy decisions.

One conclusion from these data is inescapable: although the trend within the postwar period is complicated, relative to the earlier period, presidential initiation of tax proposals has increased dramatically since World War II. This is true of both the origin and the modification of tax expenditures, although in the earlier years technical IRS rulings (coded in the "other" category) played an important role in initiating some tax expenditures.[12] Of the 18 presidential proposals, 15 have been made since 1946. Of the 60 modifications attributable to presidential proposals (19 percent of the total), all but two were enacted in these later years.

Within the postwar period there seem to be several important shifts. The peak of administrative influence occurred in the first 25 years following the war, during which time administration actions accounted for 40 percent of the new tax expenditures and 33 percent of the modifications that had calculable revenue effects. Both of those percentages declined significantly during the 1970s as Congress, particularly with Senate efforts to expand tax expenditures, regained control over tax politics. As will become clear below, this was not due to a rekindling of the earlier norm that the details of tax policy should be the exclusive prerogative of Congress, but rather the result of congressional rebellion against presidential tax proposals.

Relying on tax expenditures to measure initiative in tax legislation may understate the role of the presidents in early tax bills, although the perceived role was unquestionably different than in modern times. The reason for this is that the tendency of early twentieth-century administrations was to request total revenue needs, leaving most of the details to Congress. However, if specific proposals were made, they usually took the form of changes in the basic tax parameters and not in the specialized provisions, which were not changed as often. This was particularly true both during and after World War I. President Wilson, through Treasury Secretary McAdoo, made repeated requests for funds, specifying first a preference for tax revenues rather than bonds, and later making specific rate change proposals. Although Congress often ignored or changed these requests, the general movement of tax legislation was usually in the direction Wilson desired.

Administration tax policy under the next three Republican presidents was under the control of Treasury Secretary Andrew Mellon. So important was Mellon during these years that the standing quip in his later years was that three presidents had served under him. Mellon also increased the range and number of presidential proposals in tax policy. As with Wilson's administration, however, Congress often overruled the specific proposals, although until 1929 there was agreement on the general direction of tax legislation. Mellon worked primarily with the rate structure, although some of the most important tax expenditures, such as mineral depletion allowances and modern treatment of capital gains, were passed during his tenure in Washington.

Congress was less kind to Roosevelt's prewar tax proposals. Initially he also claimed that tax details should be left to Congress. This changed with his inheritance tax proposals of 1935 (labeled the "wealth tax") and his income tax proposals of 1936. Roosevelt was only partially successful in each, and several of the major proposals in each bill were repealed when Congress turned against the president in the late 1930s. As with Wilson, however, on the first revenue bills during the war, there was general agreement between Congress and the administration, and the president got most of the revenue he requested.

The early decades of the income tax set the stage for presidential involvement in tax legislation. The growing role of the federal government in macroeconomic policy and presidential influence on war taxation eroded the earlier norm that the details of tax legislation were the province of Congress. However, with a more active role in initiating structural as well as rate changes, the important question shifts from that of initiation to the relative success of presidential tax programs.

Presidential Success in Postwar Tax Legislation

Systematic analysis of policy success of presidential programs is another area in which scholarly research is sparse and generalizations are difficult to make. However, for a specific policy field, and particularly one in which recommendations are as exacting as in tax policy, it is possible to assess presidential success at least in relation to actual bills that are passed.[13] Although in some instances the relationship of a final provision to an administration proposal requires some judgment and allocation of partial successes, provision-by-provision analysis of the legislation allows for a relatively accurate assessment of presidential success. The tabulated results of administration proposals, broken down in terms of the direction of changes recommended, are contained in Table 8-4. The calculations are based on counting significant, nontechnical changes in both the individual and corporate tax codes. For these computations changes include both structural and rate changes as defined previously, but excludes weighting based on the magnitude of revenue effects. Although the measure is somewhat crude, the success rates conform to more descriptive analysis contained in *Congressional Quarterly* reports and secondary sources.[14] For purposes of comparison the structure of the final bills, including only those provisions that change revenue, are listed at the bottom of the table.

A number of interesting patterns emerge. The first, which confirms the trend toward tax reduction and thus adds credibility to the measures, is the structure of the final bills. Excepting the war years of 1950 and 1951, the only bills in which more provisions were enacted which raised revenue than reduced it were in 1962, 1969 and 1976. The latter two bills are usually depicted as the major tax reform efforts of the postwar period, with the 1969 bill also coinciding with a minor war. The 1962 bill was stimulated by the early efforts of Stanley Surrey, who was Kennedy's Assistant Secretary of the Treasury for taxation, and was a minor bill in relation to the 1964 act. A second and more important result is the varying pattern of presidential success. There are a number of interesting twists which can best be explained by briefly outlining the strategies and successes of each administration.

TABLE 8-4. Presidential Success on Postwar Income Tax Bills

Presidential Proposals

	1948	1950	1950*	1951	1954	1962	1964	1969	1971	1975	1976	1977	1978	1981	Total
Tax Reductions:															
Proposals	1	1	0	0	28	1	27	6	5	3	15	4	9	17	117
Successes	0	1	0	0	21	1	16½	6	4	2½	1½	1	6½	14	75
Successes/Proposals	0	1.0	—	—	.75	1.0	.61	1.0	.80	.83	.10	.25	.18	.82	.64
Tax Increases:															
Proposals	1	6	2	10	6	12	19	13	0	0	8	0	14	0	91
Successes	0	3½	1½	3¼	3	5½	4	11	0	0	1½	0	4	0	37¼
Successes/Proposals	0	.58	.75	.33	.5	.46	.21	.85	—	—	.19	—	.29	—	.41
Neutral Changes:															
Proposals	0	1	0	0	7	1	3	0	0	0	0	0	0	0	12
Successes	0	½	0	0	7	1	2	0	0	0	0	0	0	0	10½
Successes/Proposals	—	.50	—	—	1.0	1.0	.66	—	—	—	—	—	—	—	.87
Total Changes:															
Proposals	2	8	2	10	41	14	49	19	5	3	23	4	23	17	220
Successes	0	5	1½	3¼	31	7½	22½	17	4	2½	3	1	10½	14	123
Successes/Proposals	0	.63	.75	.33	.76	.54	.46	.89	.80	.83	.13	.25	.47	.82	.56

Final Legislation

	1948	1950	1950*	1951	1954	1962	1964	1969	1971	1975	1976	1977	1978	1981	Total
Tax Reductions	5	1	0	8	26	3	24	15	9	13	20	9	30	29	187
Tax Increases	0	4	2	17	6	11	14	27	0	5	30	0	7	2	125
% Reductions	100	20	0	32	81	21	63	36	100	72	40	100	81	94	61

*Excess Profits Tax Bill of 1950.

In the euphoric months following V-J day in August 1945, a very simple administration tax reduction bill, which eliminated World War II excess profits taxes, cut excise taxes and slightly reduced income taxes, was easily passed. That was the last easy tax victory for President Truman. With Republicans in power in Congress following the 1946 elections, a congressional drive to reduce taxes was undertaken. However, citing macroeconomic and inflationary effects and equity concerns, President Truman twice vetoed the efforts of Congress. However, with bipartisan support, the latter veto (in 1948) was overridden, and it appeared that the country was on the road to major tax reduction similar to that following World War I. Korea intervened with the immediate result being the reinstatement of the World War II tax structure. While as in previous wars the early tax measures passed in a state of crisis were consensual, Truman's efforts in 1951, not only to raise more revenue, but also to enact major tax reforms, were directly rebuffed by Congress. Unlike later presidents, Truman was rigidly consistent in his stance against tax reduction and for structural tax reform measures. He was also consistently unsuccessful, whether or not his party controlled Congress.

Eisenhower, on the other hand, was successful in two respects. First, under the guidance of Assistant Secretary of the Treasury Daniel Throop Smith, his administration engineered a total rewriting of the tax code, which to this day bears the title of "Internal Revenue Code of 1954." The final legislation included hundreds of technical and language changes in addition to the substantive provision changes tabulated in Table 8-4. The relative success of the administration proposals was due in part to the lengthy and very inclusive political process through which changes were adopted, but also to the fact that most of the substantive provisions reduced taxes. The principal battle, which ended in a compromise with congressional Democrats, was to allow a partial exclusion and tax credit for corporate dividends. However, the business community and conservatives were far from satisfied with administration initiation of these provisions because earlier the administration had led a successful effort *against* reduction of war-level corporate tax rates.

The second major success of the Eisenhower administration, which cannot be gleaned from Table 8-3, is the successful resistance by the administration of later congressional efforts to reduce taxes, particularly during the 1957–58 recession. Citing the deficit and fiscal responsibility, Eisenhower persistently refused to follow the historic pattern established after World War I. Thus in one sense our progressive rate structure and the mass nature of the federal income tax are due to the resilience of a conservative, Republican president who resisted political pressure, the ideology of his party and the weight of history.

The Kennedy administration broke the moratorium on tax policy, first with a minor bill and then with a major tax reform effort. As with Eisenhower, in both cases Kennedy was more successful with his proposals to reduce taxes than with those that would have produced revenue gains. And one of the clear goals of Kennedy tax policy was to reduce taxes that hampered investment. To this end one of his successful proposals, which has grown to a tax expenditure of close to $30 billion per year, was the creation of a tax credit for new investment. Although Kennedy's success rate was relatively low, the number of proposals made in 1964 was more than any other administration has ever made.

The 1969 tax bill is something of an anomaly in terms of presidential influence and success. Lyndon Johnson had little interest in tax policy and had to struggle for months with Congress to pass a simple temporary Vietnam surcharge on income taxes. However, during his administration, Congress and the Treasury were laboriously working out a wide range of tax reform measures under the careful guidance of the conservative chairman of Ways and Means, Wilbur Mills. Thus when Nixon took office, a massive tax reform package already existed. Being aware of the mood of Congress and the work already accomplished, his administration tailored its proposals to those of Congress and was highly successful in securing their passage. Thus increasing the irony, clearly the most liberal tax reform package in our history was passed with the concerted aid of two men constantly attacked by the very liberals who most often champion tax reform and income redistribution through the tax system.[15]

Presidential involvement in the next major tax legislation in 1976 was not as successful. Simple tax reduction bills had been passed following presidential recommendations in 1971 and 1975. Also during this period a major tax reform bill was working its way through Congress, stalled by the political demise of first Wilbur Mills and then Richard Nixon. When the bill finally emerged in 1976, President Ford, unlike his predecessor, failed to ride with the sentiments that had built in Congress. Instead he proposed a lopsided tax reduction bill which was favorable both to business and to upper-income individuals. Although as the bill was debated in the summer of 1976, the first signs of congressional shifts against tax reform began to emerge, and many liberal reform proposals were struck down, Ford's proposals were almost totally disregarded.

The same fate, due this time to a reverse reading of Congress, befell the Carter administration. By 1977 and 1978 the mood in Congress and probably in the country had dramatically shifted away from tax reform and toward tax reduction. The media was alive with reports first on the effects of inflation on income taxes, then on the declining rate of capital investment in the country, and finally on the property tax revolt in June 1978. The Carter administration seemed oblivious to all of this and produced a long and classic list of tax reform proposals including everything from reduced capital gains benefits to repeal of the deduction of state and local taxes.

A relatively minor bill was passed in 1977, in which Congress quickly discarded Carter's campaign proposal for a $50 per person rebate and several other proposals. In the spring of 1978, the hostile congressional reception of Carter's major reform package sent leading tax Democrats to the White House to inform the president that little in his package was possible. Still, the administration held out, not changing their proposals until late summer after Congress had written its own bill. The successes the administration did record were due more to their conforming to Congress than the other way around. Even with both houses solidly controlled by his party, the president's tax program failed miserably.

With the Reagan administration, the feelings of Congress and the president were again moving in the same direction. If anything, the president's initial proposals in February 1981 underestimated the desire of Congress to enact tax reduction. The early proposals were modest and had to be updated twice as a major "bidding war" took hold of both Republicans and Democrats.[16] Although the end result was in accord with Reagan's philosophy and campaign promises, the final dramatic showdown between Democratic and Republican bills in the House (which Republicans won) was much more symbolic than real. The Democrats had already approved the majority of the tax reduction provisions and there was very little difference between the two bills. The longer-term historical tides toward general tax reduction and increasing benefits through special tax expenditure provisions had returned and were working in concert, and neither the president nor Congress resisted.

EXPLANATION OF TRENDS

For those seeking precise generalizations and tidy theories of the policy relationships between Congress and the president, tax policy is not the case to select. Although the evidence suggests a clear increase in executive branch initiation of tax legislation in the postwar period, the ultimate influence of the president is much less certain and varies from administration to administration. Although the earlier notion that presidents should set only general revenue targets has been replaced by more detailed, almost annual tax proposals, the majority of the tax agenda is still set by Congress. Furthermore, there is no doubt that when presidential requests run counter to legislative momentum or the short-term mood of Congress, they can and are summarily dismissed by congressional actions. What follows is a brief explanation of each of these trends.

The Increasing Presidential Role

There are several possible explanations for the increasing legislative initiatives in tax policy of postwar administrations. The most obvious is simply the increasing responsibility of the president for macroeconomic performance. In recent years this has gone well beyond simple deficit management to include detailed programs to stimulate specific forms of investments, to control inflation and to aid selective industries. Beginning in earnest with the Kennedy proposals for the general investment credit and liberalized depreciation schedules, administrations increasingly turned to the tax code as a specific tool of economic policy. To cite some additional examples: Nixon attempted to stimulate exports through the creation of special tax corporations in the form of Domestic International Sales Corporations (DISCs); Carter promoted special tax credits to stimulate jobs; and the Reagan administration supported complicated proposals to provide credits and stimulation to failing or nonprofitable businesses (the Safe Harbors Leasing Provision). These general proposals are in addition to the dozens of provisions that are rationalized as beneficial to special circumstances pertaining to specific industries or businesses. While the executive branch is certainly not alone in its use of the tax code for these purposes, as government has subsumed a larger burden for economic performance, the temptation for all branches to use the tax code as an economic policy tool has grown proportionately.

The activist role of presidents in other policy arenas has also had an effect on both the general expansion of the tax expenditure system and on the more assertive role of administrations in tax policy. For example, while the Carter administration was professing a simpler tax code with fewer loopholes in its specific tax reform proposals, it used the tax code extensively to promote energy conservation policies. Similar policy proposals have been offered by other administrations to promote housing programs, charitable giving, private retirement funds, child care facilities and research and development. Thus as it became clear following World War II that the tax code could be used to reach nearly all Americans and all American corporations, and at least theoretically influence their behavior, it became irresistible as a policy tool—a tool to be used by both Congress and the president.

A final possible explanation for increasing presidential activism in tax policy lies with the parallel increase in responsibility for preparing an annual budget. Although to some degree revenue proposals remain a secondary part of this process, as deficits loom as a potential problem, and as assumptions concerning both spending and tax revenues are increasingly challenged, exact tax proposals are required and may well become increasingly a part of the budgetary cycle. If this speculation is correct, and if the executive branch remains the prime mover behind budgetary shifts, one can anticipate greater rather than less presidential activism in the future.

Varying Presidential Success in Tax Policy

Political scientists who emphasize the "science" portion of their occupational label dislike the thought that political behavior may be primarily based on idiosyncratic events, or even luck. However, a careful, case-by-case analysis of income tax politics suggests that such factors may be the most important in determining how presidential tax proposals fare in Congress. Although clearly presidential style, interest and perseverance on tax issues have some effect on final outcomes (for example, Truman's dogged delay and Eisenhower's resistance against tax reduction, or Johnson's disinterest in the subject in general), the most important factor seems to be the synchronization of presidential initiatives with both long- and short-term historical trends in tax policy.

The long-term trends are the gravitational pressure for tax reduction and the parallel growth in the tax expenditure system (both as vehicle for tax reduction and as a separate policy tool). Those presidents whose tax proposals have been consistent with these long-term forces have in general been more successful than those that have not. This result is clearly depicted in Table 8-4 in the varying success rates for proposals that either increase or reduce tax revenues. Sixty-four percent of the proposals that lower taxes are ultimately enacted, versus 41 percent for those that proposed increased burdens. Not surprisingly, the only time this differential was not the case was in 1969 when 11 of Nixon's 13 tax increase proposals were accepted by Congress. The 1969 act was the most radical tax reform legislation ever passed, occurring in the midst of one of the most liberal periods in our history. Nixon seemingly understood this mood and resisted adopting a more traditionally conservative stance. However, as is indicated by the very low success rates for the tax increase proposals of Truman, Kennedy, Ford and Carter, Nixon's success is the sole exception to the general rule.

A more difficult factor to describe and analyze is also exemplified by the 1969 case. Although there are natural political forces which shape longer-term trends in tax policy, congressional mood and policy momentum also play an important role at any given time. The Tax Reform Act of 1969 was the product of four years of proposals, counterproposals, hearings, studies and endless negotiation within Congress and between Congress and the executive branch. It also fell during a period of general liberal reform. Had Nixon attempted to derail or alter the basic thrust of this legislation, he would have failed, much like his predecessor failed when he misread congressional intentions in 1976, or Carter failed to read the shift in mood in 1978. Although one could interpret this synchronization in terms of political skill or understanding, it probably has much more to do with the pliability of presidential beliefs and simple luck. If, for example, Ford had defeated Carter in 1976, his success rating in tax policy would undoubtedly have risen significantly in that his beliefs would have fit the altered mood of Congress.

CONCLUSION

A common tendency in the reincarnated study of political economy that is currently popular in political science is to analyze partisan effects on macroeconomic outcomes. Unfortunately these studies rely only on economic outcomes as dependent variables (unemployment, inflation, etc.) and do not analyze the legislative efforts or results which more accurately reflect the intentions of political actors. As it turns out for tax policy, the latter is more difficult and produces more complex results, and indeed much less satisfying results in terms of general theory.

This chapter has argued that presidential actions and successes depend much more on nuances of belief and emphasis than on party or ideology, and that presidential success in tax policy depends more on the relationship of the president's tax proposals to long-term trends in tax policy and short-term shifts in congressional sentiment than to party control. What this suggests is that the best predictor of future directions or successes in tax policy is an understanding of those long-term trends, and even those predictions will be greatly limited.

NOTES

1. *Congressional Record* 50 (Washington, D.C.: U.S. Government Printing Office, 1913), p. 1246.

2. The personal exemption for a joint return was reduced from the initial $4000 to $2000 from 1917 to 1920.

3. Top bracket rates had risen during the depression, peaking at 81 percent. However, this action was somewhat symbolic because the top bracket only affected incomes over a million dollars, with the 81 percent bracket beginning at $5 million. By lowering the top bracket to $200,000, many more taxpayers were affected.

4. The term "tax expenditure" is meant to express a notion of government subsidy through the tax system that has similar characteristics and parallels direct government spending. They include deductions, excluded income, exempt income, tax credits and special rates for different types of income. The term itself is controversial. Those who object argue that the distinction between tax reductions that are labeled as tax expenditures and those that are not is arbitrary, and the very notion of labeling these provisions as "expenditures" implies an assumption that all income inherently belongs to the government. The term is used here because it is convenient and widely used and because decisions to grant specific tax reductions do have a logical parallel with decisions to grant positive government subsidies.

5. A full list of the tax expenditures employed in the analysis is available in John F. Witte, "The Distribution of Federal Income Tax Expenditures," *Policy Studies Review* 11 (September 1983), pp. 131–153. See also John F. Witte, *The Politics and Development of the Federal Income Tax* (Madison: University of Wisconsin Press, 1985), Chapter 13.

6. *Congressional Record* 122 (Washington, D.C.: U.S. Government Printing Office, 1976), p. 1246.

7. See the testimony presented by Alice Rivlin, Director of the Congressional Budget Office, before the U.S. Senate Budget Committee Hearings on the "Tax Expenditure Limitation and Control Act of 1981," November 24, 1981, pp. 24–45 (Washington, D.C.: U.S. Government Printing Office, 1982).

8. See, for example, Samuel Huntington, "Congressional Responses to the Twentieth Century," in David B. Truman, ed., *The Congress and America's Future* (Englewood Cliffs, N.J.: Prentice-Hall, 1965); James Sundquist, *Politics and Policy* (Washington, D.C.: The Brookings Institution, 1968); and Steven L. Wayne, *The Legislative President* (New York: Harper & Row, 1978).

9. Lawrence Chamberlain, *The President, Congress and Legislation* (New York, 1946). His study included 90 major legislative acts passed from 1890 to 1940. In tracing the origins for economic legislation, he attributed nine to presidents and 10 to Congress with eight more being joint.

10. In addition to Wayne, *The Legislative Presidency*, Sundquist, *Politics and Policy*, and Huntington," Congressional Responses in the Twentieth Century," see John R. Johannes, "Where Does The Buck Stop? Congress, the President, and the Responsibility for Legislative Initiation," *Western Political Science Quarterly* 25 (1972), pp. 396–415; and Ronald C. Moe and Steven C. Teel, "Congress as Policy-Maker," *Political Science Quarterly* 85 (1970), pp. 443–70.

11. See Witte, *The Politics and Development of the Federal Income Tax.*

12. Examples include exclusion of benefits for Social Security, unemployment benefits, public assistance and AFDC, the exclusion of employer paid benefit programs, and even the deduction of interest on consumer credit, the treatment of which was unclear in the original 1913 law.

13. A number of sources were used to check whether or not tax proposals originated with the president. The annual report of the Secretary of the Treasury, which predates the income tax, includes a section on presidential tax proposals. In addition all speeches of the president and official communications with Congress were reviewed for tax proposals. Similarly, congressional hearings, which for revenue matters usually open with an appearance by the Secretary of the Treasury, were reviewed for new or changed proposals. Chronologies in journals such as the *Congressional Quarterly* were also useful and, given the importance of revenue legislation, quite complete.

14. If bias exists in these estimates, it favors Congress because all tax proposals eventually appear in committee reports. If such proposals could not be traced to another source, they were attributed to the congressional committee. Although this may introduce a small amount of error, there is no reason to suspect that there is any appreciable bias over time.

15. Wilbur Mills and the Ways and Means Committee were the distinct target of congressional reform efforts that were largely successful in the early 1970s. See, for example, Ralph Nader's introduction to the Nader Congress Project Report, *The Revenue Committees* (New York: Grossman Publishers, 1975), written by Richard Spohn and Charles McCollum.

16. The Reagan administration tax reduction proposals actually began quite modestly, concentrating on a three-year, 30 percent rate reduction and

liberalization and an overhaul of depreciation. The Democrats increased the stakes considerably throughout the negotiations, being the initiators of proposals to eliminate the distinction between earned and unearned income, to provide a deduction for a working spouse, to increase the investment credit, to expand and increase Individual Retirement Accounts (IRAs) and to liberalize oil provisions, which had been tightened up in 1980. The Reagan administration happily accepted most of these provisions. Strong opposition to such provisions as Safe Harbors Leasing and the more liberal oil amendments came from the Republican Finance Committee Chairman Robert Dole, who in the next year led the effort to increase taxes through minor provision changes and tighter compliance requirements. See Witte, *The Politics and Development of the Federal Income Tax*, Chapter 11.

The Politics of
Federal Tax Policy

SUSAN B. HANSEN

Ronald Reagan is by no means the first president to propose cuts in
federal taxes. Every postwar election campaign platform, Democratic
as well as Republican, has included at least one plank pledging lower
taxes, tax reform or income tax reduction. Raising revenue through
tax "cuts" has become a major emphasis of twentieth-century public
finance at both the state and federal levels since tax increases are
almost universally unpopular. Tax cuts are not only favorably received by the electorate, but have been advocated by economists as
divergent as John Maynard Keynes and Arthur Laffer as a means to
stimulate the economy and ultimately enhance revenues.

Campaign promises are one thing, the exigencies of government
finance quite another. Once elected, presidents sooner or later must
confront the need for more revenues. The source of this grim news
may be members of their Council of Economic Advisers or their
budget director; it may be representatives of financial markets; it may
be foreign governments worried about American trade deficits or the
value of the dollar. It may even be members of the president's own
party (more likely the Republican), concerned about the deficit, the
debt ceiling or long-term budgetary trends.

As we shall see, such considerations have prevailed over public
preferences. Presidents, despite their own good intentions, have had
to deal with revenue constraints in one of three ways: raising taxes,
inflation, or deficit finance (and sometimes all three). Ultimately, the
American taxpayer has ended up paying more. Tax cuts have not only

186

failed to live up to the claims made for them; in several ways they have had serious negative consequences for public finance, the office of the presidency and the representation of public preferences.

The purpose of this chapter is to provide some perspective on the role of tax cuts in presidential politics. We will first consider the basic dilemma of public finance in a democracy: taxes are economically necessary but politically unpopular. We will then consider some of the major trends in federal tax policy since 1900. These trends include changes in tax reliance, a variety of fiscal illusions, new conceptions of budgetary balance, and advances in economic theory about the impact of the federal budget on the economy. In this context, the scholarly evidence will be summarized on the economic as well as the revenue consequences of post-World War II tax cuts, including a preliminary assessment of those adopted by the Reagan administration. The chapter concludes with a discussion of the political implications of tax cuts for the presidency and for economic policy.

TAX POLICY AND POLITICAL RISK

In 1900 very few Americans paid direct federal taxes. Indirect taxes such as tariffs, which constituted the majority of federal revenues, affected most people marginally. By 1980, however, over 90 percent of all Americans were required to file federal income taxes, and Social Security taxes were withheld from most paychecks. A federal bureaucracy hundreds of times larger than that of 1900 is required to collect these taxes, and individuals and corporations must expend considerable resources on attorneys and accountants in order to pay (or avoid) income taxes. Federal tax revenues have risen from about 3 percent of Gross National Product in 1900 to over 21 percent in 1983.

This growth in revenue has provided a far larger role for the federal government, as well as greater opportunities to use tax monies for political advantage. But higher, direct taxes on incomes are far more visible than tariffs ever were, and impact directly on a much larger proportion of the population. Thus the political risks of tax policymaking have been heightened. Since the Depression, the government's role in the economy has increased dramatically, but with this has come greater responsibility as well as greater vulnerability for the economic management of business cycles.

Politicians in the twentieth century thus face two dilemmas. The first is to meet revenue demands while avoiding responsibility for tax increases, or at least to reduce electoral risk if such increases are to be imposed. The second problem, however, is to maintain sufficient control over revenue and fiscal policy so as to be able to carry out their programs and manipulate government spending for their own political benefit. This has become progressively more difficult, especially for Democrats, as party strength and partisan voting have declined.

As a consequence of efforts to resolve the first dilemma, we see movement of responsibility for revenues as far as possible from the legislative or electoral arena: taxation without representation. The ancient art of "fiscal illusion" has undergone considerable refinement and institutional development. One cannot help but admire the ingenuity and survival instincts of the genus *homo politicus*, species *Americanus*, who have managed to cut tax rates and expand loopholes, yet increase federal revenues dramatically.

But such actions are risky. The president may take the blame if policies pursued by quasi-independent agencies such as the Federal Reserve Board produce inflation or unemployment. "Automatic" increases (mandated hikes in Social Security taxes or income tax "bracket creep" resulting from inflation) may be dangerous to incumbents directly or through their fiscal impacts, even if no individual elected official can be held responsible for voting for such increases. The federal budget has become largely uncontrollable due to entitlement of benefits, interest on the debt, and ongoing programs supported by entrenched subgovernments. At the same time the revenue base has eroded as tax deductions, loopholes and subsidies have increased. The huge and complex tax system is not only difficult to reform, but has become a very clumsy instrument to use for either fiscal policy or political advantage.

Citizen preferences alone cannot account for increases in revenues: the motives, resources and strategies of political leaders must be considered as well. Tax policy can of course be used to further reelection aims by providing differential benefits (expenditures or tax breaks) to political supporters in the electorate or among organized groups. While the desire to reward supporters may be a major motive, the desire of political leaders for discretionary revenue conflicts not only with the electorate's desire for lower taxes, but with efforts by entrenched bureaucracies and organized interests to guarantee that tax monies will be spent on policies advantageous to them. Thus taxes may be earmarked for certain services: sales or property taxes for education, user fees for parks and recreation, or motor vehicle fuel taxes and license fees for highway construction. Tax breaks at both the state and federal levels covary with the economic influence of certain industries.[1]

Elected officials, however, usually oppose earmarking and resort to it only if it is necessary to push through a tax proposal. Part of their reasoning is sound economics. With public goods it is difficult to predict the amount of revenue that will be raised by particular taxes, or the actual cost of providing certain goods or services. Earmarked revenues may therefore be highly inefficient, whether they provide insufficient funds for needed services or generate an excess that cannot be diverted to other purposes. Several accounts have documented the frustrations encountered by governors or the president when they assume office and discover that because of earmarking and other forms of "uncontrollable" spending (including debt retirement, entitlements and contracts with public employees) they have very little discretion over their budgets.[2] Even if legal earmarking is not a major problem, entrenched bureaucracies will fight bitterly to maintain wheatever share of the budget they already have. In order to make any policy changes, whether the motivation is personal or to reward electoral supporters, elected officials must often seek discretionary revenues. The more that existing revenues are constrained or earmarked, the more pressure on elected officials to raise taxes or devise new sources of revenues, regardless of personal preferences or campaign promises to reduce overall spending and taxes.

Another issue is that of the fiscal viability of government. Politicians who succeed in attaining office immediately find themselves faced with a multitude of legal and financial obligations concerning the debt, the budget, contracts, payrolls and entitlements for more government services. Taxpayers and voters are unlikely to share these concerns, but certain financial obligations must still be met to avoid economic disaster and its probable electoral repercussions. Although much creativity in the use of inflation, borrowing, budgets and legal requirements has been displayed, in most cases revenues must ultimately be raised through taxes, however unpopular these are likely to be.

Is it realistic or useful to describe political actors as striving to maximize revenues, specifically discretionary revenues? One could certainly point to numerous politicians (up to and including Ronald Reagan) who would disclaim any such motive. But a party's stand on tax issues may depend less on ideology or public opinion than on whether or not it controls the government. Several recent pieces of evidence suggest support for this view. In the late 1960s, congressional Democrats supported the Vietnam surcharge under Lyndon Johnson, but switched to oppose it when Richard Nixon became president.[3] Republicans in Illinois opposed an income tax in 1965 because they feared the Democratic governor would use the revenues to his (and Chicago's) advantage, but they switched views after the incoming Republican governor promised considerable highway and bridge construction money to downstate Republicans in exchange for their support of his administration's income tax passage.[4] Such partisan switching is normal politics and has appeared in connection with such issues as education, foreign aid and debt extensions among others.

This perspective is quite different from the usual association of ideology with party stands on taxes. Democrats supposedly prefer higher taxes (to finance more government services) and more progressive forms of taxation; Republicans have historically opted for lower taxes, especially on business, and flat rate or regressive taxes. Nevertheless, the income taxes of the Civil War era and the Sixteenth Amendment (1909) were passed under Republican governments, while the highly regressive Social Security system set up during the New Deal was the responsibility of the Democrats. In the states as well party ideology has been a poor predictor of tax structure.[5]

It should not be surprising, therefore, if a party's ideological coherence while in opposition were replaced by a more pragmatic outlook on taxes as on other policy areas once control of government was attained. During the debate over Reagan's 1982 tax increase proposal, sophomore Republican Congressman Newt Gingrich of Georgia was quoted in a *Washington Post* article on "Taxes: Republican Identity Crisis":

> I find myself in the most confusing situation of my short career in Congress. . . . Everything junior Republican members fought for was designed to cut spending and cut taxes, not to pacify big government and raise taxes. But now I listen to decent, honorable, well-intentioned men say the exact opposite of what they said before they went into government.[6]

Brennan and Buchanan see modern government as a Leviathan whose goal is revenue maximization. The motives of individual political actors may differ, and not all may be interested in maximizing revenue. Rather revenue maximization "emerges from the interaction of the whole set of governmental decision-makers even if no person explicitly sets maximum revenue as the goal of his own action."[7]

Certainly pressures on government to expand revenues have far exceeded those urging contraction; politicians' attempts to cut revenues have been quickly frustrated. Many factors, such as war, economic growth, territorial expansion and population increase, have contributed to these upward pressures on revenues. Not all politicians have been revenue maximizers; Jefferson, Jackson and most Republican governments since the Civil War have made some attempt to reduce the rate of government growth, and even FDR was constrained by the ideology of the balanced budget and the need to encourage private sector investment. But all have been pragmatists, beginning with Jefferson's approval of the Louisiana Purchase and culminating with Reagan's concern for the deficit. Ideology has therefore been a poor predictor of both levels and sources of revenue. So the politics of taxation has involved attempts to shift the tax burden rather than to reduce it, although the rhetoric has often been that of tax reduction. "Tax revolts" in American history have been revolts of the "haves,"[8] but none of these to date has been successful in reducing taxes.

The history of tax policy in the twentieth century can be read as a series of unsuccessful attempts to resolve the dilemmas of responsibility and control. Thus on the one hand we see highly politicized, partisan debate on tax policy, although such partisanship depends far less on party philosophy than on shifts in power, votes, and control of major governing institutions. On the other hand, there has been considerable evidence of party collusion to produce flexible instruments of fiscal policy which are deliberately set as far as possible outside the bounds of political influence. Both because of the greater electoral risks and because of the decline of political parties, tax policy is seldom a partisan zero-sum game as it was in nineteenth-century politics.[9] But even Republican administrations have been unable to reduce taxes, deficits, or levels of federal spending. Tax-reform efforts by both parties have foundered in "Christmas tree" bills which convey benefits on many social groups but give neither party a clear advantage. Nevertheless, new revenues have been found to permit discretionary spending.

FISCAL ILLUSION AND REVENUE GROWTH

Let us now consider how federal revenues have increased so markedly since 1900. The 1913 income tax (even as its opponents feared) was a stroke of genius. Taxes on incomes, even flat-rate or proportional ones, tend to be elastic; revenues thus increase as population grows and incomes rise, as has been the case throughout the century except for the Depression era. An even better revenue-producing device was the progressive rate structure built into the first income-tax law and continued, in varying degrees, ever since. During "boom" periods, people's incomes are inflated into higher tax brackets. This automatically dampens take-home pay and spending, without any need for overt political action to cool off the economy by raising tax rates. In addition, of course, this fiscal dividend (estimated recently at 1.5 percent for each 1 percent increase in income) produces additional revenues, sufficient to meet the rising costs of inflaticn and leave some remaining for discretionary political use. Not surprisingly, Congress has steadfastly resisted any attempts at indexing tax rates, despite appeals from tax reformers, economists, and conservatives concerned about the increase in the size of the public sector.[10]

No public vote is necessary for Congress to reap the benefits of the fiscal dividend of "bracket creep." Rather, if revenues appear to be expanding too fast and producing economic or political difficulties, congressmen can vote for tax "cuts" and still obtain increasing revenues in periods of inflation. Indexing, on the other hand, not only reduces revenue growth but deprives politicians of the opportunity to take credit for the tax cuts which have dominated revenue policymaking since the Depression. Tax cuts have afforded congressmen ample opportunities to gain favorable publicity and political benefits while keeping tax rates as a percentage of personal income within a fairly narrow range.

In addition to well-publicized tax "cuts," increases in revenues due to inflation or collection efficiency have also been offset by a massive and fast-growing system of tax expenditures. As federal income tax coverage increased dramatically during World War II, the opportunity and the incentive arose for Congress to alleviate economic hardship, offer benefits to specific groups and encourage economic productivity and investment. Beginning in 1974, the reformed congressional budget process required that all tax expenditures be listed in the budget and their revenue impact determined for each individually; since they overlap in many respects their cumulative effect is difficult to estimate. As of 1967, tax expenditures numbered approximately 50; by 1981 this had grown to over 100 and accounted for one-quarter of the federal budget, over 40 percent of revenues and 74 percent of income tax revenues.[11]

Despite widespread evidence that tax expenditures benefit persons in upper income brackets who have the most income to offset, tax loopholes in reality benefit a staggering variety of groups and individuals and enjoy a considerable measure of popular support. Broad-scale efforts at tax reform or simplification thus run into opposition from numerous social economic groups seeking to protect their own preferred loophole and usually willing to logroll with other interests in order to do so.

Tax cuts and expenditures have so eroded the federal tax base that one can hardly describe as "revenue maximizers" the congressmen who have devised and maintained them. But revenue aggrandizement has proceeded nevertheless. Congressmen have protected the immediate economic interests of their constituents (and thus their political fortunes) through tax subsidies, but the flow of federal revenues has been maintained in several ways.

1. *Government finance by inflation,* most prominent recently in financing the Vietnam war. Increases in the money supply and monetarization of the debt allow government revenues to increase faster than expenditures, while "bracket creep" offsets tax subsidies granted in part to ease the burden of inflation. This "bracket creep" has been effectively disguised from the public. As an aid to computation, the IRS publishes tax tables rather than tax rates on their filing forms. The innocent taxpayer simply looks up the tax due for each income level, and is seldom aware of how rates change for different levels of income.

2. *Deficit spending.* As inflation increased in the 1970s to politically unpalatable levels, the federal debt as a percentage of GNP began to reverse its long-term decline, rising from 34 percent of GNP in 1974 to an estimated 37 percent in 1981. A federal deficit of 4.7 percent of GNP (the highest since World War II) is projected for 1984.[12] Tax cuts and the proposed balanced budget amendment have both been predicated on the assumption that further increases in the deficit will not occur. Recent experience suggests otherwise, as congressional Republicans were forced to vote in 1982 and 1983 to raise the debt ceiling despite their public commitment to lower taxes and reduced government spending. Additional increases in the debt ceiling will probably become necessary in the future as the 1981 tax cuts reduce revenues further.

3. *Withholding of taxes,* both to increase rates of tax collection and to disguise tax bills from the public. Withholding had been used on civil servants' salaries as early as the Civil War and was introduced on a wide scale in 1943. Economists have since recognized withholding as a prime method of fiscal illusion. Taxpayers are less likely to estimate their tax bills accurately[13] and taxes seem less onerous if they are withheld at the source at regular intervals instead of being paid in one large annual amount. For fiscal purposes, withholding has another advantage: a tax increase or decrease can be put into effect almost

immediately, whereas new taxes or major structural changes are more difficult to implement, and may not have the intended impact for months or years.

4. *Expansion of the tax base.* Highly publicized tax cuts have been used to political advantage and marginal rates have declined, but at least until 1978 revenues were maintained or increased by expansion of the tax base. The tax base (amount of income subject to tax) rose from 36 percent of personal income in 1948 to 51 percent of personal income in 1969; it slipped back to 44 percent of personal income by 1978. The earlier increase occurred in large part because of the erosion of the value of the personal exemption by inflation, because more people were required to file tax returns, and because declines in self-employment and increases in wage and salary income have increased the extent of withholding.[14] In the 1970s the Earned Income Credit and increases in the standard deduction, both undertaken in part to offset inflation, reduced the tax base somewhat, but this loss was more than compensated for by high inflation rates.

5. *Social Security.* Social Security taxes have provided a politically expedient way to expand revenues, increase taxes and extend federal spending into new policy areas. Social Security revenues have grown dramatically since 1950, while personal income taxes have remained relatively constant and corporate taxes have fallen because of changes in rates, investment tax credits and the computation of depreciation.[15] Many taxpayers now pay more in Social Security than in income taxes, and there are no deductions or exemptions available to offset the regressive impact of the tax on low-income wage earners (although the earned-income credit, part of the federal income tax since 1974, does assist those persons who file a federal tax return). The Social Security system is characterized by ample opportunities for fiscal illusion and political advantage. Tax increases have been sold to the public as keyed to increased benefits. Even though Social Security does not operate on an actuarial or insurance basis, it is widely perceived as an earmarked tax and a good investment in one's own retirement income. The most anyone retiring in 1982 could have paid into the system since 1937 is $17,000, which he or she will recover in a year or two of benefits.[16] Since 1968, Social Security has been part of the unified federal budget, although its trust fund revenues cannot be used for general purposes. Programs as diverse and controversial as Aid to Families with Dependent Children, the Work Incentive Program and energy assistance grants are legally amendments to the voluminous Social Security law (whose very complexity and the vast

bureaucracy needed to implement it provide congressmen with ample opportunities for constituency service). A regressive, earmarked tax with widespread popular support has permitted federal expansion into several domestic policy areas (such as Medicaid and Medicare) which might well have attracted greater conservative political opposition if they had been funded out of the general revenues from progressive income taxes.

These same political advantages, however, have also been responsible for many of the serious problems currently plaguing the system. Since people feel they have "earned" benefits through their payroll tax contributions, cuts in benefits or programs are nearly impossible to make. The day of reckoning, when obligations were projected to exceed current payments, came in early 1983, when Congress enacted a package of tax increases and spending cuts in Social Security. But campaign promises in the 1984 election began to erode the reform's impact.

EROSION OF PARTISANSHIP IN TAX POLICYMAKING

Two things are remarkable about these methods used to increase federal revenues. The first is their reliance on incremental, automatic or illusionary techniques. Major changes in revenue sources, such as the 1913 income tax and the 1935 enactment of Social Security, have occurred during periods of realignment. During periods of more normal politics, only incremental changes have occurred. Reagan, as of 1981, attempted the most dramatic restructuring of the tax laws in a generation, after what many observers touted as a realigning election.[17]

The second aspect worth noting is the bipartisan cooperation which has characterized tax changes outside of periods of realignment. Parties and elections significantly shaped the development of U.S. tax policy in the nineteenth century. But party strength has varied considerably throughout American history, reaching its peak during the 1890s. A major legacy of the Progressive era was a general weakening of the party system, at least partially attributable to the "reforms" they introduced (nonpartisan election, direct primaries, voter registration requirements). As a result the realignment of the 1932 was far more diffuse than its predecessors, and Burnham suggests that the "onward march of party decomposition" has made future realignments less likely.[18] Unified party control of government today has usually been far removed in practice from the "responsible party" model.

These developments have affected tax policymaking as well. The norm of nonpartisanship characterized the House Ways and Means Committee for years, due in part to Mills' leadership and in part to the insulation of its members from electoral pressures because of seniority, incumbency and their safe districts.[19] But even in the Senate and on the House floor there has been considerable bipartisan agreement on changes in Social Security and in the Internal Revenue code. Kennedy's 1964 tax cut, a major revolution in fiscal policy, passed by a vote of 335 to 18. Tax increases have been voted in wartime (World War II and Korea) with considerable bipartisan unity; the opposition party was seldom willing or able to oppose revenues needed for national defense, especially in the form of short-term tax increases or surcharges. Johnson's Vietnam tax surcharge did run into serious difficulty in Congress, but the opposition came as much from his own party in that bitter time as from Republicans, and the tax did not take effect until after Nixon took office.[20]

Presidential efforts at tax policy innovation have been stymied by lack of the party cohesion necessary to initiate effective changes or reform in the size, source or distribution of the tax burden. Even when presidents tried to reform the tax structure, the outcome was usually quite different from their intentions. President Carter in 1978 proposed tax reforms in a more progressive direction, but his $50 rebate fell victim to inflation and the final 1978 tax bill not only preserved most existing loopholes but added others, with strong support from Democrats as well as Republicans.[21]

Changes in party voting on tax policy are illustrated by Table 9-1, which shows the index of party likeness for final votes on major tax bills since the peak period of party voting in the 1890s. Partisanship was still evident in voting on the 1909 and 1913 tax bills. But the 1920s saw the beginning of hegemonic tax policymaking[22] as many Democrats came to share Treasury Secretary Mellon's view of lower, less regressive taxes as means to spur investment and generate more revenues. Partisanship reappeared during the New Deal, in particular on Roosevelt's 1935 "soak the rich" tax increase, but even Social Security had considerable Republic support. By that time the Conservative Coalition was beginning to emerge; although Democrats had high party cohesion on the final roll call, accounts of the writing of Social Security legislation detail the many compromises included in order to gain support from Southern Democrats.[23]

TABLE 9-1. Party Votes on Major Tax Bills, 1894–1982

		Index of Party Likeness*	
		House	Senate
1894	Income tax	98	99
1909	Tax amendment	94	91
1913	Income tax law	96	82
1921	Revenue Act	92	78
1935	Social Security Act	19	23
1954	Tax Reform Act	34	27
1964	Tax cut	28	14
1969	Vietnam surcharge	05	24
1972	Social Security indexation	11	02
1975	Tax cut	30	42
1978	Tax reform	14	0
1981	Economic Recovery Tax Act	44	20
1982	Tax increase	03	60

*The index is the absolute value of the difference between the percent of each party supporting each tax bill, with 100 indicating complete polarization.

Party voting fell even further during the 1950s and 1960s. Most Republicans came to accept Social Security, and votes to expand benefits and raise payroll taxes were consistently bipartisan. Goldwater's political difficulties in 1964 because of this stand on Social Security no doubt contributed to this bipartisan approach to an issue so universally popular with the electorate. The 1975 tax cut was moderately controversial because of Republic concern about the deficit, but the 1978 tax reform found both parties strongly in favor of what emerged as a "Christmas tree" bill, in part attributable to the demise of Chairman Mills and the decreasing influence of the House Ways and Means Committee.

Throughout the 1970s party unity was consistently higher within the Republican minority. This culminated in passage of the 1981 Economic Recovery Tax Act with only one dissenting Republican vote in either House. The Democrats, divided into "gypsy moths" and "boll weevils," were unable to counter President Reagan's popularity, his effective legislative liaison, and his willingness to deal in order to gain passage of the centerpiece of his economic program. But the Republicans split badly on the 1982 tax increase, which passed only with Democratic votes in favor of what one Democratic senator termed the "best liberal tax-reform package in years." Democratic gains in the House in the 1982 Congressional elections and the economic difficulties facing Reagan's economic policy will insure continued partisan debate, but any new tax bills are unlikely to pass without bipartisan support.

Taxes remain party issues in debate and campaign rhetoric; many final roll calls are still partisan.[24] But bipartisan cooperation on tax policy has emerged in this century for at least three reasons. The first is broad acceptance of the use of tax policy to spur investment; Democrats compete with Republicans to offer tax breaks to corporations. Herbert Stein has stated that because of near universal concern with recent declines in economic growth and productivity, "we are all supply-siders now."[25] Second is the degree of internal division within the parties, partly ideological, partly a consequence of structural changes such as the spread of primaries. Parties lack the incentives for cohesion and only through compromise can they make even limited changes in a complex revenue structure reflecting so many vested interests. Chances for comprehensive reform—in either liberal or conservative directions—are increasingly remote; even Reagan's tax cuts were so thoroughly compromised in Congress that they failed to provide a test of supply-side economic theory.

Finally, although politicians of both parties have much to gain from increased discretionary revenues, the hazards of tax policymaking have increased along with government revenues. Tax increases, however advantageous these might be for fiscal policy or budget balance, are too hazardous to be enacted in the absence of party cohesion—unless they are disguised as tax cuts.

INNOVATIONS IN ADMINISTRATION AND IDEOLOGY

Let us now consider two administrative changes which have been essential to twentieth-century practices of increasing revenues by cutting taxes. The first of these is the Bureau of the Budget. Before the creation of the Budget Bureau in 1921, no institutionalized means for budgetary planning and balance existed. If in 1900 budgets were balanced by accident, after the Keynesian revolution they were unbalanced by design. Despite rhetoric to the contrary, budgeting procedures were *not* set up in order to cut taxes or reduce the scope of government. Rather they were a means to permit additional government spending by introducing efficiency and improved managerial practices into government finance. This would produce more discretionary revenues without the necessity to raise taxes.

A second administrative change in fiscal policy is all too familiar to taxpayers: the increase in policy responsibility by the agencies with authority for the collection of taxes. The Internal Revenue Service and the Social Security Administration, like many other Washington bureaucracies, have grown dramatically in terms of revenue collections, proportion of the popular taxes, number of employees, administrative costs, paperwork and involvement in litigation. More important for our purposes, however, is the latitude explicitly granted to the IRS to implement legislation, prepare detailed regulations, and handle disputes between taxpayers and the government. With taxes, as with tariffs and the budget, Congress had absolved itself of much of the risk of tax policy implementation. As insiders' accounts show, IRS staff and agents take their role as guardians of the public purse far more seriously than most Congressmen do. The paradox is nicely illustrated by the 1982 tax increases; the repeal of tax leasing and the adoption of withholding of interest on savings and dividends had long been favored by the IRS and the Treasury. Because of the looming deficits they were able to prevail over supply-siders in the administration who were concerned that such reforms would discourage investment.

Partisan battles have occasionally erupted over the Bureau of the Budget, its successor OMB, and the IRS when they became too closely identified with the political interests of the presidency or certain members of Congress. But on the whole both have enjoyed bipartisan support. Who, after all could oppose efficiency, economy and limits to uncoordinated raids on the Treasury by special interests? And at least some members of Congress have come to realize how necessary both IRS and OMB have become in order to offset their own tax-cutting proclivities.

Changes in tax laws and administrative procedures since 1900 have extracted steadily increasing amounts of revenues from American taxpayers.[26] The World Wars, Korea, the Cold War and Vietnam provided some rationale for such increases. But an expanded role for government in the peacetime economy required further intellectual justification to be palatable to citizens as taxpayers, voters and businessmen. Further, classical economics and public finance held that budgets should balance and that taxes should be raised to cover projected deficits. How, then, could tax cuts produce anything but economic and political disaster? The economic ideas of John Maynard Keynes and Arthur Laffer provided politically appealing answers.

Keynes argued that decisions as to levels and sources of taxes could be made quite independently of decisions concerning expenditures. Governments could borrow money to finance expenditures during market downturns. Such borrowing would stimulate the private markets and maintain consumer demand. In theory bonds could easily be paid off in the future when the economy was functioning better, so that today's debts would not constitute a burden on tomorrow's taxpayers.

American governments, liberal as well as conservative, have long intervened in the economy; Keynes' theory offered an economic justification in addition to the political one. Deficits are not only permitted, but are positively beneficial during recessions, and can otherwise be justified by the "full employment budget" strategem (that government revenue and expenditure levels should be based on the amount of goods and services the economy would produce if all who sought work were gainfully employed). In Buchanan and Wagner's terms, Keynesian economics "destroyed the effective constraint on politicians' ordinary appetites. Armed with the Keynesian message, politicians can spend and spend without the apparent necessity to tax,"[27] especially if such spending maintains a healthy economy.

As of 1900, U.S. politicians and voters were generally committed to balanced budgets, fiscal restraint and a limited role for government in the economy. Even during the New Deal the acceptance of Keynes' ideas was a lengthy and difficult process.[28] Roosevelt, for political far more than economic reasons, upheld the ideal of the balanced budget well into his presidency. It was not until the 1940s, when younger economists from prestigious academic departments found wartime positions in Washington, that the new economics gained hegemony. The ideal of the balanced budget was buried when it became apparent even to fiscal conservatives that deficits incurred during war and depression led to economic growth (and greatly increased revenues), not public bankruptcy.

Congress, by passage of the Employment Act in 1946, appeared to endorse Keynesian ideas concerning governmental responsibility for regulation of the economy. But public and political acceptance of Keynes' ideas concerning taxation was slower in coming. Eisenhower's pursuit of a balanced budget led to three recessions during his two administrations. Not until Kennedy pushed for a tax cut in 1962 did Keynesian ideas concerning taxation gain official acceptance, and then principally among Democrats. Republicans, usually philosophically inclined toward lower taxes on business, opposed the 1964 cut, publicly because of concern over the budget deficit, and privately because they were unwilling to give the ruling Democrats credit for a policy the GOP had backed under Eisenhower.[29] The 1964 tax cut appeared to be a resounding success as the economy boomed and revenues increased, and the "new economics" was widely hailed. By 1970 Keynesian ideas (vastly expanded and elaborated from his original *General Theory* by a generation of economists) dominated fiscal policy. Even a Republican president could proclaim, as Nixon did, that "We are all Keynesians now."

As deficits mounted, polls persistently showed most Americans committed to the idea of a balanced budget, and by the mid-1970s Keynes had few remaining adherents among politicians or economists. The fiscal tools developed since the Depression were not sufficient to cope with new economic challenges: structural unemployment, OPEC, declining productivity and inflation due to cost rather than demand factors.[30] Keynesian economics had emphasized demand management. If people had money to spend (even if, as Keynes once urged, the government merely paid them to dig holes and fill them up again), the wages they received could buy goods and services, keep other persons employed and thus fuel the economy, of course generating revenue in the process. During the Depression excess grain had to be destroyed and plants stood idle because of lack of purchasing power. But the current problem for fiscal policy is to add to productive capacity.

An alternative "supply-side" approach stressed America's low rates of investment, savings and productivity, which have aggravated inflation, limited economic growth, and diminished our ability to compete with the Germans and Japanese. Conservative economists and businessmen argued that if government spent less on welfare and regulation, government growth would be slowed and inflation reduced. Government borrowing to finance deficits (which have become the hallmark of Keynesian policies) would no longer compete with the private sector in capital markets, interest rates would fall, and corporate investments and profits could increase.

For politicians the revenue impact of supply-side economics lies in the paradoxical "Laffer curve." In theory too-high marginal tax rates discourage work and investment; people choose more leisure over additional income which would only flow to the government. But if taxes are reduced, people will find additional work and savings more worthwhile than leisure, and government revenues will therefore increase sufficiently to balance the budget. Advocates pointed to the economic growth (and revenue increases) following Andrew Mellon's tax cuts in the 1920s, the economic boom produced in part by the 1964 tax cut, and more rapid growth in the sunbelt states and Puerto Rico, where taxes were generally lower than the national average. Keynes' supporters favored progressive or proportional taxes in order to stimulate consumer demand; private savings were not to be encouraged because they would reduce spending and thus discourage economic expansion. Supply-siders are far more likely to advocate less government spending and lower taxes, especially for those who are presumed to save higher proportions of their incomes.[31]

Despite considerable differences in economic theory and political support, Keynesian and supply-side theory are similar from the taxpayers' viewpoint in two crucial respects. Both permit revenue aggrandizement, although by different routes: Keynesians by deficit spending during economic downturns, supply-siders by cutting marginal tax rates in order to encourage economic growth and thus higher tax revenues. And neither philosophy is greatly concerned about deficits. Keynesian deficits in bad times will in theory be paid off by higher taxes on the economic growth they stimulate. Many supply-siders assume deficits would be self-financing; lower taxes would not only encourage saving, making government borrowing easier, but would also generate more revenues. Because of their optimistic predictions of GNP growth rates following the 1982 tax cuts, the Reagan administration projected higher future revenues than did the Congressional Budget Office,[32] and even promised to balance the federal budget by 1984.

But revenue growth failed to materialize, and spending cuts proved more difficult than anticipated. As deficit projections approached the $200 billion level for fiscal 1984, Reagan had little choice but to support tax increases. In practice, therefore, theories as divergent as Keynes and supply-side have led to the same results: continued high taxes and tax increases. But economic theories have also been used to justify shifts in the tax burden *away* from the supporters of the party in question. Changes in tax sources have been gradual over the past 75 years, but their cumulative impact has been considerable, in particular the decline in corporate taxes and the increase in Social Security as a percentage of total federal revenues. As Stein notes, Roosevelt was "glad to use economic arguments for something he wanted to do on other grounds."[33]

EFFECTS OF FEDERAL TAX CUTS ON REVENUES AND THE ECONOMY

We have considered the variety of methods used to raise federal revenues and the administrative and ideological changes involved. In this context let us turn now to the actual impact of postwar cuts in federal taxes on the economy (savings, consumption, productivity, growth in GNP, inflation, unemployment), on revenues and on presidential politics.

One point to be stressed early on is that these are very difficult questions to answer. Once a policy is put into effect, can't we simply look back and see what happened? The problem is that

> Only one economic path is known: the path the economy followed after adoption of the policy. The path the economy would have followed in the absence of policy action, and therefore the effects of the policy, are unknown and can be estimated only through use of an econometric model.[34]

The U.S. economy is not a laboratory operating under experimental controls; any changes that occurred in historical trends may have been due to a multitude of other factors in addition to the tax policy at issue. Moreover, the econometric models used in most economic research are basically Keynesian in structure. Alternative supply-side or monetarist models might account for economic trends equally well, but there is no critical test or unique event which we can use to differentiate between them. Economic models are constantly being revised over time as new information is gained and new theories are developed. David Stockman had some sound theoretical reasons (in addition to the more obvious political ones) for changing key parameters of OMB's computer program.[35] But such changes make comparison and assessment more difficult. Finally, the time element is a major issue. Supply-siders in particular have argued that the benefits they anticipate from tax cuts are long-term; Keynesians look for more immediate short-term impacts (and, their critics charge, ignore the long-term adverse implications of countercyclical policy). In American political history, short-term effects (particularly those immediately preceding the next election) are more likely to be salient, but do not necessarily indicate the best policy.

When politicians are faced with such complex methodological considerations and conflicting advice among experts, their likely response is to make decisions based on political considerations such as ideology, campaign commitments or the actions they can most readily control. They may also hedge their bets by adopting only marginal changes in policy in the hopes of averting any adverse impacts, which can easily mean that their policy has little measurable impact at all. This is a charge that supply-siders are currently leveling against Reaganomics; Reagan's pledged 30 percent tax cut was reduced to 25 percent by Congress. Since the latter two years were to be figured on a lower base, the actual cut amounted to only 23 percent, and less than 2 percent for Reagan's first fiscal year. Even so, deficits were so large by 1982 that Reagan was forced to ask Congress for what George Will termed a "loophole-closing compliance-inducing revenue enhancer,"[36] otherwise known as a tax increase.

Given these political facts of life it is hardly surprising that the impacts of tax cuts have been fairly minimal. Exact estimates are difficult to make because different scholars have used different econometric models and different time periods, and have focused on different economic sectors or indicators. When the 30 percent Kemp-Roth tax cut bill was being debated in Congress, however, the Congressional Research Service was asked for an evaluation of the economic evidence of the effects of the tax cuts of 1964 and 1975 and the surcharge of 1968; the summary given here will rely on their reinterpretation of the economic literature.[37]

The 1964 tax cut reduced individual and corporate income tax rates from 5 to 20 percent. It had an initially strong impact on GNP, but the full effect was not reached until nearly three years later, and by that time was actually less than the size of the tax cut itself. There were significant early favorable effects on employment, but unfavorable effects on inflation even before the Vietnam war changed the political scene as well as the economy. Savings rates increased to a postwar high as a percentage of GNP, but productivity and business investment had already begun their long-term decline. Vietnam and the 1968 tax surcharge intervened before larger changes could make themselves felt on the supply side. But it is still not clear whether such changes as did occur could be attributed to the tax cut's supply-side or demand-side stimulus.[38] Further, an expansive monetary policy and wage-price guidelines were adopted simultaneously. These no doubt contributed to the subsequent period of economic prosperity, but make analysis of cause and effect more difficult.

In contrast to the 1964 tax cut, the 1968 Vietnam tax surcharge has become almost a textbook example of how not to make economic policy. It took effect nearly three years after the Council of Economic Advisers had recommended it, by which time inflation had already built up steam. Moreover, it was billed from the start as a "temporary" measure, which meant that individuals and businesses discounted its effects in advance. Savings did not decrease and consumption did not decline because of anticipation of future high inflation rates. Although the surcharge exacerbated the effects of the 1966–67 business downturn, it was not sufficient to counteract higher

Vietnam spending and an expansionist monetary policy. Both GNP and inflation continued to rise. But the repeal of the surcharge in 1971–72 was likewise discounted in advance and had little effect on rising unemployment.

The 1975 tax cut took the form of a rebate, a 10 percent cut in 1974 tax payments, as a stimulus to reduce the impact of the 1974–75 recession. This was coupled with an increase in the investment tax credit from 7 to 10 percent, changes in the standard deduction and exemption allowances, and $50 cash payments to recipients of Social Security or Railroad Retirement Benefits. Most of these provisions were continued and then made permanent between 1975 and 1978. The net fiscal impact totaled $23 billion, but this was not large relative to GNP. Research estimates of the economic impact are mixed, but the results were certainly not large. They were further diluted by the temporary nature of the rebate and the fact that the maximum impact of a tax policy change is experienced in the second or third year after enactment. This rendered it of little use as an effective anti-recession measure; instead it may have augmented the inflation of the late 1970s. When President Carter proposed another $50 per person rebate in 1977, it died in the Senate for just this reason.

Ronald Reagan and the 1980 Republican party platform promised a 30 percent, across-the-board income tax cut (the Kemp-Roth proposal). The Economic Recovery Tax Act of 1981 was hailed as a dramatic reversal of the previous decades of increased federal spending, deficits and taxes. This included 25 percent cuts in individual and corporate income taxes over a three-year period and adoption of tax indexing in 1985. The Reagan administration pledged to reduce government spending as a percentage of GNP and to balance the budget by 1984. A strong economic recovery, increased investment and lower inflation were also promised. But as early as spring 1981, ominous projections of future deficits emerged from the Congressional Budget Office and private economic forecasts. By later in that year the administration had to admit publicly that its projections for budgetary balance could not be met. As David Stockman was quoted in his celebrated *Atlantic* interview, "Sometimes confrontation with reality can have a sobering effect."

What had gone wrong? A major problem was that the economy had not responded as predicted. The world economy differed considerably from conditions in 1962, when the Kennedy investment tax credit and subsequent income tax cuts had indeed stimulated growth and thereby revenues. Reagan's policies had produced a sounder American dollar on world markets, but although that encouraged foreign investment, it discouraged trade. Except for agriculture, American exports continued to decline.[39] Moreover, as inflation declined (largely because of the oil glut and two years of bountiful harvests), revenues rose less rapidly than OMB had anticipated because people's incomes were not inflated into higher tax brackets at the anticipated rate. Expected increase in investment and productivity did not occur; in fact capital formation rates were at a ten-year low and the savings rate did not increase as expected because of the recession.

Other problems, however, were political. Congress did manage to make dramatic cuts in the current-services budget for domestic spending, but defense and entitlement programs such as Social Security were politically sacrosanct. Because of problems in cutting spending and concern for the projected deficit, the promised tax cuts were delayed and reduced by Congress, but the Federal Reserve's policy of monetary restraint was implemented almost immediately. The result, not surprisingly, was a serious recession. Strict supply-siders within the administration argued that deficits were only temporary and should not be a cause for concern; as former administration official Paul Craig Roberts noted, "the large tax increase, which the administration believes will lower interest rates by reducing the deficit, may actually keep them high."[40] But in light of Reagan's campaign promises, high inflation and fears of "crowding out" in financial markets, more traditional economic views prevailed. The soaring deficit became the major focus of attention.

Despite supply-side theory and Reagan's own rhetoric, the immediate solution appeared to be a tax increase. The planned income tax cuts were left untouched, and the variety of administrative reforms enacted instead included many (such as withholding of income from dividends and interest on savings) which had long been advocated by liberals. By the summer of 1982, President Reagan was forced to sign into law the Tax Act of 1982, which was intended to raise over $90 billion in revenues through administrative reforms, closing of loopholes such as the 1981 tax-leasing provisions, introduction of tax withholding on interest and dividend income, and increases in federal excise taxes. Economists of all persuasions worried that a tax increase during a recession, accompanied by tight money, could lead to a thirties-style depression. Unemployment soared and both the economy and the deficit became major issues in the 1982 elections. Reagan signaled a change after Republican losses in those elections by proposing higher federal gasoline taxes earmarked for highways. He signed a major Social Security tax increase and opposed attempts by banks and many in Congress to repeal withholding on interest income. An alternative solution, according to the *Wall Street Journal* and fiscal conservatives, was to cut taxes and government spending further. But that path is most unlikely to be chosen by any party in power—Democratic or Republican. Pressures for increased spending far exceed those for lower taxes, particularly when unemployment is high and the Soviet Union appears to be ahead in the arms race.

Shifts in income distribution have also been difficult for politicians to manage, whether by tax cuts or any other means. In the 1960s, higher-income groups paid larger amounts of revenues as a result of cuts in marginal tax rates.[41] But these same groups paid less after the Reagan policy changes, which some AFDC and Social Security recipients paid marginal tax rates as high as 100 percent.[42] A striking feature of the U.S. revenue system has been the stability of the tax burden and income distribution over time. Data from the U.S. Census indicates a shift of less than 1 percent in the share of income held by the highest and lowest quintiles over the period from 1947 to 1974.[43] Some moderate income redistribution occurred between 1932 and the end of World War II, but certainly not what Roosevelt's opponents would have been able to call a "soak the rich" policy. The measurement of trends in inequality is of course a difficult one conceptually and methodologically; if one considered non-money income or wealth, quite different distributions can be suggested.[44] But the lack of change in the distribution of money income indicates the limits of ability of any party or administration to shift tax burdens, despite its campaign rhetoric or its dominant economic theory. Horizontal inequality is so large, owing to the maze of tax loopholes and the complexities of tax administration, that vertical equity is difficult to obtain.[45]

We turn now to an estimate of the effects of these tax policy changes on revenues. The 1982 Reagan tax increase was the first peacetime tax increase since the ill-timed Depression measure of 1932 (likewise intended to balance the federal budget regardless of the condition of the economy). All other major peacetime changes in the income tax have been billed as tax cuts and were projected to *reduce* federal revenues, according to figures prepared by the Joint Committee on Internal Revenue Taxation (see Table 9-2).

Reality, however, has differed from those projections. The 1954 tax cut, under a Republican Congress, substantially reduced revenues from their Korean war highs, but revenue as a percentage of GNP rebounded by 1958. The 1964 tax cut reduced revenues by only 0.2

TABLE 9-2.   Estimated Revenue Changes in Major Postwar Revenue Acts

Revenue Act	Fiscal Year	Revenue Change ($ billions)*	Personal, Corporate Income Tax as % GNP	Total Revenue as % GNP
1954	1955	− .2	− 2.0	−2.7
1964	1964	− 7.3	− 1.3	−0.2
	1965	−11.3	− 0.8	−0.7
1969†	1969	+ 5.7	+ 2.7	+2.4
	1970	− .5	− 2.4	−0.5
1975†	1974	− 8.1	− 0.8	+1.0
	1975	−12.8	− 2.5	−0.4
1976	1977	−15.7	+12.3	+1.3
	1978	−11.7	+ 0.9	0.0
1978	1979	−19.3	+ 1.5	+0.7
	1980	−37.5	− 2.5	+0.5
1981	1982	−37.5	− 4.8	−0.4
	1983	−90.8	+ 0.7	−1.0

Source: Estimates of Joint Committee on Taxation following final passage.
*Includes rate schedule and bracket changes, general credits and surcharges, exemptions, low-income allowances, earned income credits and standard deduction.
†Calendar year estimates.

percent of GNP in its first year and 0.7 percent in its second. The 1968 Vietnam surcharge led to a modest and temporary increase, but the tax cuts of the 1970s had only a marginal impact on revenues as a percentage of GNP because of high inflation rates. Personal and corporate income taxes showed an *increase* as a percentage of total federal revenues in 1977, 1978 and 1979, despite tax cuts.

Even as far back as 1924, Treasury Secretary Andrew Mellon was urging cuts in the marginal rates on high incomes in order to reduce tax avoidance and increase revenues. The economic stimulus resulting in part from the Kennedy tax cuts of 1962 and 1964 did produce additional revenues, but subsequent tax cuts have barely offset the fiscal dividend arising from inflation. The 1964 tax cut was credited with a modest increase in inflation and real GNP growth (and thus in bracket creep and federal revenues) over the next three years.[46] Over half of the 1981 Economic Recovery Tax Act was expected to offset "bracket creep."

The 1964 example, however, does not mean that U.S. revenue policy can easily move up the Laffer curve—that cuts in tax rates will be self-financing in terms of revenue gains. An analysis of the relationship between tax rates and revenues in the U.S. for the period 1930 to 1980 shows, not a smooth curve, but a scattered pattern which

Martin Gardner dubbed the "technosnarl." Several different tax rates can produce the same amounts of revenues; there is no simple relationship.[47] None of the post-World War II tax cuts can be considered self-financing. As Keifer notes, "for a tax cut to increase federal revenues, rather than add to the deficit, it would have to increase GNP by a multiple of five times its original size or more. No analysis of fiscal policy in the U.S. economy has concluded that such a high multiplier for an overall tax cut is possible." Thus, despite any other beneficial effects, "one inevitable result of a tax cut with undiminished spending is an increase in the deficit."[48] In the same vein, the Office of Tax Analysis concluded that the tax rates would have had to be 70 times higher for the Kemp-Roth 30 percent tax cuts to be self-financing in terms of revenues.[49]

One major reason that tax cuts have not been self-financing is that cuts in individual or corporate income taxes have been accompanied by increases in other taxes, notably Social Security and federal excises. At least until 1979, Federal Reserve policies permitted expansion of the money supply and monetarization of the debt, which augmented inflation, increased bracket creep and thus enhanced revenues. The particular targets of tax cuts and their timing can make a big difference in results, as supply-siders who argued for higher cuts in marginal rates clearly recognize. Politically, however, it has been easier to pass across-the-board cuts.

The impact of tax cuts has been further confounded by adverse timing, and they have also been countered by a steady increase in state and local taxes, whose rates have risen faster than federal revenues since the 1950s. No institutional mechanism exists to coordinate state and federal fiscal policy; OMB and CBO have only occasionally made mention of state revenue trends in their forecasts. In the mid-1970s the Council of Economic Advisers did recommend a larger federal deficit to counter the deflationary impact of high state surpluses, but Reagan's official economic policy has taken no notice of the large increases in state taxes, borrowing and deficits resulting from cutbacks in federal aid and the 1981–82 recession.[50]

POLITICAL EFFECTS OF FEDERAL TAX CUTS

If tax cuts have not had the anticipated effects on the economy or on revenues, what has been their political impact? One short-term gain can be noted: a modest increase in presidential popularity in years when taxes are cut, even when other influences on trends in presidential support scores are considered.[51] But from the point of view of the presidency, most of the other implications are adverse and have tended to limit his scope of action in revenue policy. His role in this area has come more to resemble that of state governors than that of the "imperial presidency."

The proportion of the federal budget that is earmarked has increased. Earmarked taxes (including Social Security, airport construction and most recently the gasoline tax for highways) have risen, but this has reduced overall budgetary flexibility. Moreover, earmarked and regressive revenue sources are less elastic than are progressive income taxes and thus do not respond as readily to changing economic conditions. The utility of revenue as an instrument of fiscal policy is correspondingly reduced. Monetary policy has become increasingly important as a tool of macroeconomic policy, but this is even less subject to presidential discretion than is revenue policy. Since the 1974 reforms, Congress has played a larger role in budgetary matters; the expertise of the Congressional Budget Office can (and has) challenged revenue, expenditure and economic estimates emanating from OMB. Opportunities to use impoundment have been restricted. Although President Reagan has made some use of the budget reconciliation process to accomplish the objectives of impoundment,[52] presidents still lack a potent fiscal tool available to most American governors—the item veto. By accepting major cuts in one of his most powerful instruments of fiscal policy, the discretionary political power of the president has been diminished even as he is being held increasingly responsible by the voters for management of the economy.

Yet there has been no corresponding decrease in pressures to increase spending. State and local governments have joined PACs in pressing Washington for maintenance of budgetary allocations, if not increases in them. The portion of the budget going to transfer payments has risen from 18 percent in 1960 to close to 45 percent today, and persons receiving such benefits are not likely to be reticent in urging their continuation. Short of a supply-side miracle, unprecedented in earlier tax cuts, the prognosis can only be for continued deficits. It is no longer possible (if it ever was) to raise revenues by cutting taxes.

This discussion has stressed differences in points of view between the president and Congress. The conventional wisdom of American politics stresses the importance of constituency influence, the strong role of interest groups in legislation and the parochialism of Congress. As the phenomenal growth of the tax expenditure system illustrates, Congressmen seek special tax privileges for key district industries, local or regional interests and major campaign contributors. The effect of special loopholes, subsidies or exemptions on total revenues is of far less concern to them than their own electoral fortunes and the economic prosperity of their districts. It is therefore left to the executive branch, the president, and to some extent the majority party leadership to maintain sufficient revenues to meet spending demands without pushing levels of debt, borrowing or inflation above tolerable limits.

A study of revenue trends in the American states found that state governors were most likely to spearhead drives for expanded revenues and to initiate proposals for new taxes,[53] despite the not inconsiderable risk to themselves. Requests for new or increased taxes rarely if ever came from state legislators or interest groups (with the exception of public employees, notably teachers). At the federal level, the president has seldom been forced to spearhead drives for new taxes; the revenue-generating power of the progressive federal income tax has usually been sufficient to meet most contingencies short of financing a war. However, the president must contend with the proclivities of Congress to reduce tax rates and add yet more tax expenditures. If he is to have any discretionary revenues for his own policy priorities, if he is to control inflation, if borrowing is to be limited and foreign investment encouraged, the executive branch must constrain the hemorrhage of revenues.

To a considerable extent the president tries to do this through improved administration. The Department of the Treasury and the IRS have for years testified on Capitol Hill about the revenue loss due to tax expenditures, and are likely to oppose any additional ones (including those urged by the president himself). The IRS has argued for expansion of its own budget for enforcement and auditing. On a comparative basis the U.S., with its self-reporting income tax system, spends less per capita on tax administration ($1.50 per $100 in tax dollars collected compared to more than $5 in Germany).[54] Nevertheless, the auditing expenses of the IRS more than pay for themselves, bringing in $180 in additional revenues for each $100 spent for auditors. Although the Reagan administration cut the IRS budget as part of its general reduction in government expenditures for fiscal 1982, it moved to restore those funds in subsequent years.

With regard to Social Security, Congressmen deal with many requests from constituents and are disposed to be sympathetic. The Social Security Administration, on the other hand, has tightened eligibility requirements, cut Medicaid funds to states whose rate of erroneous payments exceeded federal guidelines, and has been re-checking disability qualifications.

The 1983 debate over withholding of taxes on interest and divi-dend income is likewise instructive. This provision had been ad-vocated for years by the IRS and tax-reform groups, and was included by a close vote in the August 1982 tax cut. Banking interests, how-ever, were vehemently opposed, and generated a massive letter-writing campaign. They had strong support in Congress, but the Republican party leadership, which had been instrumental in passage of the 1982 tax increase, held firm. President Reagan threatened to veto a bill which included withholding repeal and vigorously de-nounced the "selfishness" of the banking industry in a March 1983 speech. Even though withholding has been estimated to add $4 to $6 billion a year to federal revenues, Congress repealed the withholding provision in August 1983 with a vote strong enough to override a veto.

During the 1980 election campaign, George Bush accused Reagan of advocating "voodoo economics" when he promised to cut taxes, balance the federal budget and increase defense spending simulta-neously. But Reagan is not the first president to find that promises made in the heat of campaigns, however appealing ideologically, are difficult to keep. Such promises create further problems by support-ing the cherished hope of many voters that we can have something for nothing and can enjoy the benefits of public goods without paying for them. Presidential administrations can be evaluated in part by how fast they learn that they cannot provide a "free lunch," and that they will either have to raise revenues or cut politically popular pro-grams in order to pursue their own priorities. Even if a president learns this hard lesson fairly quickly (as Reagan seemed to do by his second year in office), he must confront the resulting decline in sup-port from the public and from his own party; his second-term chances may suffer accordingly. The net result is a loss of political capital and an increase in public cynicism: the political bankruptcy of the "wel-fare state" so ably described by Rose and Peters.[55] But a campaign to raise taxes and maintain revenues is not likely to be politically viable unless threats of war or serious economic difficulties can be made credible. The prognosis is for a continuation of fiscal illusion, inflation and deficit finance, unless a major reform such as a balanced-budget amendment can be adopted. It remains to be seen whether the cure would be worse than the disease.

This analysis should not be construed as an argument against cuts in the federal income tax. The system as it has evolved contains many inequities, and its very complexity imposes considerable excess burden on corporations and individuals. Both liberals and conservatives have mounted worthy arguments for reform, including cuts in both rates and coverage. But presidents should be forewarned that the results they anticipate may not be those they get. Tax cuts are no panacea for hard questions of budgetary priorities and fiscal management.

NOTES

1. The more influential the petroleum refining industry in a state's economy, the less likely that motor fuel taxes would be imposed; if they were imposed, they were earmarked for highway construction. See Lester Salamon and John Siegfried, "Economic Power and Political Influence: The Impact of Industry Structure on Public Policy," *American Political Science Review* 71 (September 1977), pp. 1026–43.

2. See discussions by Lance Leloup, *Budgetary Politics* (Brunswick, Ohio: Kings Court, 1977), pp. 52 ff., and Ira Sharkansky, *The Politics of Taxing and Spending* (Indianapolis: Bobbs-Merrill, 1969), pp. 83ff.

3. John Kingdon, *Congressmen's Voting Decisions* (New York: Harper & Row, 1973), p. 175.

4. *Chicago Tribune* (July 1, 1969), p. 1.

5. For a fuller discussion of politicians' goals and strategies, and of why ideology is such a poor predictor thereof, see Susan B. Hansen, *The Politics of Taxation* (New York: Praeger, 1983), Chapters 3 and 4.

6. *Washington Post* (August 8, 1982), p. C8.

7. Geoffrey Brennan and James M. Buchanan, *The Power to Tax: Analytical Foundations of a Fiscal Constitution* (New York: Cambridge University Press, 1980), p. 29.

8. See discussion of the 1978 tax revolt in historical context in Robert Kuttner, *Revolt of the Haves: Tax Rebellions and Hard Times* (New York: Simon & Schuster, 1980).

9. On nineteenth-century partisanship, see David W. Brady, *Congressional Voting in a Partisan Era* (Lawrence: Kansas University Press, 1973).

10. See George F. Break and Joseph Pechman, *Federal Tax Reform: The Impossible Dream?* (Washington, D.C.: The Brookings Institution, 1975), pp. 36–43, for discussion of inflation and indexing proposals.

11. Testimony by Alice Rivlin, Director of CBO, before the U.S. Senate Budget Committee, November 24, 1981 hearings on "Tax Expenditure Limitation and Control Act of 1981."

12. Figures on the deficit as a percentage of GNP from the *Budget of the United States Government, Fiscal Year 1983* (Washington, D.C.: U.S. Government Printing Office), Table 21, pp. 9–60.

13. Joseph Van Wagstaff, "Income Tax Consciousness Under Withholding," *Southern Economic Journal* 32 (1965), pp. 73–80.

14. Charles R. Hulten and June A. O'Neill, "Tax Policy," in John L. Palmer and Isabel V. Sawhill, eds., *The Reagan Experiment* (Washington, D.C.: The Urban Institute, 1982), pp. 101–102.

15. Historical and projected data from Council of Economic Advisers, *Economic Report of the President, 1982*, Tables B-69, B-72. See Hulten and O'Neill, "Tax Policy," pp. 104–111, on changes in corporation taxes.

16. Andrew Tobias, "How to Fix Social Security," *Parade* (October 31, 1982), p. 12.

17. James Douglas, "Was Reagan's Victory a Watershed in American Politics?" *Political Quarterly* 52 (1981), pp. 171–183.

18. Walter Dean Burnham, *Critical Elections and the Mainsprings of American Politics* (New York: Norton, 1970), pp. 110ff.

19. John F. Manley, *The Politics of Finance: The House Committee on Ways and Means* (Boston: Little, Brown, 1970).

20. For detailed history of the politics of the Vietnam surcharge, see Lawrence Pierce, *The Politics of Fiscal Policy Formation* (Pacific Palisades, Cal.: Goodyear, 1971).

21. Harold Kenski, "Partisanship and Ideology in the Revenue Act of 1978," in Warren J. Samuels and Larry Wade, eds., *Taxing and Spending Policy* (Lexington, Mass.: D. C. Heath, 1980).

22. Ronald F. King, "From Redistributive to Hegemonic Logic: The Transformation of American Tax Politics 1893–1954," *Politics and Society*, 1983.

23. Barbara Deckard Sinclair, "Party Realignment and the Transformation of the Political Agenda in the House of Representatives, 1925–1938," *American Political Science Review* 71 (September 1977), pp. 940–953; Edwin E. Witte, *Development of the Social Security Act* (Madison: University of Wisconsin Press, 1962).

24. Thomas J. Reese, *The Politics of Taxation* (Westport, Conn.: Quorum Books, 1980), pp. 135–42, finds partisan votes on half the tax bills since 1947, most since the expansion of Ways and Means after 1974.

25. Herbert Stein, "What Happened to the Supply Side?" *AEI Economist* (September 1982), p. 4.

26. See Hansen, *Politics of Taxation*, Chapter 4, for analysis of the revenue impact of changes in budgetary and administrative procedures in the IRS.

27. James Buchanan and Richard E. Wagner, *Democracy in Deficit: The Political Legacy of Lord Keynes* (New York: Academic Press, 1977), p. 4.

28. Herbert Stein, *The Fiscal Revolution in America* (Chicago: University of Chicago Press, 1968), offers an excellent historical account of changes from Hoover to Johnson.

29. King, "Hegemonic Logic," James Sundquist, *Politics and Policy* (Washington, D.C.: The Brookings Institution, 1968), 3–56.

30. For changing views on Keynes, see Robert Skidelsky, ed., *The End of the Keynesian Era* (New York: Penguin Books, 1980).

31. For a summary of basic ideas, see Jude Wanniski, "Taxes, Revenues, and the Laffer Curve," *Public Interest* (Winter 1978); pp. 3–16; and Richard H. Fink, ed., *Supply-Side Economics: A Critical Appraisal* (Frederick, Md.: University Publications of America, 1982).

32. See Committee on the Budget, U.S. House of Representatives, analysis of "President Reagan's Fiscal Year 1983 Budget" (Washington, D.C.: U.S. Government Printing Office, 1982), p. 27.

33. Stein, *Fiscal Revolution*, p. 105.

34. Donald W. Keifer, "A Review of Research on the Economic Effects of the 1964 Tax Cut, the 1968 Surtax, and the 1975 Tax Cut" (Washington, D.C.: Congressional Research Service, July 1980), p. 6.

35. William Grieder, "The Education of David Stockman," *Atlantic Monthly* 248 (December 1981), pp. 27–54.

36. *Newsweek* (August 30, 1982), p. 76.

37. The following paragraphs are drawn from Keifer, "Economic Effects," pp. 12 ff.

38. A good current account is Thomas Reese, *The Politics of Taxation.*

39. On international economic trends in post-industrial societies, see Roger Benjamin, *The Limits of Politics* (Chicago: University of Chicago Press, 1980); and David H. Blake and Robert S. Walters, *The Politics of Global Economic Relations* (Englewood Cliffs, N.J.: Prentice-Hall, 1983).

40. Paul C. Roberts, "The Stockman Recession," *Fortune*, February 22, 1982, p. 70.

41. Bruce R. Bartlett, "The Kennedy Tax Cuts," pp. 276–285, in Fink, *Supply-Side Economics.*

42. Joseph Pechman et al., *Setting National Priorities: The 1983 Budget* (Washington, D.C.: The Brookings Institution, 1982), p. 111.

43. See Michael K. Taussig and Sheldon Danziger, "Conference on the Trend in Income Inequality in the U.S." (Madison: University of Wisconsin Institute for Research on Poverty, 1976), pp. 4–16, for basic census data and critical discussion of alternative interpretations. See also dis-

cussion by John Witte, "Incremental Theory and Tax Policy," paper presented at the annual meeting of the American Political Science Association, Denver, 1982

44. Timothy M. Smeeding, "The Anti-Poverty Effects of In-Kind Transfers," *Policy Studies Journal* 10 (March 1982), pp. 499–521.

45. See discussion in Break and Pechman, *Federal Tax Reform*, pp. 16–18.

46. Keifer, "Review of Research," p. 45.

47. Martin Gardner, "The Laffer Curve and Other Laughs in Current Economics," *Scientific American* 245 (December 1981), pp. 18–31.

48. Donald W. Keifer, "An Economic Analysis of the Kemp/Roth Tax Cut Bill," (Washington, D.C.: *Congressional Research Service*, July 1978), pp. 45–46.

49. Don Fullerton, "Can Tax Revenues Go Up When Tax Rates Go Down?" U.S. Department of the Treasury, Office of Tax Analysis Paper 41, September 1980.

50. For further discussion of fiscal federalism and tax policy, see Susan B. Hansen, "Fiscal Federalism and Fiscal Crisis," paper presented at the European Consortium for Political Research, Salzburg, April 1984.

51. For detailed analysis of the Gallup Poll time-series, see Susan B. Hansen and John M. Carroll, "Public Opinion and Tax Policy, 1947–1976," paper presented at the annual meeting of the American Political Science Association, Chicago, 1978.

52. Allen Schick, *Reconciliation and the Budgetary Process* (Washington, D.C.: American Enterprise Institute, 1981), pp. 38–39.

53. Richard Bingham et al., *The Politics of Raising State and Local Revenue* (New York: Praeger, 1978), pp. 203 ff.

54. Arnold Heidenheimer, Hugh Heclo and Carolyn T. Adams, *Comparative Public Policy* (New York: St. Martin's, 1975), p. 235.

55. Richard Rose and Guy Peters, *Can Governments Go Bankrupt?* (New York: Basic Books, 1978).

4

MONETARY POLICY & THE FEDERAL RESERVE

Monetary Policy and Monetary Theory: The Poverty of Choice

ALBERTA SBRAGIA

One of the less considered limitations on economic policymaking is intellectual—the lack of choice in basic strategies. At any time a few ideas may be in fashion, but the number of those out of fashion—the alternatives—is equally small. Even if a chief executive *wants* to make a radical change of course, his or her boldness is unlikely to be rewarded by a flood of exciting, untried ideas. The similarity between the policies of President Reagan and those of Britain's Prime Minister Thatcher stems partly from an intellectual poverty which stretches across the spectrum of states and ideologies. Even newly established governments, such as those of Zimbabwe and Nicaragua, find their choices limited conceptually as well as politically. The global "intellectual inventory" for economic policy is thinly stocked. Choice may be polarized, with little between the poles, and even if policymakers enjoy the latitude bestowed by a large electoral victory, they cannot readily convert this advantage into a corresponding strategic discretion. Usually the choice is one between tinkering with existing policy and plumping for the sole competing "grand strategy." This is not to say that the outcomes will be similar whatever is tried, but only that the initial choice is constricted.

The focus of this chapter is on the limitations imposed by lack of conceptual choice, not on constraints of a political and institutional

219

kind. The latter are, of course, important and numerous, originating from interest groups, Congress, the president, the Federal Reserve System and elsewhere. But the main purpose of this discussion is to suggest ways in which the assumptions and concepts of economists have influenced and channeled thinking about one type of economic policy—monetary policy.

Monetary policy, in fact, provides a good example of the limitation of political choice by intellectual poverty. It is all the better as an example (and all the worse as a dilemma) in view of the importance of monetary policy in determining the direction and success of other aspects of public policy. Even when the president and the Federal Reserve disagree about policy, their disagreement occurs within an intellectually confined space, neither side having many alternatives upon which it can draw. Indeed there are only two basic alternatives at present: a "money supply approach" and an "interest rate strategy." All others currently conceived involve some combination of these two.

The main reason for the narrowness of choice is the lack of theory in monetary economics. This deficiency bears on policymaking in an unusually direct manner because the political community itself finds monetary policy an intimidating subject. Monetary policy resembles a mountainous island, difficult of access, known to few and inhabited by people speaking an arcane and fiercely complicated language. Experts—in this case economists—have exceptional influence over the inhabitants, for they are the major shapers of the intellectual paradigms within which monetary policy options are conceived.

Such privileged access has not been limited to the field of monetary policy. As James Q. Wilson has pointed out, intellectuals exercised a similar monopoly over social policy in the 1960s:

> Intellectuals provided the conceptual language, the ruling paradigms, the empirical examples (note that I say *examples*, not evidence) that became the accepted assumptions for those in charge of making policy. Intellectuals framed, and to a large degree conducted, the debates about whether this language and these paradigms were correct.[1]

Similarly, in the 1970s, arguments between economists about the value of alternative paradigms shaped debates about monetary policy. The trouble is that the monetary economists have had only two such paradigms to communicate—hence the problems of policymaking.

MONETARY POLICY: AN OVERVIEW

Monetary policy is "the process whereby the monetary authority attempts to achieve a desired set of economic goals by controlling either the money supply, the cost and availability of credit, or the allocation of credit to its various uses."[2] It is public policy concerned with interest rates, the creation of money and credit generally. Usually the goals which monetary policy has tried to reach are price stability, high employment, economic growth and the management of exchange rates.

Institutional Organization

Monetary policy in the U.S. is the province of the Federal Reserve System. The Fed, as this system is commonly called, consists of 12 regional Federal Reserve banks which are under the jurisdiction of a seven-member Board of Governors. The members of the board, which is the main policymaking body within the system, are appointed by the president and approved by the Senate for 14-year staggered terms; the chairman of the Board, however, is appointed by the president for a four-year term. The president of each regional reserve bank is elected by the bank's nine-member Board of Directors (three members of which, including the chairman, are appointed by the Board of Governors) and is then approved by the Board of Governors.

Federal Reserve banks differ from ordinary banks in that they earn money primarily by holding U.S. Treasury debt rather than by loaning out money as ordinary banks do. The only loans Federal Reserve banks make are to the commercial banks which are members of the system. Moreover, Federal Reserve banks are owned by those commercial banks which are members of the Federal Reserve system.

The Federal Reserve System, then, is a mixture of public and private control. It is a privately owned system, but the President of the United States, through his appointments to the Board of Governors (particularly his appointment of the Chairman of the Board) and that Board's influence on the various regional banks, exercises considerable (although usually indirect) public control.

Policy Implementation

The Federal Reserve influences the country's monetary system by increasing or decreasing the *reserves* (ready cash and deposits with the

Federal Reserve System) of member banks. Reserves are important because they determine how much money the banking system can lend, and the more money the system lends, the more money has been created. It is important to remember how the banking system creates money: your bank, for example, lends out most of the money you have deposited with it, money which is then redeposited in the borrower's checking account, the process continuing through several cycles. Those borrowers have money they did not have before. Banks do not create money by printing it; they merely change balance sheets. Because the banking system creates money, and because the level of reserves largely determines how much money can be created, *monetary policy is focused on increasing or decreasing reserves.*

Instruments

The Federal Reserve has three major instruments by which it affects the monetary system. The most rarely used one involves changing the legally required ratio of cash reserves to deposits in the bank. Commercial banks which are members of the Federal Reserve System are required to keep a certain proportion of the money deposited with them in "reserve" rather than lending it out; most of such required reserves are deposited in the banks' reserve accounts at the appropriate Federal Reserve bank. If the Fed increases the reserve requirement, banks must put a higher proportion of their deposits into their reserve account which in turn limits their lending. In this case the money supply would contract; the reverse also holds.

The second instrument available to the Fed is the setting of the discount rate—the rate at which a member bank can borrow from its Federal Reserve bank. The Fed considers borrowing from it a privilege and not a right, and member banks, in order not to be seen as abusing that privilege, will often borrow from each other (in what is known as the "federal funds market") rather than from their Federal Reserve bank's "discount window." Changes in the discount rate are thought to indicate whether the Fed is tightening or loosening its policy—that is, whether it is trying to add to or subtract from the money in the monetary system.

The most important of the Fed's three instruments is known as open-market operations. These involve either the purchase or the sale of U.S. securities (bills, certificates, notes and bonds). When the Fed buys such securities, the reserves of member banks increase, since the Fed is putting money into the monetary system; when it sells securities, reserves decrease. When a bank's reserves increase, as mentioned, it can loan out more money; when reserves decline, it can lend less money. In the first instance, the money supply will grow, while in the latter it will decline.

If we take a closer look at open-market operations, we quickly see how and why they are so important:

> The actual buying and selling of securities is conducted at the New York Fed under the direction of the account manager. All of the system's transactions are with a set of 25 approved dealers in government securities, all of whom are located in New York. When the manager of the Open Market Account buys securities from a dealer, he pays for them by crediting the reserve account of the commercial bank which serves as the dealer's agent. The bank in turn credits the demand deposit account of the dealer. Member bank reserves rise by the amount of the purchase. By this simple act of changing the ownership of government securities between private corporations (the securities dealers) and the Federal Reserve System, the Fed can quickly and easily engineer whatever changes in the supply of reserves it desires. It is a powerful weapon: the System has the power to acquire whatever volume of government securities it wishes simply by *creating* member bank reserves.[3]

The Federal Reserve does not create money by operating the printing presses; it simply changes balance sheets. If we remember that an increase in banking reserves increases the amount of money that banks can lend, we see how affecting bank reserves through open-market operations affects banks' lending activities and therefore the creation of money.

Since the most important policy instrument by which the Fed affects bank reserves is open-market operations, the committee within the Fed that handles that activity is the most important of its various committees. Known as the Federal Open Market Committee (FOMC), its members include the seven members of the Board of Governors and five of the twelve presidents of the regional banks. The chairman of the Board is also the chairman of the FOMC, and he is therefore the single most important figure in the system. The vice-chairman of the FOMC is always the president of the Federal Reserve Bank of New York, so that the other four seats are rotated annually among the eleven other Federal Reserve bank presidents. All of the regional bank presidents usually attend FOMC meetings, but only the five official members are allowed to vote.

MONETARY POLICY IN
THE ERA OF CONSENSUS

From the 1950s until the mid-1960s, Keynesian economic theory held undisputed sway over most experts concerned with credit. Such theory was preoccupied with interest rates, for interest rates were seen as an extremely important and as perhaps the primary channel for transmitting monetary policy to the banking system.[4] Policymakers therefore assumed that interest rates should be the focus of attention, and the basic question as defined by the president and the Federal Reserve was how best to keep interest rates at a level which maximized employment and achieved an equilibrium in the balance of payments. The question of controlling the money supply was not seen as relevant (at least in the short-term), and debate focused on whether long-term or short-term interest rates should be controlled by the Federal Reserve.

The debate therefore centered on techniques. In concrete terms, should the Fed *directly* influence only short-term markets (those markets in which debt instruments maturing in less than a year are bought and sold), or should it also intervene in long-term markets (those dealing with securities with maturities of over a year)? From 1953 until early 1961, those who favored intervention only in the short-term markets prevailed; the so-called bills-only policy was established. The policy's proponents argued that the Fed, through its open-market operations, should influence banking reserves by buying and selling only short-term securities and should not buy and sell securities maturing in over a year. As the Commission on Money and Credit reported in 1961:

> The argument advanced in support of the bills-only policy is that it minimized the *direct* influence of open market operations on the structure or pattern of interest rates without sacrificing any of the total impact of these variables . . . Investors and dealers in Treasury securities are thus assured that "free market forces" will determine the structure of security prices and this, in turn, will prove the 'breadth, depth, and resiliency' of the market.[5]

Critics challenged the bills-only policy, for they thought it reduced the potential effectiveness of the Federal Reserve. They questioned the idea that the impact of the Fed's intervention in the short-term securities market (also known as the money market) spread quickly and completely to markets concerned with longer-term securities. At the beginning of the 1960s, the critics won, and the bills-only policy was effectively dropped. Although there was controversy during this period over what the Federal Reserve should do, for our purposes it is important to note that the debate was exclusively concerned with various issues related to interest rates. This focus on interest rates was accepted by most monetary economists.

Most, but not all. A few academic economists, Milton Friedman prominent among them, were busy refurbishing and revising the "quantity theory of money." Their theories and lines of argument did not immediately affect American policymakers, but it was perhaps inevitable that the "monetarists" would become a force to be reckoned with.

Manipulating interest rates did not seem to dampen inflation, and the policy climate became ever more receptive to new approaches. However, there were no approaches to consider—rather there was only one relatively well-worked-out and argued new approach. That approach was monetarism. As the theoretical challenger to Keynesian monetary policy, monetarism did not instantly dissipate the Keynesian preoccupation with interest rates. Milton Friedman, for one, did not expect to be listened to even in the medium term. Writing in 1964, he clearly understood the intellectual sociology of economic policymaking:

> There is almost invariably a long cultural lag before developments in theory manifest themselves in policy . . . The policy proposals that are being made in the U.S. today are all reflections of the ideas of the late 1930s or at the latest of the early 1940s. That is natural and widespread. The people who make policy, who are involved in policy formation, are inevitably people who got their training and their education and their attitudes some 20 or more years earlier . . . I expect that monetary policy will in the course of the next 20 years show some radical changes as a result of the changes I have described in monetary theory.[6]

As it turned out, Friedman was too pessimistic about his own influence, for the monetarists were going to have a significant influence on monetary policy within only 15 years of this statement.

MONETARISTS VS. KEYNESIANS

Monetarist theorists in the 1950s and early 1960s often saw themselves as besieged on all sides by economists who simply rejected the notion that the quantity of money had any significant impact on aggregate demand and inflation. Philip Cagan expressed this feeling of isolation well:

> No one who was not in touch with the economics profession in the 1940s and early 1950s can quite imagine the state of thinking then in the profession at large on monetary theory and policy. The quantity of money was not considered important, indeed was hardly worth mentioning, for questions of aggregate demand, unemployment, and even inflation. Peruse the journals of that period! . . . textual discussions of theory and policy in article after article hardly mentioned the quantity of money at all. Textbooks in basic economics and even in money and banking mentioned the quantity theory of money, if at all, only to hold it up to ridicule. If you traveled among the profession at large, mention of the quantity of money elicited puzzled glances of disbelief or sly smiles of condescension.
>
> Monetarism is a reaction to that earlier inhospitable environment. Indeed, if there had not been a time when most of the profession said 'money does not matter,' it would never have occurred to anyone to say 'money does matter.'[7]

That feeling of isolation intensified their sense of belonging to the "monetarist school"—a group set apart from mainstream economies.

Although there is a great deal of debate within the monetarist school, there are certain ideas which identify an economist as a monetarist rather than as a Keynesian. Such ideas are inspired by the core idea that "money matters"—that is, that changes in the money stock affect economic activity, including inflation. To quote Cagan again:

> Monetarism has gained such attention that its opponents have feared that it might sweep away everything else. They have raised the spectre that monetarists claim that 'only money matters.' That was never claimed. What the opponents mistook for such a claim, perhaps, was the lesser one implied by some monetarists' writing that, among the list of influences on aggregate demand, money should stand at the top.[8]

Karl Brunner, one of the major figures associated with the monetarist group, in a widely cited article characterized monetarist theoretical work as concluding that:

> First, monetary impulses are a major factor accounting for variation in output, employment, and prices. Second, movements in the money stock are the most reliable measure of the thrust of monetary impulses. Third, the behavior of the monetary authorities dominates movements of the money stock over business cycles.[9]

By contrast, Keynesian economists see the money stock as having, at most, only a weak influence on economic activity, inflation included. Monetary policy for them is therefore much less important overall than fiscal policy. When Keynesians do analyze monetary policy, they tend to emphasize interest rates as the important target of the policy. For them long-term interest rates are crucial, but they use short-term rates (which are more directly under the Fed's control) as indicators of the impact of Fed policy.

Monetarists, on the other hand, are not concerned with interest rates. They focus on the money stock—the growth in the money supply, as indicated for example by bank reserves—as that which must be steadily controlled. Thus Keynesians argue that the Fed should pursue an "interest rate strategy," while monetarists view the Fed's role as one of controlling various *monetary aggregates.* Monetary aggregates, simply put, "are various measures of the nation's stock of money."[10] Since money can be measured differently, each aggregate measures one type of money.

Thus, as the monetarists gained prominence, so too did the general notion of the "money supply," as measured by monetary aggregates. But since no consensus exists on what money or the money stock is, the Federal Reserve has had to define, and as conditions changed redefine, various monetary aggregates which it thought would be useful in formulating and implementing monetary policy. Each aggregate is indicated by the letter M and a number; the higher the number, the broader the definition of money being measured by that aggregate. As of February 1982, M1 was a basic measurement of cash in circulation and deposits in all types of checking accounts, whether they pay interest or not; M2 consisted of M1 plus savings deposits under $190,000, most money market funds and some bank borrowings; and M3 consisted of M2 plus large negotiable certificates of deposit issued by banks, institutional money market funds and certain types of bank borrowings. M1 was the most widely discussed figure, as it measured money intended for spending and not saving.[11]

Various other positions distinguish the Keynesians from the monetarists. Keynesians worry about the costs associated with unemployment, while monetarists emphasize the perils of inflation. Monetarists tend to dislike government intervention, for they view the private sector as inherently stable, whereas Keynesians are much more interventionist. Monetarists tend to accept a much smaller discretionary role for the Fed (arguing for relatively stable or even fixed money supply growth) than that favored by Keynesians. Monetarists tend to stress, and Keynesians to ignore or reject, the "crowding-out effect"—the notion that if government finances a budget deficit by borrowing from the public rather than by expanding the money supply, private sector investment will decline because private borrowers will be "crowded out" of the financial markets.[12]

Policy Implications

What are the broad policy implications of stressing monetary aggregates rather than interest rates? Does it make a difference if monetarists rather than Keynesians dominate monetary policy, and if so to whom?

One of the main differences is that Keynesians are more likely to be concerned with the impact of interest rate changes on specific sectors, such as housing. This concern grows out of an important distinction between monetarists and Keynesians. As Thomas L. Mayer put it,

> One of the points of distinction between the monetarists and the Keynesians is that in trying to determine short-run changes in income the Keynesian, unlike the monetarist, typically focuses on what happens in particular sectors of the economy. For example, a rise in the interest rate may have different effects on residential construction, and hence on total output, at a time when mortgage lending institutions are already short of liquidity than at a time when they have a large liquidity buffer. More fundamentally, the Keynesian predicts, or explains, income by looking at expenditure motives in each sector. Hence, he has to analyze each sector.

> By contrast, in explaining short-run changes in income, the monetarist usually expresses little interest in allocative detail. His belief in the stability of the private sector and the absence of a need for government intervention gives the monetarist little incentive to focus his attention on developments in various sectors.[13]

Although it is not suggested here that a direct causal relationship exists between the Keynesians' more sectoral concern and government credit programs, it is interesting that as the monetarists made inroads at the Fed and interest rates became higher and more volatile, the sectoral approach was enshrined in federal credit policies. Some sectors of the economy seem to have been protected from the monetarists by federal credit programs. Between 1977 and 1981, loans and guaranteed loans climbed from $71.6 billion to roughly $147 billion, and loans outstanding rose from $315 billion to roughly $624 billion in 1981.[14] Although there were many political reasons for the growth in federal credit programs (which are usually "off-budget" and not subject to much public or congressional scrutiny), the idea that government has a right to intervene in the interest rates of various sectors is given theoretical legitimacy by many Keynesian economists. Monetarists, on the other hand, are much more likely to be critical of such programs.

Thus Keynesian monetary policy is much more sensitive to the impact of the level and volatility of interest rates on housing, utilities, state and local borrowers and pension funds than are monetarists, who focus on the money supply and do not worry about the impact of policy aimed at controlling the money supply on the level and volatility of rates.

MONETARY POLICY IN TRANSITION

In the 1950s and 1960s, Keynesian thought dominated monetary policy: interest rates were the central focus. Accordingly, only a very few monetary aggregates, the symbols of monetarism, were used.[15] Attention was focused instead on the "federal funds" rate, the rate at which banks lend money to one another. That rate was seen as the indicator which most accurately reflected the impact of Federal Reserve decisions aimed at controlling interest rates.

The Fed's actions during this period were designed to keep interest rates stable and low; they passively accommodated the demand for money and credit. The "accommodative" policy of the 1960s meant that

> increases in interest rates caused by higher borrowing demands would result in the Federal Reserve's increasing bank reserves. The borrower would then be determining growth in both bank reserves and bank deposits. *This would then permit the money supply to grow in a manner desired by the users of money.* Under these conditions, it was difficult to argue that Federal Reserve monetary policy was really an exogenous policy, i.e., external to forces operating in the economy.[16]

As the inflation rate kept climbing in the late sixties and into the seventies, however, the Federal Reserve gradually came to feel that it had to try something different. "Accommodation" was obviously not being effective in keeping inflation down. Such ineffectiveness was not surprising. It may well be that controlling interest rates would have been sufficient if the Fed had been willing to increase interest rates more sharply and more quickly than it did. However, both political reasons and the Keynesian concern with the impact of high interest rates on various sectors discouraged the Board of Governors from making large changes. Looking back at that period, Frank Morris, president of the Federal Reserve Bank of Boston, summarized well the Fed's dilemma:

> Given . . . the awareness of FOMC members of the impact that sharp interest rate changes have on both the domestic and foreign economies, there was a systematic tendency on the part of the committee to raise (or lower) interest rates in smaller increments than the situation required. The action taken was frequently too little and too late and, as a consequence, monetary policy was frequently more procyclical in character than any Committee member would have thought appropriate.[17]

Changing interest rates significantly, especially when the curve was upward, was in fact consistently problematic for the Fed. Although the Fed is not usually subject to direct congressional intervention or oversight and although it does have a certain detachment from the president, it is nonetheless operating in a democratic society where the potential always exists for more direct intervention by elected officials. It has to be sensitive to criticism and increases in interest rates lead inevitably to protests, especially from interest-rate-sensitive sectors such as the housing industry. Moreover, because of these anticipated protests, it was difficult to develop a widespread consensus within the Fed in favor of sharp increases in rates. The Fed does not usually take action in the absence of consensus, for it feels it would be making itself vulnerable.[18] Interest rates, therefore, tended to be adjusted only cautiously. This caution helped keep the Fed united, silenced criticism for the time being (until inflation began to climb), and helped ensure that the U.S. Treasury was able without undue cost to find investors willing to buy its debt.

The Federal Reserve's policy in the late 1960s, however, began to be seen as ineffective in controlling inflation. The concern with inflation gradually made the Fed more receptive to a less accommodating policy than it had chosen previously. At the beginning of 1970, therefore, the FOMC began placing more emphasis on monetary aggregates. In other words, in making decisions about open market operations, it analyzed what was happening to the monetary aggregates as well as what was happening to the federal funds rate.[19] By 1972, that focus became more pronounced. Nonetheless, the Federal Reserve still kept a very watchful eye on interest rates, so much so that many monetarists accused the Fed of paying only lip service to controlling money supply growth.[20]

It was not until October 1979 that the Federal Reserve officially affirmed that it would now emphasize the quantity of bank reserves—treated as an indicator of the money stock—rather than interest rates. The "money supply approach" had been adopted. However, interest rates were still followed with some interest.[21] By 1981, however, interest rates had diminished still further in importance: the Fed now was aggressively trying to control the money supply regardless of what impact its policies had on interest rates. At that point interest rates became increasingly volatile.[22]

The focus on monetary aggregates allowed FOMC members to accept a volatility in rates they would have found inconceivable under the "interest rate strategy." They were able to accept such fluctuations because the focus on aggregates allowed them to avoid explicitly changing rates; they merely accepted the consequences for interest rates of controlling the monetary aggregates. As the president of the Federal Reserve Bank of Boston put it, "it has proven much easier for the FOMC to agree on a monetary growth path and to accept the interest rate consequence of that path than it has for the Committee to make explicit decisions to change interest rates to the extent required."[23]

By 1982 the "interest rate" strategy had very few important supporters. Even a prominent critic of the way monetary aggregates were used and defined said that there was "no support within the FOMC and very little outside of it to return to the pre-October 1979 practice of . . . controlling the federal funds rate."[24]

MONETARISM'S SHORT LIFE

In late 1979, the Federal Reserve adopted an explicitly monetarist position. Monetarist theorists occupied center ring; scholars such as Milton Friedman and Allan Meltzer became household names in economic circles. Monetarism seemed to be well on the way to becoming established public policy. Clouds, however, soon appeared. As early as one year after the adoption of a focus on monetary aggregates, John Davenport, writing in *Fortune,* could state that "oddly enough, the people who attach so much importance to the Fed's statistics do not agree on what they mean. There are disputes about which figures are the truly significant ones and confusions about the yo-yo performance that some of them put on."[25] Monetarists were already criticizing the way the Fed was implementing "their" theory as well as debating with one another as to how the Fed should be implementing monetarist theory. It soon became clear that there was not an overwhelming consensus within the monetarist camp when it came to applying the theory to the complex financial world.

New monetary aggregates were defined, measured and reported as the Federal Reserve gradually came to realize how complex controlling the money supply actually is. By late 1980, the complexity was already clear:

> . . . all efforts to monitor the process of money creation are now running into our multiplying confusions about which indicators to watch. Money is fungible and protean, and the form it takes is endlessly influenced by the inventiveness of bankers. With the rise of NOW accounts (the customer can write a check against his savings balance) and automatic transfer accounts (money moves back and forth between savings and checking accounts), the definitions used [previously] had to be discarded. If you read the financial columns, you now see an array of new classifications including not only 1-B, which gets the most attention, but also M1-A (basically, currency and demand deposits), M2 (currency, all checkable deposits, savings certificates and money market mutual funds), and M3 (M2 plus large certificates of deposit and certain other temporary deposits).[26]

By 1982, money had changed its shape once again and the use of M1-A and M1-B was discarded. The aggregates were once again redefined; the Fed was desperately trying to figure out, in other words, how to measure the money supply so as to know whether it was controlling it.

The monetarist strategy at the Fed resulted in extremely high interest rates, especially in 1981 and part of 1982. The prime rate in mid-1981 rose as high as 20 percent. The money supply aggregates also fluctuated, sometimes widely. As the inflation rate fell, interest rates failed to follow suit, and many critics argued that such high rates would abort any potential for economic recovery. The theory came under increasingly heavy fire as the unemployment rate rose and bankruptcies spread.

The monetarists, on the other hand, argued that the problem was not with their theory, but with how the Fed had implemented it. They argued that it was the variability of money growth that had kept interest rates high, and that if the Fed would only adopt certain technical procedures so as to be able to control money supply more effectively, interest rates would fall. The financial markets would not suffer the high degree of uncertainty they experienced during periods of fluctuating money supply growth, would not be afraid that the Fed's ineptitude would lead to further inflation, and interest rates would consequently decline. They also argued that the Fed should use only one aggregate and abandon the "incompatible, multiple monetary targets"[27] which were being monitored and factored into the Fed's policymaking.

By 1982, however, skepticism about focusing on aggregates had penetrated too deeply in even the neo-conservative intelligentsia to keep monetary aggregates legitimate. The monetarists' argument that monetarist theory was not really being tried by Paul Volcker, chairman of the Board of Governors, fell on increasingly deaf ears. Influential analysts who had earlier defended monetarism began to express their doubts more and more publicly. In effect those in economic circles who previously had been disillusioned by the ineffectiveness of Keynesian monetary policy in dampening inflation started into another cycle of disillusionment—this time with the theory which many of them had embraced wholeheartedly as *the* alternative to Keynesianism. The former supporters of monetarism joined other critics in accusing monetarism of keeping interest rates extremely high while inflation was declining and of therefore checking any economic recovery.

This disillusionment was perhaps best expressed by Irving Kristol, who identified himself as one who had taken it "for granted until recently that one could leave monetary policy to the monetarists." It is worth quoting Kristol at length, for he expressed the skepticism about monetarism that by early 1982 was sweeping through the neo-conservative intelligentsia which previously had marshalled public support for monetarism. As Kristol put it:

> Mr. Volcker's loyalty to the official monetarist policy is being called into question by the Fed's inept execution of this policy, specifically by its resistance to various procedural reforms—involving such arcana as lagged reserve accounting, open market operations, etc.—that monetarists have long advocated. It is this slovenly execution, monetarists insist, that explains the wild swings in the money supply—which, in turn, by creating anxiety and uncertainty in the financial markets, keeps interest rates unduly and "inexplicably" high.
>
> It is all quite unconvincing. One does not have to believe Mr. Volcker when he says that the proposed reforms would in fact create even wilder swings in those weekly monetary statistics in order to be skeptical that such relatively minor procedural changes could have such consequential, substantial effects. Nor can it be these wild swings

in money numbers, and uncertainty about those numbers, that explain the present high level of interest rates. The financial markets are used to uncertainty and anxiety, and are perfectly capable of discounting these short-term swings.

In truth, our monetarist economists do not have an explanation for the present high level of interest rates, at a time when inflation is rapidly receding. Milton Friedman says he doesn't understand it; and if he doesn't, then either no one can or else there is a flaw in his monetarist theory.

That the latter is the case, I believe, becoming more evident every day. I say this with reluctance and regret, since I took it for granted until recently that one could with confidence leave monetary policy to the monetarists. This can no longer be taken for granted. In our present condition, it is monetarism that is on trial, not Mr. Volcker. Or to put it more accurately: Mr. Volcker is on trial to the degree that, for a year and a half now, he has pursued monetarist policies—not because he has deviated from them in some subtle and obscure way.

Monetarism is an elegant and persuasive economic theory that is not working.[28]

Not surprisingly, in mid-1982 the Federal Reserve began backing away a bit from its previously strong focus on the money supply aggregates, and in October 1982 it publicly decided not to restrain money supply growth, even though the supply was above the target range. The stock market soared—in one week, it gained over 100 points.

The exuberant reaction of the capital markets to this loosening of monetary policy seemed to confirm Kristol's conclusion that "anyone who actually spends time talking to living members of this financial community quickly finds out that fear of inflation is minimal as compared with fear of tighter money resulting from monetarist economic policies."[29] The new-found confidence of investors, which spelled hope for the end of the deepest recession since the Great Depression, was due, it was clear, to the abandonment of at least the "pure" monetarist position. In turn monetarism as public policy was reappraised by many who earlier had seen it as the only cure for ever-escalating inflation. An editorial in the *Wall Street Journal* expressed the opinion of many observers who had initially been sympathetic to monetarism:

. . . after watching M1 these last few years, we can't believe that it is a bad thing to move it aside as the centerpiece of monetary policy. We are deeply indebted to the monetarists, and to Milton Friedman in particular, for keeping alive classical economics pending the collapse of the simple-minded and pretentious doctrine that Keynesianism had become; by now nearly everyone understands that money certainly does matter. Certainly, too, the monetary aggregates are one useful way of looking at monetary policy. But in making them the overriding focus of policy, we failed to understand how the aggregates themselves would be undermined by the high inflation environment we had not previously experienced.[30]

The implementation of monetarist theory, then, proved to be too tough a medicine for the economy. Although inflation was reduced, its costs in the form of an extremely deep recession were very high. It was not surprising that monetarist theory was moved from center stage. The question that was left hanging, however, was "what next?" As the *Wall Street Journal* put it, "The suspension of M1 does leave us with a problem. If the Fed does not follow the aggregates, what will it follow?"[31] The answer seemed to be eclectism. The Fed began considering numerous indicators, including "real" interest rates, the strength of the dollar, nominal GNP, monetary aggregates and the growth of total credit, in formulating its policies, but it had not yet found a systematic theoretical framework by which to guide its actions.

In fact the move away from monetarism left a void which still exists. In mid-December 1982, the *Wall Street Journal* carried a front-page news story which neatly summed up the confusion that followed "eclectism":

The Federal Reserve System, which traditionally has operated in an air of secrecy, seems to be going a step further: it now is operating in an air of confusion. Probably the most confused about what the Federal Reserve's policy might currently be are the people who scrutinize the Fed the hardest. Many prominent economists more or less admit that they don't know what is going on . . . And right now, there are indications that the Fed itself doesn't know precisely what it is up to. Recently, some Fed officials and academic economists gathered to ponder the usefulness of M1 and just what, if anything, should replace it as a guide to monetary policy. Some participants at the conference, which was sponsored by the Federal Reserve Bank of San Francisco, seemd a bit confused.[32]

By 1983 both the "interest rate strategy" and the monetarist approach to monetary policy had been discredited as primary guides to policy. While both interest rates and monetary aggregates would still be used, they would not be the sole indicators by which the Fed would decide policy.[33] But there was no obvious alternative waiting in the wings; no new monetary theory appeared as the new theory which the Federal Reserve should implement.

Policymakers concerned with monetary policy could only combine various elements of the two theories which alone had been tried and subsequently discarded and hope that by combining these components in an eclectic and quasi-intuitive fashion, policy would be more effective than it had been when either theory had been tried in isolation.[34]

CONCLUSION

Discussion of monetary policy often centers on the degree of "autonomy" enjoyed by the central bank from chief executives or legislative bodies. What may be even more important, however, is the richness of choice available to whomever is in charge of monetary policy—whether it be the president or the Federal Reserve Board. This chapter has argued that, at least since 1945, choices concerning monetary policy have been extremely limited, and has attributed such lack of choice to the state of theory in the field of monetary economics.

Ideas matter in policymaking, and in respect of monetary policy they matter a great deal. The weaknesses of theory show up rather clearly when theory is implemented as policy, and the absence of alternative theories shows up as well when old theories are discredited but no alternatives are available to be considered by policymakers. Monetarism as public policy lasted a much shorter time than did Keynesian monetary policy, and it may well be that whereas the monetarists had time to formulate, debate and refine their theory before capturing public policy, potential challengers to monetarism did not have enough time to formulate and test new theoretical propositions. The unprecedented stagflation that afflicted many of the industrialized countries may have forced economic policymakers to experiment with—and then discard—economic ideas much more quickly than economists could devise new ones. The "lead time" that is necessary for the emergence of new theories may now be too long for the needs of policymakers. The latter may increasingly be forced to experiment with theories which have not undergone the same degree of testing and development which previous theories have had.

In sum, monetary policymakers have had to deal with extremely trying times, and with rather limited help from the so-called experts in the field of monetary economics. Perhaps policymakers, presidents included, never do have many choices. Even so, in the case of monetary policy, the poverty of choice is especially evident.

NOTES

1. James Q. Wilson, " 'Policy Intellectuals' and Public Policy," *The Public Interest* (Summer 1981), p. 33.

2. James M. Boughton and Elmus R. Wicker, *The Principles of Monetary Economics* (Homewood, Ill.: Richard D. Irwin, 1975), p. 342.

3. Boughton and Wicker, pp. 130–132.

4. Thomas Mayer, ed., *The Structure of Monetarism* (New York: Norton, 1978), p. 29.

5. The Report of the Commission on Money and Credit, *Money and Credit: Their Influence on Jobs, Prices, and Growth* (Englewood Cliffs, N.J.: Prentice-Hall, 1961), p. 63.

6. Milton Friedman, "Postwar Trends in Monetary Theory and Policy," in Alan D. Entine, ed., *Monetary Economics: Readings* (Belmont, Cal. Wadsworth, 1968), p. 323.

7. Phillip Cagan, "Monetarism in Historical Perspective," in Thomas Mayer, ed., *The Structure of Monetarism* (New York: Norton, 1978), pp. 85–86.

8. Cagan, p. 86.

9. Karl Brunner, "The Role of Money and Monetary Policy," *Review* (Federal Reserve Bank of St. Louis), July 1968, p. 9.

10. Alfred Broaddus, "Aggregating the Monetary Aggregates: Concepts and Issues," *Bank Deposits and the Money Supply: Concepts, Measurement and Interpretation* (Federal Reserve Bank of Richmond, February 1982), p. 7.

11. For various definitions of the aggregates, see *Bank Deposits and the Supply*, p. 96, and "Defining the Money Supply," *New York Times*, February 11, 1982, p. D19.

12. See Karl Brunner, "Issues of Post-Keynesian Monetary Analysis," p. 72, and Helmut Frisch, "Monetarism and Monetary Economics," pp. 120–21, in Thomas Mayer, ed., *The Structure of Monetarism;* and John T. Woolley, "Monetarists and the Politics of Monetary Policy" *Annals* (January 1982), p. 151. Woolley's article makes the important point that there are links between economic ideas and ideology. As Woolley puts it, "Monetarists should be understood as pressing specific elements in a neo-liberal political program" (p. 152).

13. Mayer, pp. 15–17.

14. Clifford M. Hardin and Arthur T. Denzau, *The Unrestrained Growth of Federal Credit Programs* (Center for the Study of American Business,

Washington University, St. Louis), p. 5. See also William Barry Furlong, "America's Other Budget," *New York Times Sunday Magazine*, February 2, 1982, p 32ff.

15. John A. Cochran, *Money, Banking, and the Economy*, 4th ed. (New York: Macmillan, 1979), p. 247.

16. Cochran, p. 246.

17. Frank E. Morris, "Do the Monetary Aggregates Have a Future as Targets of Federal Reserve Policy?" *New England Economic Review* (March/April 1982), pp. 8–9.

18. See Robert J. Shapiro, "Politics and the Federal Reserve," *The Public Interest* (Winter 1982), p. 128.

19. Richard F. Janssen, "How the Reserve Board Decided to Put Stress on the Money Supply," *Wall Street Journal*, July 3, 1970, p. 1.

20. See, for example, James Pierce, "A Difference of Opinion: An Interview," *Fortune* (March 27, 1978); and Sanford Rose, "Why the Fed is a Flop at Managing Money," *Fortune* 98 (October 23, 1978), pp. 53–59.

21. John A. Davenport, "A Testing Time for Monetarism," *Fortune* 102 (October 6, 1980), p. 44. For a discussion of why the Fed began to emphasize bank reserves in October 1979, see John T. Woolley, *Monetary Politics: The Federal Reserve and the Politics of Monetary Policy* (New York: Cambridge University Press, 1984), pp. 103–105.

22. Michael Quint, "Running in the Money Supply: The Fed's Unwieldy Mission," *New York Times*, May 6, 1981, p. D7.

23. Morris, p. 9.

24. Morris, p. 8.

25. Davenport, p. 42.

26. Davenport, p. 43.

27. Lawrence K. Roos, "The Attack on Monetary Targets," *Wall Street Journal*, February 3, 1982, p. 24; see also Warren L. Coats, Jr., "How to Improve Control of the Money Supply," *The AEI Economist* (March 1981).

28. Irving Kristol, "The Focus is on the Fed," *Wall Street Journal*, February 12, 1982, p. 20.

29. Kristol, p. 20.

30. "What has Paul Wrought?" *Wall Street Journal* October 12, 1982), p. 32.

31. *Wall Street Journal* (October 12, 1982), p. 32.

32. Lindley H. Clark, Jr., "Economy May be Hurt as Analysts Wonder What the Fed is Doing," *Wall Street Journal* (December 16, 1982), p. 1.

33. For a sophisticated discussion of why and how the Federal Reserve policy should be informed by both monetarism and Keynesianism, see Ralph C. Bryant, "Money and Monetary Policy," *The Brookings Review* 1 (Spring 1983), pp. 6–12. For a discussion of the extent to which some of

the central tenets of the monetarist school have been accepted by economists generally, see Bruno S. Frey, Werner W. Pommerehne, and Friedrich Schneider, "Are We All Monetarists Now? An Empirical Inquiry," *JPKE, Journal of Post-Keynesian Economics* 6:1 (Fall 1983), pp. 89–96.

34. The Fed previously adopted policies which, while shaped by the thinking of economists, were not considered theoretically consistent by them. As Woolley states (*Monetary Politics,* p. 102), "an examination of decision making in the early 1970s found that the FOMC did not choose among the consistent alternatives presented by the staff, but instead combined inconsistent specifications from competing alternatives."

The Federal Reserve and the Politics of Monetary Policy

JOHN T. WOOLLEY

MONETARY PROBLEMS AS POLITICAL PROBLEMS

One need not read far in the economic literature on inflation to learn that inflation is ultimately a monetary phenomenon. It is not easy to conceive of the conditions under which inflation could continue at a high level or could accelerate for sustained periods unless the money supply also grew or accelerated. The most vigorous statement of this position has come from monetarist economists. Some have seemed to believe that the solution to the problem of inflation is rather simple: instruct the monetary authority to control the money supply. From that point of view monetary authorities appear to be perverse or ignorant—else why haven't they done the right thing already? The more sophisticated monetarists recognize that the reasons for the

An earlier version of this chapter was prepared for the Brookings Conference on the Politics and Sociology of Global Inflation. Research for this chapter was supported in part by a grant from the National Science Foundation. Special acknowledgment is made to the Brookings Institution, the editors of the Brookings Project, and to Ralph C. Bryant and William Poole for their comments.

behavior of the monetary authority are not obvious. Thus, for example, Karl Brunner has suggested that "one chapter on the political economy of inflation" should deal with the central banks—with how they conceive of their task and how their behavior relates to the government budget.[1]

For political scientists it is obvious to begin an analysis of monetary policy with the assumption that monetary policy, just as much as fiscal policy, reflects the judgment of members of the dominant political coalition about their preferred political outcomes. If the inflation of the past decade is "the problem," then the answer is not to be found by examining the Federal Reserve in isolation. Rather the Federal Reserve must be viewed in its larger political and economic context.

This means that monetary policy choices have to be explicitly conceptualized as political choices. There are several kinds of political choices faced in monetary policy, and each kind of choice includes options tending toward more inflation. We shall briefly examine several choices in the following sections. First, monetary policy plays an important role in achieving the aggregate economic performance desired by elected officials and their core constituencies. These officials and their constituencies may prefer some combination of outcomes that involve more rather than less inflation.

Second, the use of monetary policy to achieve macroeconomic objectives may be constrained by a desire to avoid harming politically important but economically vulnerable groups. Protecting those groups may require tolerating inflation. Finally, policy choices in related but apparently separate arenas can constrain monetary policy or make monetary control more difficult. Thus, innovations in the financial sector which have been tolerated or promoted by policymakers for reasons unrelated to economic management may have made precise economic management more difficult. To advance a social and political explanation of inflation, we need to understand how policymakers might see inflation as a solution to their political problems or how inflation might be an undesired consequence of their policy choices.

Monetary Politics at an Aggregate Level

As conventionally viewed, monetary problems involve aggregate balances—keeping interest rates, exchange rates and bank credit in some appropriate relationship to inflation, employment, economic growth, and international payments flows. There are, to be sure, important political consequences associated with these macroeconomic quantities. There is a large literature demonstrating the relationship between these quantities and government popularity and electoral success. Many studies now convincingly show that citizens' evaluations of governments and their voting decisions are influenced by macroeconomic performance.[2] However, as we shall see in the case of U.S. monetary policy, it is far from certain that macroeconomic policy decisions are in fact guided by some narrow attempt to maximize government popularity in the short run.

Monetary Policy and Accommodations of Distributive Conflict

Political problems and political conflict typically involve distributive questions, and these are more likely to be obscured than clarified by the terminology of economic aggregates that economists use to discuss monetary issues. One can readily understand that inflation could be regarded by many policymakers as attractive second-best choices if the alternative involves damaging some economically important or politically powerful sector. Moreover, inflation-tolerating choices may be more likely if policymakers believe that they are confronting temporary "shocks" or disequilibria which will subside in the future. Such a belief on the part of policymakers seems to have been widespread in the 1970s. Following Robert J. Gordon, we can characterize policy that accepts inflation in order to avoid undesired distributive consequences as "accommodative policy."[3] Inflation in the United States has been, in part, the consequence of several kinds of accommodation.

A quite common argument along this line focuses on government demand for credit. If government demands for loans in credit markets are increasing (for example, because of deficits), then some private borrowers may be unable to borrow at prevailing interest rates because governments, which are relatively insensitive to interest costs of borrowing, will receive available funds at the margin. When such conflicts occur, monetary authorities may wish to provide sufficient funds to accommodate some substantial portion of the demands of borrowers who would otherwise be excluded. When the economy is near full employment the result will predictably be inflation, and neither government nor the private sector will get the real value of the nominal quantity borrowed.

Despite the fact that this is the most commonly offered interpretation of how politics affects central bank behavior and thus inflation, there is a striking lack of confirmation for the notion that the primary source of inflation has been in monetary accommodation of deficits. However, for at least some periods in some countries, it is clear that this kind of accommodation has been significant. The most obvious and perhaps the most important example is the case of the United States and the financing of the Vietnam war in the late sixties. There seems to be substantial agreement that at least this one episode of accommodating deficits accounted for a burst of inflation in those years. No one argues, of course, that one such episode is sufficient to produce a prolonged period of continuing inflation.

A second and important kind of accommodation is related to shocks, both real and monetary. A sudden restriction in supply of some important commodity or some rapid movement in exchange rates may have distributive consequences which policymakers wish to diminish. A sudden or sustained exchange rate increase, for example, may disadvantage or threaten the existence of a favored export industry. Returning the rate to a low level may involve tolerating a level of domestic price inflation higher than would otherwise seem desirable. A similar problem might be confronted in the case of a supply shock. Of course, supply shocks can, and have, caused a temporary burst of inflation independent of monetary policy.[4] However, policymakers may choose to responds to the shock by an accommodative monetary policy in order to shift the burden of adjustment. Such a policy would reduce the degree to which real resources were transferred from one sector to another or from the domestic economy to a foreign economy. Something like this probably occurred in several Western European countries in response to the OPEC price shocks, but this seems to have happened to a somewhat lesser degree in the United States.[5]

A third kind of distributive problem arises from the attempts by societal groups to regain lost ground following inflationary shocks or other unanticipated monetary accommodation. It is to be expected that groups within the economy will attempt to recoup their past losses. They may also attempt to avoid future losses if they expect similar inflation to occur again. Under such conditions, fighting inflation through monetary policy alone—which in the U.S. has often proved to be the only means available—requires a willingness to accept whatever pattern of distributive consequences flow from existing patterns of economic vulnerability. Unemployment and bankruptcies in the most vulnerable sectors—housing and consumer durables—is very unpopular, perhaps more unpopular than inflation itself. For this reason policymakers have sometimes choosen to forsake the fight against inflation before victory was consolidated. In this case political problems arise because only one effective, but rather blunt, instrument is used to fight inflation—aggregate monetary policy. With such an approach there is no assurance that the burdens of fighting inflation are borne equitably. Indeed, in such circumstances, considerations of equity can scarcely be entertained at all, or only with considerable difficulty. At the same time, there is the certain assurance that individuals, groups, and organizations will do all they can to reduce their own vulnerability and to shift the burden of adjustment onto somebody else.

Financial Innovation and Monetary Control

One consequence of inflation, of previous financial regulation and of previous monetary policy decisions has been financial innovation. Novel means such as money market mutual funds have been developed for managing money for individuals, corporations, and financial institutions. This kind of innovation has itself made anti-inflationary monetary control more difficult. In the United States it is precisely in the era of increased inflation that a variety of financial innovations have occurred. All serve to decrease the precision of control that can be exercised by monetary authorities and thus have increased the probability that inflation-accommodating errors will occur. Indeed recent studies suggest that this outcome may be even more likely when monetary authorities are concentrating their attention on achieving monetary aggregate targets—as has been true in the U.S. since late 1979.[6]

MONETARY POLITICS AND FEDERAL RESERVE INDEPENDENCE

Rather than castigating the Federal Reserve for permitting inflation, students of inflation need to understand why it is that the Fed does what it does. What is its role in economic policymaking? What kinds of political constraints are there on its choices? How plausible is the widely held notion that the Fed has some meaningful form of independence from politics and thus behaves in ways not fundamentally shaped by politics?

In a formal sense, monetary policy is controlled by the Federal Reserve. The most important of its policy decisions are made in the twelve-member Federal Open Market Committee, composed of all seven members of the Federal Reserve Board and five of the district bank presidents. The Federal Reserve was not created for the purpose of macroeconomic stabilization. On the contrary, as in other Western settings, it emerged in response to the need for a central institution to serve other banks. Like other central banks, the Federal Reserve has a long and conservative heritage. It has been closely linked to the major financial institutions of the day, and its organizational ethos has been one of stressing stability.

To understand the economic events of the late 1970s and early 1980s, it is crucial to know more about why monetary policy has been conducted as it has. If the Federal Reserve is fundamentally free from political constraints, then it is clear that we have to study its behavior separately from other political actors. However, if its policy choices are substantially constrained by other political actors, then we should treat monetary policy as being the product of larger political and economic coalitions. Studying monetary policy and the Federal Reserve in isolation could lead to a vast overestimation of the degree to which monetary policy reflects the separate, independent preferences of a set of autonomous actors.

Many writers who are concerned about the independence of the Fed would prefer that no monetary policy choices be made because of political pressure. They hope that the monetary authority will have sufficient political power to resist pressures. Commonly, this view is held by those who fear inflation and who see the Federal Reserve as being disposed to fight inflation. They welcome Fed independence—"depoliticizacy" of monetary policy—because they hope it will lead to realization of their preferred macroeconomic outcomes. Under such conditions there would presumably be no effective way of pressuring the Federal Reserve to accommodate government deficits, for example. On the other side are those who regard Federal Reserve independence as undesirable if it thwarts democratic control of policy, even if that entails a policy considered to be suboptimal by standards of economic efficiency. Still others argue that the functional interdependence of monetary and fiscal policy requires that there be full coordination of macroeconomic policy instruments and thus no independence for monetary policy. This position could be consistent with the view that all economic policy choices should be relatively depoliticized.

Since the effects of monetary and fiscal policy cannot be known separately from each other,[7] one may reasonably expect monetary and fiscal authorities to be in close contact in order to learn what their counterparts are doing. One may further anticipate that they will at least occasionally be in conflict. They may disagree about how to carry out policy or about what objectives should be sought. Moreover, since both authorities control political resources, each may attempt to force the other to behave in the way he prefers. The problem confronting any outsider who attempts to understand this relationship is the limited opportunity to observe the actual bargaining that exists or to know with great confidence what resources each participant tries to use to influence the other's behavior. Behavior which is very interesting and very important is also very inaccessible to observers.

As an initial response to this problem one can attempt to establish a benchmark for evidence indicating some minimal level of Federal Reserve "behavioral independence." At a minimal level the Fed demonstrates independence if it sets policy instruments without prior approval from outside authorities, and if, for some minimal time period (say a month) the instrument settings clearly differ from those preferred by the president.[8] This is an explicitly political, rather than statutory, definition of independence. It does not rule out the possibility that in periods when conflict is not observed, one actor is forcing the other to comply. This definition means simply that for some short but significant period of time the resources of the fiscal authority do not guarantee that its preferences dominate in monetary policy. From such observed conflict one infers that the monetary authority has determined its own preferred policy.

Institutional Structure and Central Bank Independence

The notion that central bank independence is primarily a question of appropriate organizational design is implicit in various discussions. Some prominent economists have suggested that depoliticizing monetary policy may be a solution to the problems of economic instability that they see resulting from democratic control of economic policy.[9] It is possible that organizational devices hold the key to depoliticizing agencies such as central banks. However, available evidence overwhelmingly indicates that, at best, organizational features are necessary but not sufficient for central bank independence. Independence in a formal legal sense may be better conceived of as revealing the existence of strong support by other political actors for fighting inflation. Behavioral independence reflects the fact that the central bank controls important political resources—such as the support of a sympathetic constituency.

In the United States, the Banking Acts of 1933 and 1935 consolidated power in the Federal Reserve Board and defined a relationship for the Fed to the rest of the national government which was both more "governmental" *and* more removed from short-term influence by other national-level actors than had formerly been the case. An annual report to Congress was required; the Secretary of the Treasury and Comptroller of the Currency were removed as members of the Board of Governors; funds assessed member banks were defined not to be government funds and were therefore no longer subject to Treasury audit; the Board was given new policy instruments and members' terms in office were lengthened. All of these should have increased the independence of the system from the president. Such was not the result. System policy was very passive during the period. The Fed helped maintain an "orderly market" for government securities—as the Treasury desired. This continued through World War II and was not a source of controversy.[10]

After the war, the Federal Reserve did not establish any scope for meaningful independent action until the early 1950s. Then independence resulted from a negotiated agreement—the famous "accord" with the Treasury in 1951—not from organizational changes. In the accord the Treasury agreed that the Fed did not have to maintain a fixed, low-interest rate for Treasury debt. At the time, when the government was running deficits to finance the Korean war, the Federal Reserve feared that the obligation to keep interest rates fixed at low levels would lead to inflation. In fact the process of achieving flexibility in monetary policy followed a long period of discussion and dispute, facilitated by congressional hearings. The clear exercise of Federal Reserve independence in 1953 was marked by cautious probings within a region of discretion regarded as being acceptable to the Treasury.[11] Only subsequently did independence as defined here become evident.

Compared to the demands for cooperation during periods of crisis, the cooperation entailed by policy interdependencies and the political resources that government controls, specific organizational features can make only a marginal contribution to central bank independence.

Kinds of Disputes, Instances of Independence

The definition of independent action advanced above directs our attention to instances of conflict recognized as such by the participants. Judging from published accounts, from interviews, and from documentary evidence, there have been only a few instances of conflict in recent years.[12] Even those few conflicts have not all been of the same kind, and many have been viewed as relatively unimportant by the participants. This does not mean, of course, that there have not been some other conflicts, which, for some reason or another, have not become publicly known. Nonetheless, it is more than clear that whatever independence the Fed may have, it does not very often result in policy clearly considered to be objectionable by the president. Consider three different kinds of conflict.

The first kind involves conflict over objectives. By this is meant disagreement that flows from the fact that one group of actors (say elected officials) believe that one policy problem is "the problem," and another group—for example, the Federal Reserve—believes that some other problem is "the problem." Policymakers who are "satisficers"[13]—that is, whose attention shifts from problem to problem in searching for conditions that they consider to be unsatisfactory—are likely to be in conflicts of this sort occasionally, even if they basically agree.

Disagreements on what constitutes satisfactory economic performance might flow from some ideological difference. Liberal Democrats would be more likely to perceive that unemployment is the policy problem than is the conservative Federal Reserve, which would be more sensitive to the concerns of the financial community. Conflicts might also reflect the different incentives policymakers face. Thus elected officials are likely to be more sensitive to the employment issue because of its influence on their electoral prospects. The Fed does not face this kind of constraint, and thus may be less sensitive to unemployment than elected officials.

The likelihood of conflict about objectives depends on the movement of the economy and on the degree of divergence between the two actors. If there is any divergence at all, one might expect conflict to be evident around the peaks and troughs of business cycles. As a period of expansion lengthens and evidence accumulates that full employment is being reached or that inflation is accelerating, the Federal Reserve would perceive a problem with inflation more quickly than would elected officials. The Federal Reserve would want to begin to tighten policy before elected officials would be ready to, and conflict would be particularly likely at that time. The reverse would occur at the trough when elected officials would perceive an employment crisis more quickly than would the Fed.

In fact this kind of conflict is relatively rare, or at least it rarely leads to overt disagreement. One case where it did lead to conflict was in 1965, when the president and the Federal Reserve tangled over whether or not the Fed should start fighting inflation by raising the discount rate. Similarly, there were repeated tensions between Jimmy Carter and the Federal Reserve during the first year of his administration when the president was concerned about an employment situation that was not viewed as critical within the Fed.

The second kind of conflict, which is more common, is not so much about objectives as it is about the degree of policy action required given that a problem exists. If the objective of policymakers is to return unsatisfactory economic performance to satisfactory levels, then they must decide how rapidly to try to accomplish that change. The speed of movement into the satisfactory region is usually considered to be inversely related to the ability to stay in that region. However, for reasons related to electoral politics, officials may sometimes want to move the economy as rapidly as possible to the satisfactory region despite the risks involved. And this, in turn, may provoke conflict with the Federal Reserve. This has occurred in both Republican and Democratic administrations. In 1971, for example, the Nixon White House quarreled with the Fed over whether stronger stimulus should be provided in order to produce a more rapid recovery during the election year of 1972.

There has also been conflict related to the method of implementing policy. This conflict has pitted monetarists against Keynesians. Monetarists argue that the sole and overriding objective of monetary policy should be to achieve a steady, slow rate of growth in the money supply—and that any other policy is not satisfactory. Keynesians, by contrast, argue that an exclusive view to the money supply ignores important problems caused by high or fluctuating interest rates. For complex historical reasons, the Federal Reserve has tended to find itself more in the Keynesian than the monetarist camp. Thus, when a president is advised by monetarists, as is the case with Reagan, there is a high probability of conflict emerging over the way policy is conducted. In the early Reagan years, one could perceive two different kinds of conflicts going on. Despite the nominally more monetarist policy adopted in October 1979, the Fed was criticized from within the Reagan administration for allowing the money supply to fluctuate too much. At the same time it was strongly attacked in Congress for failing to perceive the true dimensions of the unemployment problem—a conflict of the first kind.

It should be noted that in interviews, members of the Council of Economic Advisers under Nixon, Ford and Carter were unable or unwilling to cite specific instances of any significant disagreements with the Federal Reserve that occurred during their tenure.[14] In particular they tended to play down conflicts over the speed of policy adjustment (the second kind of conflict) as being relatively unimportant. They stressed that there was generally good agreement both on the definition of the problem and on the correct method for addressing it.

The Federal Reserve and the Political Business Cycle

Few research enterprises have captured the imagination of political scientists in recent years like that of demonstrating the linkage between the timing of presidential elections and macroeconomic policy.[15] Most of the research has been guided by a single, central, and rather simple hypothesis: that the president wants "good" economic conditions at election time, and he achieves this by stimulating the economy beforehand. After elections he undoes the inflationary damage by instituting restrictive policy. The result is a politically generated economic cycle referred to as the "political business cycle" (PBC).

It has not always seemed obvious to observers that things work this way with monetary policy. Many observers have believed that the system was likely to create *recessions*, not booms, at election periods. This President Nixon firmly believed, and thus were Lyndon Johnson's economic advisers warned about the Federal Reserve by outsiders.[16] In short the insider view in the mid-sixties was that monetary policy could not be counted on to support stimulative fiscal policy.[17]

The PBC hypothesis has been subjected to vigorous criticism, based both on the weakness of the empirical findings which are cited in support of the theory and on conceptual shortcomings in the theory itself.[18] Different studies have produced contradictory results concerning the same countries and even the same elections. Only the 1972 election unambiguously fits the expected pattern in the United States. One possible reason for the absence of good fit may be the institutional obstacles to rapid change of fiscal and monetary policy that limit the degree to which the president can manipulate the economy for electoral purposes. The independence of the monetary authority is one such obstacle. Edward Tufte deals with this by suggesting that monetary policy is a participant, however unwilling, in election-year economic manipulations.

Evidence on Monetary Policy. William Nordhaus presented no evidence bearing specifically on monetary policy. Still it is interesting to
note that Nordhaus discovered evidence of "very marked" electoral
cycles only in Germany, the U.S. and New Zealand.[19] Since the central
banks of Germany and the U.S. are often characterized as being independent, Nordhaus's suggestion that it may be possible to diminish
PBCs by depoliticizing central banks is somewhat baffling.[20] Tufte
presented data on observed growth rates of M1 over the two years
before and after presidential elections. He reported that in six of
seven post-election biennial periods from 1948 to 1976, M1 grew more
slowly after the election and in four of seven, grew more rapidly
before the election—apparently in confirmation of his expectations
about political business cycles.[21]

The author's attempt to reproduce Tufte's findings using a
slightly different measure, the compound annual rate of change in
the detrended monetary base,[22] completely failed to reveal Tufte's
pattern.[23] Golden and Poterba estimated reaction functions for the
inflation-adjusted money supply to see if it varied in a pattern consistent with the PBC and found no statistically significant results.[24]

It is more appropriate, surely, to test the PBC hypothesis by
looking at the instruments policymakers actually control rather than
at variables like the money supply, which they cannot control in the
short run. Results of this sort are generally quite negative as well. For
example, the appropriate PBC hypothesis would probably be that in
election years interest rates should decrease or should increase at a
rate slower than or equal to the rate of increase in the previous year. If
reserves are being used as an "operating target," they should grow at
a rate faster than or equal to the growth rate in the previous year. The
author's examination of monetary instruments shows that trends are
about as likely not to fit the PBC hypothesis as to fit it. On the
contrary there is some evidence that policymakers are as willing to
begin a policy of restriction in election years as in non-election years.[25]
This may reflect the fact that policy effects involve lags. In another
reaction function study, this one focused on policy instruments, Beck
reports that for the 1972 election there is no evidence of consistent
with the PBC hypothesis.[26]

Lying Low. Sherman Maisel wrote that "Federal Reserve policy
has always been to avoid, if possible, taking any major monetary
actions as elections approach."[27] This conclusion was echoed in several interviews with Fed officials. As Governor Partee put it, "if you
were to ask a central banker about what he would want to see in a

period prior to an election, he would say he wanted to have stability." Stability in interest rates and money supply would presumably keep the central bank from being dragged into partisan politics.

No discussion of the PBC hypothesis known to the author has used this idea to explain why monetary policy might contribute to an observed cycle, even though monetary policy instruments do not reveal a strong policy thrust. This might have the consequence of supporting the PBC pattern if fiscal policy were simultaneously shifting to a very expansionary stance, as occurred in 1972. Such a pattern would clearly demonstrate the sensitivity of the Federal Reserve to partisan politics—and that is relevant both to the PBC hypothesis and to questions of behavioral independence.

The federal funds rate has been slightly more stable in presidential election years than in non-election years. Over the years 1958 to 1981, the average within-year variation in the monthly average federal funds rate as measured by the standard deviation has been 0.819 in presidential election years as opposed to 0.892 in odd-numbered years. If observations for 1980 and past are excluded on grounds that the Federal Reserve was following a new operating regime, the difference would be greater—0.415 in presidential years vs. 0.814 in odd-numbered years. Obviously, whatever the reality underlying the PBC hypothesis, recent periods are not adequately captured by any relatively simple behavioral expectations.

THE IMPORTANCE OF FEDERAL RESERVE INDEPENDENCE

Can the findings that there is little conflict between the president and the Federal Reserve be reconciled with reports and documents revealing relationships that are often tense, marked by mistrust and by attempts by one actor to pressure the other? Although clear-cut conflict, observable from the outside, is rare, it is not necessarily the case that policymaking is primarily harmonious. If there really is no disagreement between fiscal and monetary policy authorities, why is the Fed's independence so carefully preserved? If there is disagreement, why again is central bank independence so carefully preserved? We will consider two partially competing interpretations of the findings just presented.

Version One. This interpretation emphasizes the existence of a consensus among major policy participants that monetary policy must be protected from the pressures of "pluralistic" political processes, especially the demands of interest groups for pork-barrel benefits and protection from the costs of stabilization policy. The relationship between the Federal Reserve and the president is characterized as largely one of agreement—a tacit conspiracy to keep other political actors, especially legislators, out of the monetary policy game. Formal independence and occasional independent action are welcomed by presidents because:

1. all major actors recognize the desirability of having one macroeconomic policy instrument which can respond solely, more or less, to the "technical requirements of the economy";
2. the political costs of unpopular policy choices can to some degree be deflected onto an "independent" the Federal Reserve and away from elected officials;
3. the government and the Federal Reserve agree on the undesirability of much legislative influence on monetary policy.

The last flows naturally from the first due to the shared perception that the legislature is most likely to reflect narrow, particularistic pressures. This perspective is little more than the assertion that the president and the Federal Reserve collude to overcome congressional irresponsibility and delay. This relationship is actually a rather fragile one and contains pressures which can simultaneously undermine both the political and economic rationales which support it. However, considerable evidence can be marshalled to support this interpretation.[28]

Although the Federal Reserve is, technically speaking, a "creature of Congress," Congress has never devised an effective means of closely influencing monetary policy—unlike the president and the Treasury. In part this has been due to a lack of interest and self-confidence on the part of key congressmen. Nonetheless, by tolerating occasional public disagreements with the Fed, the president and the Treasury have been able to keep monetary policy relatively flexible and not subject to congressional delay in changing policy direction.[29]

The specific facts of the reestablishment of the Federal Reserve's independence in the early 1950s may seem not to fit with this interpretation. The standard version is of a bitter struggle between the Treasury and the Fed which was settled by treaty in the accord of 1951. The settlement was encouraged by Congress, particularly by Senator Douglas, rather than being impeded by an obstructionist Congress, as this interpretation might suggest. An alternative view holds that the drama of intra-administration battle has blinded ob-

servers to more fundamental continuing cooperation between the
Federal Reserve and the president. The actual increase in the flexibility of monetary policy coincided with the change from Truman to
Eisenhower administrations. With a new Republican majority in Congress, Eisenhower moved to adopt a series of strong anti-inflationary
policies.[30] A more active monetary policy fit comfortably with this
general policy direction.

Congressional support for Federal Reserve independence has for
the most part been a symbolic exercise "defending Congressional
prerogative." Members of Congress seem to believe that Federal Reserve independence from the Treasury enhances its responsiveness to
Congress; the converse may well be true. Such independence may
remove a potentially effective way of defining policy responsibility
more clearly. It is certainly clear that congressional attention to Federal Reserve policy (as opposed to the trappings of independence) are
as cyclical as conflict between the president and the Fed. When interest rates increase and the housing industry is hurt, Congress—or at
least some of its members—quite predictably threatens to begin running monetary policy itself with the objective of securing lower interest rates. This happened in 1969–70, in 1975 and again in 1982–83.

In any case there is much to indicate that there is more meaning
to the notion of Federal Reserve independence when it comes to
Congress than it is with the Treasury and the president. A high level
of agreement between the Fed and executive branch economic policy
officials has been enhanced by exchanges of personnel and by
similarities in outlook which are supported by a careful process of
recruitment to top positions.[31] Top policy officials in most administrations have included at least some prominent figures who have been
close to the Federal Reserve.[32] Support of the Treasury for Fed independence from closer congressional oversight has been expressed
repeatedly.[33]

It is clear that if this "facade of independence" interpretation is
accurate, then the relationship it describes is a delicate one. In order
to perform the political function of diverting criticism for unpopular
policy, the Federal Reserve must be perceived to have some genuine
degree of independence. It can, however, never be seen to be so
independent and its policies so harsh that it provokes an attack which
would destroy the illusion by formally subordinating the Fed to the
executive branch. On the other hand, the more the Federal Reserve
cooperates openly with the government, the less plausible it is for
others to "point the finger" when policy tightens. Thus the ideal
relationship would be one of studied distance and intermittent squab-

bling. Such a process would be expected to produce policy in the long run very similar to that which would result from a fully subordinate Federal Reserve subject, like the president himself, to political pressures from various groups in society. The primary difference would be that considerable energy and inventiveness would be invested in protecting a facade of independence which primarily serves a political function.

Version Two. Rather than assuming an underlying consensus between the Federal Reserve and the president, the second version assumes a persistent tension and disagreement. One might not expect to perceive overt conflict between the two actors most of the time because differences would be negotiated quietly or a solution would be imposed by one of them. One might imagine a situation in which relevant political resources are overwhelmingly controlled by the president. One who observed no conflict then might interpret his finding as indicating compromise on the government's terms. If this were true, of course, one would be surprised by the instances when some genuinely independent action has been found. Neither would one expect to see the Federal Reserve chairman unleashing vigorous and apparently successful public attacks on fiscal policy proposals. Nor would one expect to find attentive elites attributing high levels of influence to the chairman.[34] These observations, which seem to be anomalies in terms of the first interpretation, can be explained by noting that the Fed has its own political resources which may be used to support its preferred policy. What are those resources? Are they sufficient to account for some meaningful independence?

The Federal Reserve possesses two very valuable political resources. The first is expertise and a reputation for expertise. The capability to analyze complex economic events quickly and accurately and the ability to maneuver adroitly in executing policies are formidable resources. These resources are not sufficient to insulate the Federal Reserve from political pressures, but they may give it a degree of flexibility that can substantially affect policy in the short term.

The second resource available to the Federal Reserve is its relationship with the financial community. This relationship is one of long standing, and the resources of the financial community have often been effective in ordinary political commerce. There is fairly convincing evidence that Federal Reserve officials work in a milieu that is significantly shaped by the interests and concerns of commercial bankers. And there is evidence that in some settings the links are strong enough that bankers can be mobilized to support the Fed actively when that might be appropriate. However, it is not clear that the bankers are the first line of political support for the Federal Reserve in specific controversies. Indeed the political resources drawn from this relationship exist because of the importance of the financial community in economic affairs. The Fed's capacity to push or pull macroeconomic policy in a conservative direction stems from the economic, not the political, influence of the interests the central bank represents. We may refer to the interests of this constituency as "sound finance"—others may simply speak of business confidence.[35]

Substantively, the "sound finance" position is composed of several, possibly contradictory, concerns:

1. protecting "the value of the dollar" both from inflation and from international decline;
2. sustaining moderate, stable economic growth;
3. dampening sharp market fluctuations which might arbitrarily inflict losses or gains on asset holders or, more importantly, undercut investor confidence;
4. promoting the development of financial institutions which are both profitable and capable of withstanding short-term stresses and strains;
5. protecting the financial system from rippling panic in the event a major institution does fail;
6. doing all these with minimal state interference in financial markets.

These concerns are institutionalized in the Federal Reserve. The perception among the major participants in the economic system that stability is currently threatened varies from time to time, and consequently so should support for the Federal Reserve. But there is always some sound finance sentiment that the Fed can rely upon.

We know this support is not randomly distributed in the U.S. population. Wall Street, the financial establishment writ large, strongly supports Federal Reserve tight money as a means of combating inflation, even though tight money may be against the immediate interests of parts of the financial community.[36] Positive evaluations of the Federal Reserve Board chairman among the general public increase sharply with income level. They are three times as likely among Republicans as Democrats, and twice as likely among stockholders as non-stockholders.[37] At various points, particularly involving appointments to the Federal Reserve, the question of "business confidence" repeatedly surfaces in the writing of journalists discussing monetary policy.[38] Presidents and their economic advisors are continually sensitive to the need to maintain that confidence and to avoid appearing to challenge the principles of "sound finance."[39] The

Federal Reserve stands for something desirable to the groups with the greatest stake in this country's financial stability. These groups are as well identified by the label "sound finance" as any other. It is the representation of the values and preferences supported by this very important constituency that remains the Fed's greatest resource in negotiation with the president.

If the Federal Reserve can claim "sound finance" as its constituency, and if the president recognizes that in part he too is dependent on that constituency, then the president has a strong incentive to be attentive to the policies recommended by the Fed. Disputes may be resolved on terms favoring the position of the Federal Reserve because the president recognizes the need to adopt policies that engender confidence in the sound finance constituency and to avoid policies diminishing confidence—policies which one expects to be strongly opposed by the central bank. Periodic public disputes with the president may reassure the sound finance constituency that the Fed retains the freedom to represent its desires. These disputes may also reinforce the sense of identity of the Fed with this constituency. Additionally, Federal Reserve independence may usefully permit the bank to explain and defend policies to this critical group with higher levels of credibility than could be achieved by the president alone.

From this perspective, too, the relationship of the president and the Federal Reserve is fragile. Almost by definition, the sound finance community cannot mobilize swiftly and cohesively for competition in pluralist political arenas such as Congress—although specific financial groups may have this capacity—despite its continuing potential for damage in financial matters. Thus too much obvious Federal Reserve independence again threatens to provoke a potentially damaging attack in pluralist arenas, while too little evidence of independence threatens a loss of constituency support which would, in turn, make independent action even more hazardous. Loss of support would be particularly problematical if substantial sections of the sound finance community came to share a definition of appropriate policy which the Federal Reserve believed to be in conflict with its broader mandate of "stability."

CONCLUSION

Though infrequently acting independently in the terms defined above, the Federal Reserve is separately an important actor in U.S. monetary policy. It is probably more important, and more politically useful, precisely because it has its formal independence as well. The important role of Congress in policymaking enhances the value of Federal Reserve control of "flexible" and "efficient" policy instruments which are not subject to legislative control. And, ironically, because the role of Congress in policymaking is so large, it appears to be easier to sustain an independent central bank capable of absorbing political criticism. This reflects the advantage given to defenders of the status quo in legislative processes which require repeated approval of any given proposal, such as reducing central bank independence. More fundamentally, the liberal values underlying our separation of powers system, especially a fear of concentrated power, provides a ready rationale for insulating major state functions from nominal control of elected officials.

At a different level the willingness of presidents to compromise with the Federal Reserve is increased because of the dependence of presidents on the Fed's "sound finance" constituency for good economic performance. Because our government depends on private decisions regarding production and investment to insure a strong and growing economy, our independent central bank is very useful, both to represent and to reassure the private sector.

A formally independent central bank may in fact contribute to the capability of a country to respond to inflation. However this cannot be understood as flowing directly from the organizational factors which insulate the Federal Reserve. Both the central bank's organization and its contribution to fighting inflation cannot be abstracted from the larger political and economic structure. The Federal Reserve's independence reflects the values and priorities of the dominant political coalition.

NOTES

1. Karl Brunner, "Comment", *Journal of Law and Economics* 18 (December 1975); p. 851.

2. See the review and citations in Martin Paldam, "A Preliminary Survey of the Theories and Findings on Vote and Popularity Functions," *European Journal of Political Research* 9 (1981); pp. 181–199.

3. Robert J. Gordon, "The Demand for and Supply of Inflation," *Journal of Law and Economics* 18 (December 1975), pp. 807–836; "World Inflation and Monetary Accommodation in Eight Countries," *Brookings Papers on Economic Activity* (1977), No. 2, pp. 409–477.

4. Alan S. Blinder, *Economic Policy and the Great Stagflation* (New York: Academic Press, 1979).

5. Blinder, Chapter 8.

6. Donald D. Hester, "Innovations and Monetary Control," *Brookings Papers on Economic Activity* (1981), No. 2, pp. 141–189.

7. See Alan S. Blinder and Robert M. Solow, "Analytical Foundations of Fiscal Policy," in *The Economics of Public Finance* (Washington, D.C.: The Brookings Institution, 1974), and James Tobin and Willem Buiter, "Long-Run Effects of Fiscal and Monetary Policy on Aggregate Demand" in Jerome L. Stein, ed., *Monetarism* (New York: North-Holland, 1976).

8. For a discussion of this and other meanings of central bank independence, see John T. Woolley, "Monetary Policy Instrumentation and the Relationship of Central Banks and Governments," *The Annals* 434 (November 1977); pp. 170–172. A similar definition and a very useful discussion can be found in Ralph C. Bryant, *Money and Monetary Policy in Interdependent Nations* (Washington, D.C.: The Brookings Institution, 1980), Chapter 18.

9. Assar Lindbeck, "Stabilization Policy in Open Economies with Endogenous Politicians," *American Economic Review* 66 (May 1976), p. 18; William D. Nordhaus, "The Political Business Cycle," *Review of Economic Studies* 42 (April 1975), p. 188.

10. Milton Friedman and Ann Jacobson Schwartz, *A Monetary History of the United States, 1867–1960* (Princeton, N.J.: Princeton University Press, 1963), p. 520 and Chapter 10; A. Jerome Clifford, *The Independence of the Federal Reserve System* (Philadelphia: University of Pennsylvania Press, 1965).

11. Friedman and Schwartz, p. 613; James Tobin, "Discussion 3," in *Proceedings of a 50th Anniversary Symposium* (Federal Reserve Bank of Boston, 1964), pp. 30–33.

12. Sources included G. L. Bach, *Making Monetary and Fiscal Policy* (Washington, D.C.: The Brookings Institution, 1971); Arthur M. Okin, *The Political Economy of Prosperity* (Washington, D.C.: The Brookings Institution, 1970); Walter W. Heller, *New Dimensions of Political Economy* (Cambridge, Mass.: Harvard University Press, 1966); Sherman J. Maisel, *Managing the Dollar* (New York: Norton, 1973); newspaper accounts; documentary evidence in the files of the Lyndon B. Johnson Library at Austin, Texas; and personal interviews with various participants in policymaking during the years 1966–78.

13. On satisficing, see Herbert A. Simon, *Administrative Behavior* (New York: Free Press, 1957), Chapters 4 and 5; and Paul Mosley, "Towards a 'Satisficing' Theory of Economic Policy," *The Economic Journal* 86 (March 1976); pp. 59–72.

14. Arthur Okun indicated his awareness of White House/Federal Reserve friction in late 1974 and early 1975, but Ford CEA member William Fellner insisted that he was not aware of any such friction. The analysis presented here would have predicted conflict at exactly that time. Carter CEA member Lyle Gramley indicated that there was some disagreement on targets at the outset of 1978 and attributed that to the "cyclical phase." Arthur Okun interview, February 7, 1978; Herbert Stein interview, July 27, 1978; William Fellner interview, July 12, 1978; Lyle Gramley interview, June 16, 1978.

15. Tufte's *Political Control of the Economy* is probably the best known contribution to this literature, although serious writing on the topic clearly originated with Nordhaus, an economist, who claims heritage from Kalecki's recently discovered 1943 article. Edward R. Tufte, *Political Control of the Economy* (Princeton, N.J.: Princeton University Press, 1978); William D. Nordhaus, "The Political Business Cycle," *Review of Economic Studies* 42 (April 1975); pp. 169–190; M. Kalecki, "Political Aspects of Full Employment," *Political Quarterly* 14 (October–December 1943); pp. 322–331. See also, Assar Lindbeck, "Stabilization Policy in Open Economies with Endogenous Politicians, *American Economic Review Papers and Proceedings,* 66 (May 1976); pp. 1–19; C. Duncan MacRae, "A Political Model of the Business Cycle," *Journal of Political Economy* 85 (April 1977); pp. 239–263; Bruno S. Frey and Friedrich Schneider,"A Politico-Economic Model of the United Kingdom," *The Economic Journal* 88 (June 1978); pp. 243–253; James Alt and Alec Chrystal, "Modelling the Growth of Government Expenditure in Advanced Industrial Economies," paper presented to the 1978 Annual Meeting of the American Political Science Association; and Bruno S. Frey, *Modern Political Economy* (New York: Wiley, 1978).

16. Nixon, *Six Crises.* See also the exchange filed together as Letter, President to Seymour E. Harris, January 23, 1964, EXFI, WHCF, LBJ Library; Memo, Ackley to President, March 27, 1964, and attached memo of March 27, 1964, EXH19, WHCF, LBJ Library. Also bearing on this matter is Letter, George Reedy to President, August 2, 1966, CFBE 5, WHCF, LBJ Library.

17. This view almost certainly stemmed from the perception that in the election of 1960 a recession partly provoked by Federal Reserve policy had been blamed for Nixon's defeat.

18. See the excellent review and analysis in James E. Alt and Alec Chrystal, *Political Economics* (Berkeley: University of California Press, 1983).

19. Nordhaus, "The Political Business Cycle," p. 182.

20. Perhaps this is intended as irony. Perhaps it reflects Nordhaus's unstated belief that the central banks in those countries are not in fact independent, or perhaps he would point out that central banks can be political *and* independent.

21. Tufte does not report actual growth rates, so the size and importance of the observed differences are unclear. Tufte, *Political Control of the Economy*, pp. 50–51. In an unpublished work David Cameron examined the patterns in rates of growth of M1 for annual periods ending a full year prior to the election. His research also supported the PBC theory. David R. Cameron, "Taxes, Deficits, and Inflation," unpublished paper prepared for the Brookings Institution Project on the Politics and Sociology of Global Inflation and Recession, December 1978.

22. Calculated from the first quarter of odd-numbered years to the last quarter of the subsequent even-numbered year. The monetary base consists of member bank deposits at Federal Reserve Banks, vault cash held by member and non-member banks, and currency held by the public. The measure used here includes an adjustment for changes in reserve requirement ratios and is seasonally adjusted. See Albert E. Burger and Robert H. Rasche, "Revision of the Monetary Base," *Federal Reserve Bank of St. Louis Review* 59 (July 1977), pp. 13–28. Research attempting to produce an accurate measure of monetary policy impact indicates that the detrended monetary base is a substantially better indicator of monetary policy impact than in the detrended change in M1. Tufte's measures are not detrended. Using quarterly figures for the monetary base without detrending produces results marginally less supportive of Tufte's position. See Alan S. Blinder and Stephen M. Goldfeld, "New Measures of Fiscal and Monetary Policy," *American Economic Review* 66 (December 1976), pp. 780–796.

23. The rate of growth of the detrended monetary base increased in five of seven pre-election biannual periods, and also in five of eight post-election biannual periods. The growth rates of the monetary base (both detrended and not) averaged over even and odd years, presidential and congressional election years were also compared. There is a difference. For example, in presidential election years the detrended monetary base grew on average by 2.2 percent, while in all odd years it grew on average by only 1.7 percent. The difference, calculated with a difference of means test, is not statistically significant (even at the 0.10 level), although it is in the expected direction. When all even years are compared to odd years, the difference is even smaller.

24. David G. Golden and James M. Poterba, "The Price of Popularity: The Political Business Cycle Reexamined," *American Journal of Political Science* 24 (November 1980), pp. 696–714.

25. John T. Woolley, *Monetary Politics: The Federal Reserve and the Politics of Monetary Policy* (New York: Cambridge University Press, 1984).

26. Nathaniel Beck, "Presidential Influence on the Federal Reserve in the 1970s," *American Journal of Political Science* 26 (August 1982); pp. 415–445.

27. Maisel, *Managing the Dollar*, p. 117.

28. A particularly clear statement of this position may be found in Edward J.

Kane, "External Pressure and the Operations of the Fed," in Raymond E. Lombra and Willard E. Witte, eds., *The Political Economy of Domestic and International Monetary Relations* (Ames: Iowa State University Press, 1982).

29. Evidence of this is available in commentaries on economic policymaking processes in general, and the Federal Reserve in particular. Economists of various stripes mistrust and are impatient with congressional politics in economic policymaking. Okun, for example, wrote of the case in 1966 when the Federal Reserve was there to shoulder "the thankless burden" when fiscal policy adjustment was not possible. Okun, *Political Economy of Prosperity*, pp. 71, 79, 81. Congressional refusal to provide flexible tax instruments for the president is another source of criticism. The problem is outlined in Joseph A. Pechman, *Federal Tax Policy* (Washington, D.C.: The Brookings Institution, 1977), pp. 49–50. Criticism of Congress along these lines is not the special preserve of economists by any means. The various indictments are outlined in James L. Sundquist, "Congress and the President: Enemies or Partners," in Henry Owen and Charles L. Schultze, eds., *Setting National Priorities: The Next Ten Years* (Washington, D.C.: The Brookings Institution, 1976), pp. 583–618.

30. The most "political" account is in Clifford, pp. 300–303, although he accepts most of the standard account at other points. See also Weintraub, "Congressional Supervision of Monetary Policy," p. 354; and Friedman and Schwartz, *Monetary History*, pp. 624–627.

31. There are many examples, but three very prominent ones will suffice. The first post-accord chairman of the Federal Reserve, William McChesney Martin, had negotiated the agreement for the Treasury. Truman's last appointee to the Fed, James Louis Robertson, was previously a high career official with the Office of the Comptroller of the Currency, a division of the Treasury. The second post-accord Federal Reserve chairman, Arthur Burns, had served as Eisenhower's CEA and as an adviser to Nixon.

32. This has been true in both Democratic and Republican administrations. For example, under Kennedy, Dillon and Roosa (formerly vice-president of the New York Federal Reserve Bank) at the Treasury were quite close in outlook to Martin at the Federal Reserve. This closeness continued under Johnson with Fowler and Deming (formerly president of the Minneapolis Federal Reserve Bank). Carter's administration included two former top Federal Reserve staffers: Lyle Gramley at the Council of Economic Advisors and Daniel Brill at the Treasury. Others who have served in both the Federal Reserve and the Treasury include Dewey Daane, Henry Wallich, Bruce MacLaury, Stephen Gardner, Frank Morris, Robert Mayo, Paul Volcker, Emmett Rice, Sidney Jones, Samuel Chase and Peter Sternlight.

33. See, for example, the statement by Treasury Secretary Douglas Dillon in *The Federal Reserve After Fifty Years*, Hearings before the Subcommittee on

Domestic Finance of the House Committee on Banking and Currency, 88 Cong. 2 sess. (1964), pp. 1231–1232; and the statement of Deputy Treasury Secretary Stephen Gardner in *Financial Institutions and the Nation's Economy "Discussion Principles,"* Hearings before the Subcommittee on Financial Institutions Supervision, Regulation and Insurance of the House Committee on Banking, Currency, and Housing, 94 Cong. 1 and 2 sess. (1975–76), p. 604.

34. An example of apparently successful criticism of fiscal policy by the Federal Reserve chairman is the case of Burns's criticism of Carter's proposed $50 tax rebate early in 1977. Influence is regularly attributed to the chairman of the Federal Reserve in the *U.S. News and World Report* annual surveys of top leaders to identify "the most influential individuals" in the United States generally and in particular fields. *U.S. News and World Report*, April 22, 1974, p. 30; April 21, 1975, p. 28; April 19, 1976, p. 24; April 18, 1977, p. 28; and April 17, 1978, p. 30.

35. A provocative analysis of structural power in which business confidence figures prominently is Fred Block, "The Ruling Class Does Not Rule: Notes on the Marxist Theory of the State," *Socialist Revolution* 33 (May/ June 1977); pp. 6–28. This is also central to the analysis of Charles E. Lindblom, *Politics and Markets: The World's Political-Economic Systems* (New York: Basic Books, 1977).

36. Sidney Weintraub, "Wall Street's Mindless Affair with Tight Money," *Challenge* (January/February 1978), pp. 34–39.

37. Opinion data collected by Sindlinger and Company, Inc., reported in "The Statistical Romance Covering First 14 Weeks of Fed Chairman Miller's Honeymoon" (Media, Pa.: S&C, 1978).

38. This has been prominent in analysis of appointments to the Federal Reserve as well as discussion of policy. With respect to specific appointments, see the following, as from the *New York Times:* Concerning Dewey Daane, October 30, 1963, p. 53; October 31, 1963, p. 1; November 9, 1963, p. 24. Concerning William Sherrill, April 23, 1967, p. 1. Concerning William McChesney Martin, March 26, 1967, IIV, p. 3; March 30, 1967, p. 1. The appointment of William Miller was preceded by a considerable flap in the financial press about Arthur Burns' value as a generator of confidence; see Charles Walker, "The Economic Case for Reappointing Burns," *Washington Post* (November 10, 1977), p. A23; Ira R. Allen, "Key Group in Senate Urges Carter to Reappoint Burns as Fed Chief," *Washington Post* (November 5, 1977), p. A5; William Safire "While Burns Roams," *New York Times* (December 1, 1977), p. 39; and "After Burns the Fed Will Lean to the Left," *Business Week* (November 21, 1977), pp. 108–116.

39. See Woolley, *Monetary Politics,* Chapter 5.

Index